WEST ACADEMIC PUBLISHING'S LAW SCHOOL ADVISORY BOARD

SPECIAL EDUCATION LAW

IN A NUTSHELL®

RUTH COLKER
Distinguished University Professor and
Heck-Faust Memorial Chair in
Constitutional Law
Professor of Law
Moritz College of Law
The Ohio State University

WEST ACADEMIC PUBLISHING

444 Cedar Street, Suite 700
St. Paul, MN 55101
1-877-888-1330

Printed in the United States of America

ISBN: 978-1-68328-589-2

PREFACE

The objective of this *Nutshell* is to help law students, parents, lawyers and others recognize and understand the federal laws that protect students with disabilities. Students taking courses related to special education or education law, as well as education clinics, are among the intended beneficiaries. The book will also assist lawyers as well as parents of children with disabilities who want to learn more about this complex area of the law.

When appropriate, this *Nutshell* includes the statutory and regulatory language relevant to each topic. Each state has their own IDEA regulations so readers should be sure to consult their own state's regulations when learning about this area of the law. Further, regulations are frequently amended; thus, regulations should be checked for possible updates.

As with all Nutshells, a word of caution is required. This *Nutshell* presents an *overview* of the relevant federal statutes and regulations pertaining to the field of special education. It is not intended to provide a comprehensive analysis of those laws. Case citations are provided but the citations are not exhaustive as might occur with a Treatise. With a few exceptions, there is little discussion of policy issues, although the relevant statutes, regulations, and case law are often placed in historical perspective for clarity.

This *Nutshell* reflects updates as of July 2017 in a changing area of the law. Where appropriate, this *Nutshell* notes areas of uncertainty but it is too early to predict how the current administration may seek to make further changes in this area of the law through regulatory changes or changes in enforcement strategies. This *Nutshell* is descriptive rather than predictive of the law of special education.

This *Nutshell* was made possible by a generous research grant from the Michael E. Moritz College of Law at The Ohio State University, and the research assistance of Lauren Sabo (Moritz '18) and Moritz Reference Librarian Stephanie Ziegler. I would also like to thank Dr. Nicole Ofiesh, Director, Schwab Learning Center and Professor Nancy Mather, University of Arizona, College of Education, for their assistance with providing some of the examples used in this *Nutshell*. Any errors, of course, are my own.

RUTH COLKER

August 2017

OUTLINE

TABLE OF CASES

References are to Pages

SPECIAL EDUCATION LAW

IN A NUTSHELL®

CHAPTER 1
HISTORY AND ENACTMENT OF IDEA

§ 1.1 EARLY TWENTIETH CENTURY

Until the mid-1970s, attempts by parents to challenge the exclusions of their children with disabilities from school were largely unsuccessful. One of the earliest reported cases is from the state of Massachusetts. A young boy was excluded from school in Cambridge in 1885 because he was "too weak-minded to derive profit from instruction" and was deemed "troublesome to other children" because he made "uncouth noises," pinched others, and was "unable to take the ordinary decent physical care of himself." A court upheld the school committee's conduct, in excluding this child from instruction, as coming within their "good faith." *See Watson v. City of Cambridge,* 32 N.E. 864 (Mass. 1893).

The first states to adopt laws requiring the education of children with disabilities were New Jersey in 1911, New York in 1917, and Massachusetts in 1920, but enforcement of those (and other similar) laws were generally ineffective. Merritt Beattie's case was typical of children from that era who were even able to bring a legal challenge. The school district excluded him from regular public school in Antigo, Wisconsin, in 1919, although he had normal cognitive functioning, because "his physical condition and ailment produces a depressing and nauseating effect upon the teachers and school children." As a result of some paralysis that had affected his vocal cords, he had "slow and hesitating in speech," "a peculiarly high, rasping, and disturbing tone of voice," and "an uncontrollable flow of saliva, which drools from his mouth onto his clothing and books, causing him to present an unclean appearance." The court upheld the right of the public school to insist that Merritt attend a day school that had been established for the "instruction of deaf persons or persons with defective speech" out of consideration for the sensibility of others who might feel "depressing and nauseating" by his presence in a regular classroom. *See State v. Board of Education of City of Antigo*, 172 N.W. 153 (Wis. 1919).

Even though Wisconsin had a constitutional provision requiring a free public education "to all children between the ages of four and twenty years," the court ruled: "The right of a child of school age to attend the public schools of this state cannot be insisted upon when its presence therein is harmful to the best interests of the school." *Id.* at 154. Merritt Beattie's exclusion from the public schools and placement in a separate facility was typical of the way children with disabilities were segregated and excluded from public education in the early twentieth century. His paralysis was equated with deafness to exclude him from public education and provide him a substandard education in another facility, although his educational placement had nothing to do with his actual needs or abilities.

Exclusion and segregation were, in part, a story of good intentions gone awry. Thomas Hopkins Gallaudet and Samuel Gridley Howe were early disability rights activists who sought special public day schools for children with various disabilities, specifically children who were deaf, blind, or intellectually impaired at a time when there was enormous public skepticism about whether such children deserved any education at all. Despite the purported humanitarian rationale for these schools, they were often grossly substandard. Hence, Merritt Beattie's parents preferred that he attend the regular public school rather than one of these segregated institutions.

The schools created by Gallaudet, Howe, and others were not for all categories of children with disabilities. These schools did not seek to educate children who used wheelchairs, were not toilet-trained, or were considered uneducable. Nor did they seek to educate children with mental health impairments, who often were placed in residential facilities that were later described as deplorable, offering no education whatsoever.

Meanwhile, hostility toward students with disabilities was ideologically linked to hostility toward immigrants and a developing interest in intelligence testing. Concurrently, as a progressive gesture to increase the availability of public education, states began to enact compulsory education laws in the late nineteenth century. When large influxes of immigrants began to move to urban areas in the early twentieth century, some schools began having class sizes of eighty or ninety students, and schools were hard-pressed to find a way to reduce enrollment in the face of the new education laws. "Mental retardation"[1] soon became an excuse to reduce class size. Some of the immigrant students were not literate and with the advent of intelligence testing, were soon classified as "morons" and placed in special classes for children with intellectual impairments or what was then called mental retardation. Special schools or classes for the so-called mentally retarded were largely an urban phenomenon; in comparison, rural school districts typically sought to exclude or expel children who presented problems as a way to get around compulsory education laws.

§ 1.2 JUDICIAL RESPONSE: THE 1960s AND EARLY 1970s

As schools were forced to racially integrate in the 1960s, some judges found that tracking and special education became a vehicle to maintain racial segregation. In 1967, Judge Skelly Wright found that the District of Columbia School District unconstitutionally used tracking as a way to relegate African American students to inferior schools and classrooms. The "Special Academic" track was for students who had "emotionally disturbed behavior, an IQ of 75 or below, and substandard performance on achievement tests."

---

[1] The term "mental retardation" is no longer used to classify students as disabled for the purpose of the special education laws. Today, school districts would use terms such as "intellectual disability" to describe students who may have previously been classified as "mentally retarded." This *Nutshell* uses the term "mental retardation" for historical accuracy, not to suggest it is a term that is accepted for usage today.

Tracking attained segregation on the basis of race because the students in the "Special Academic" track were disproportionately African American. *See Hobson v. Hansen,* 269 F. Supp. 401 (D.D.C. 1967). Judge Wright found that students placed in the special academic track received a segregated and inferior education.

The educational psychologist Lloyd M. Dunn strongly praised Judge Wright's legal conclusions. In a seminal article published in 1968, Dunn documented what he saw as a crisis in special education. The number of segregated "special day classes" for the "retarded" was increasing by "leaps and bounds" with about 60 to 80 percent of those pupils coming from "low status backgrounds—including Afro-Americans, American Indians, Mexicans, and Puerto Rican Americans; those from nonstandard English speaking, broken, disorganized, and inadequate homes; and children from other non-middle class environments." Dunn argued that we must "stop labeling these deprived children as mentally retarded" and "must stop segregating them by placing them into our allegedly special programs." *See* Lloyd M. Dunn, *Special Education for the Mildly Retarded—Is Much of It Justifiable*?, EXCEPTIONAL CHILDREN 5 (September 1968).

In 1972, a federal district court similarly criticized the way school districts used standardized intelligence tests to place children in classes for the so-called mentally retarded in California. *Larry P. v. Riles*, 343 F. Supp. 1306 (N.D. Cal. 1972), *aff'd,* 502

F.2d 963 (9th Cir. 1974). The court concluded that racial bias was the only rational explanation for the tracking program because it was used to take African Americans out of the regular classroom and place them in dead-end classes that did *not* try to teach them the regular curriculum or prepare them to reenter mainstream classes.

In the same year, Judge Cornelius Waddy ruled that the District of Columbia violated the Constitution by excluding various children with disabilities from the educational system. *Mills v. Board of Education,* 348 F. Supp. 866 (D.D.C. 1972). Once again, the plaintiffs were African American, but the court's ruling was not dependent on that fact. Instead, the court concluded that denying an education to children with disabilities while offering it to children who were developing typically was a denial of equal protection. The District of Columbia case coupled with a case from Pennsylvania, *see Pennsylvania Association for Retarded Children (PARC) v. Pennsylvania,* 334 F. Supp. 1257 (E.D. Pa. 1971), helped draw national attention to the millions of children who were denied an education altogether because of their disability status.

Both the *PARC* and *Mills* courts approved judicially-enforceable consent decrees that would serve as the foundation for the Education for All Handicapped Children Act (EAHCA). These enforceable agreements required all school-age children to receive a free public education (although the *PARC* decree was technically limited to children who were "mentally retarded"). The *PARC* decree stipulated that each "retarded child [be] placed in a program of education and training appropriate to his learning capacities." The *Mills* decree used similar language and also specified that any child who was suspended for more than two days was entitled to a hearing (and education during the suspension). The *Mills* decree also created an extensive Hearing Officer system and provided that parents would be supplied with information concerning free diagnostic services as well as legal counsel.

Both decrees created a presumption that a child classified as disabled should be placed in a regular public school class rather than in a segregated public school class or a special public or private school. This language was based on the integration mandate from *Brown v. Board of Education*, 347 U.S. 483 (1954). Congress was quite aware of both consent decrees (and other court decisions) when it considered and enacted into law the Education for All Handicapped Children Act in 1975. These consent decrees were responsive to Dunn's work in presuming that children should be placed in integrated rather than segregated environments, but they nonetheless did further the practice of using the classification "mentally retarded" (or some other label) as a condition of receiving special assistance.

§ 1.3 EARLY CONGRESSIONAL RESPONSE

By the early 1970s, Congress was aware of the cases in which courts concluded that the constitutional rights of children with disabilities were being violated by their exclusion from school or by their receiving inferior education in segregated classrooms. Even before passage of the landmark Education for All Handicapped Children Act in 1975, Congress began to increase federal funding for special education.

In the 1950s, Congress used its appropriation authority to develop programs for subgroups of individuals with disabilities. On July 26, 1954, Public Law 83–531 authorized Congress to provide 1 million dollars in grants to support educational research for students with mental retardation. It subsequently took Congress several years to finally appropriate $650,000 of those funds in 1957. Nonetheless, for the next several years, other laws supported students who were deaf or mentally retarded.

With the election of President John F. Kennedy in 1960, more attention was directed towards the need to educate children with disabilities. (John Kennedy and his sister, Eunice Kennedy Shriver, reportedly were concerned about this issue because they had a sister, Rosemary Kennedy, who had intellectual disabilities. Rosemary was forced to have a lobotomy and live in an institutional setting for much of her life.) President Kennedy helped establish the Division of Handicapped Children and

Youth that brought new significance and strength to the education of children with disabilities under Public Law 88–164. This division dealt with a broad range of children with disabilities, not just a subset of the population. It set the foundation for the approach to fund special education services through grants directly available to the states. (A few years later Eunice Kennedy Shriver helped establish the Special Olympics, which today is the world's largest sports organizations for children and adults with intellectual disabilities, providing year-round training and competition to more than 5.2 million athletes and Unified Sports partners in nearly 170 countries.)

In 1965, Congress enacted the Elementary and Secondary Education Act (ESEA). The primary purpose of this Act was to assist disadvantaged children. In 1966, an ad hoc subcommittee of the House Education and Labor Committee held hearings on the need to support the education of children with disabilities. In response to those hearings, Congress added Title VI to the Elementary and Secondary Education Act in order to provide grants to the states for the education of handicapped children. The grants did not go to school districts but rather to "schools for handicapped children operated or supported by [the state's educational agency]." Instead of the modern "full inclusion" model, this funding supported only segregated programs for children with disabilities. However, Congress did not actually appropriate the funds until 1966. The funding then, and now, was only a portion of what states might spend on special education through what the Supreme Court has characterized as a model of cooperative federalism.

The ESEA amendment process continued in 1970 when Congress amended the Act with Public Law 91–230 to include 200 million dollars in funding to the states, conditioned on their willingness to "initiate, expand, and improve programs and projects, including [special education] preschool programs and projects." This allocation, 15 percent of the total amount earmarked for "innovative and exemplary local programs," represented a significant commitment. Public Law 91–230 repealed Title VI of the ESEA as of July 1, 1971, and created a separate Act called the Education of the Handicapped Act (EHA). This was the first freestanding special education statute.

Rather than targeting a small subset of children with disabilities, the 1970 amendment reached children who were "mentally retarded, hard of hearing, deaf, speech impaired, visually handicapped, seriously emotionally disturbed, crippled, or other health impaired." It also created support for special programs tailored to children with "specific learning disabilities."

The 1970 statute was path breaking in that it provided money to educate children with disabilities on a broad scale, but it did not create extensive substantive rights. Notable, no right of action was specified in the statute so that parents could enforce these statutory requirements. The statute also did not mandate the education of all children with disabilities, so children who were disabled but not considered "educable" were still denied an education. Its statutory terms also were fairly ambiguous, with terms such as "reasonable promise" and "substantial progress" to describe programs that could be funded.

Although the 1970 statute seems modest by today's standards, it was a very important beginning because it mandated children with disabilities be educated and that they should receive the "special education and related services" they need to make progress. The term "special education and related services" is still part of the statutory framework today.

Congress adopted Public Law 93–380 in 1974, extending the EHA for another three years. It was aware that a broader response was necessary and enacted an emergency one-year authorization provision for greatly increased aid to the states for fiscal year 1975. It also created the first procedural safeguards for parents, modeled after the consent decrees in several of the successful court cases, particularly the *PARC* litigation. These safeguards required school districts to give "prior notice to parents or guardians of the child when the [school district] proposes to change the educational placement of the child" and to give parents a chance to "examine all relevant records with respect to the classification or educational placement of the child" and have an opportunity to seek "an impartial due process hearing" that is "binding on all parties subject only to appropriate administrative or judicial appeal."

The second set of procedural safeguards created the "least restrictive rule." This rule created the presumption that children with disabilities should ideally be educated with children who are not disabled "and that special classes, separate schooling, or other removal of handicapped children from the regular educational environment occurs only when the nature or severity of the handicap is such that education in regular classes with the use of supplementary aids and services cannot be achieved satisfactorily." This rule—which was borrowed directly from *Brown v. Board of Education*—has been a part of special education law since 1974.

The amendments also created what today is called the Child Find provision. States were required to have in place a program to identify, locate, and evaluate which children need special education and related services. A part of this new requirement was the explicit statement that there should be a goal of "full educational opportunities to all handicapped children." The era of educating only a subset of children with disabilities was coming to an end.

§ 1.4 EDUCATION FOR ALL HANDICAPPED CHILDREN ACT

In 1975, there was enough political momentum for Congress to mandate that states receiving federal special education funds educate *all* handicapped children. It enacted the Education for All Handicapped Children Act on November 29,

1975, by an overwhelming majority. The EAHCA received extensive consideration by Congress before being enacted into law. This consideration reflected its landmark importance as signaling a change in U.S. education policy—that all children should receive an adequate education irrespective of their disability status.

After extensive hearings, Congress enacted a statute that sought to provide an appropriate education for all children with disabilities. The addition of the word "All" to the name of the Act reflected this intention. There was also a minor change to the definition of disability. The term "crippled," which was included in prior law, was replaced with "orthopedically impaired." And, instead of "specific learning disabilities" having separate statutory coverage, it became part of the definition of disability. In other words, "specific learning disabilities" made the list as a covered disability under the Act.

The funding scheme also sought to assist states in funding students with disabilities. Congress authorized appropriations equal to 5 percent of the Average Per-Pupil Expenditure (APPE) in public elementary and secondary schools for the 1977–78 fiscal year, 10 percent for 1978–79, 20 percent for 1979–80, 30 percent for 1980–81, and 40 percent for 1981–82 for each child identified as handicapped under the statute. That level of funding, however, never survived the appropriations process. It tended to range from 8 to 12 percent of APPE. Furthermore, Congress sought to encourage identification of children as disabled by linking funding to the number of children identified rather than to the number of children overall in the school district.

The 1975 statute created two important and interconnected concepts that are still basic to federal disability education law: the concept of a Free and Appropriate Public Education (FAPE) and the concept of an Individualized Education Program (IEP). A FAPE was defined as "special education and related services which (A) have been provided at public expense, under public supervision and direction, and without charge . . . and (D) are provided in conformity with the individualized education program." An IEP was established as a written statement developed by a school district representative, the teacher, the parents or guardian of the child, and the child, when appropriate, to help the child attain a FAPE. This written statement must include five elements: (1) present levels of performance, (2) annual goals, (3) specific services and whether the child will participate in regular educational programs, (4) projected date of services, and (5) criteria for assessing whether objectives have been met.

It also repeated the least restrictive educational environment rule contained in the 1974 amendments. Children with disabilities should be educated with nondisabled children "to the maximum extent appropriate." Supplementary aids and services should be provided, if necessary, to keep children in the regular classroom.

Further, it expanded the procedural safeguards established in the 1974 Act. Congress expanded the list of when parents should be provided written explanations (in what is described as "prior written notice"). Under the new language, parents should get written notice when a school district "(i) proposes to initiate or change, or (ii) refuses to initiate or change, the identification, evaluation, or educational placement of the child or the provision of a free appropriate public education to the child." That notice was labeled "written prior notice," as it had been under the 1974 amendments, although it no longer always encompassed situations in which a school district needed to provide notice before taking action.

Finally, it created the "stay put" rule. Under this rule, the current educational placement stays in place during the pendency of any proceedings under the Act. That rule would be helpful in a situation in which the school district wants to change a child's placement and the parent disagrees. The original placement would stay in place during the pendency of the due process hearing and various appeals (assuming a parent is sufficiently well informed to take advantage of the rule).

§ 1.5 1977 AMENDMENTS

Because the original funding formulas only lasted through July 1, 1977, Congress had to enact its first amendments to the Act by that date. On June 17, 1977, Congress enacted a two-page public law to set new appropriation levels for some discretionary grant programs. The 1977 amendments reflect quite modest increases in funding levels for certain projects. Congress made no substantive changes to the Act.

§ 1.6 1983 AMENDMENTS

The 1983 Amendments made some minor substantive changes. The term "speech impaired" was amended to read "speech and language impaired." The change was made upon the recommendation of speech and language pathologists who reported that many of the children they served had significant language impairments.

These Amendments also broadened the right of children attending private schools to receive special education resources. They authorized the Secretary of Education to bypass the State Educational Agency (SEA) in order to provide special services to children with disabilities in private schools. Today, private schools get what is often called their "equitable share" of money from the state to provide some special education services, such as speech therapy. Students are not entitled to a full IEP if they attend a private school but can obtain some publicly-funded assistance, subject to how the private school decides to spend those resources.

§ 1.7 1986 AMENDMENTS

Congress was quite busy in 1986 with respect to the special education laws. On August 5, 1986, it enacted an amendment to the EAHCA to provide for attorney's fees. Then, on October 8, 1986, it amended the EAHCA to provide for a new title that would cover infants and toddlers with disabilities.

In *Smith v. Robinson*, 468 U.S. 992 (1984), the Supreme Court had held that school districts need not reimburse parents when they prevailed in EAHCA proceedings. Congress partially overturned the holding in *Smith* by enacting Public Law 99–372, the Handicapped Children's Protection Act of 1986, which was an amendment to the EAHCA. The 1986 Act provided: "In any action or proceeding brought under this subsection, the court, in its discretion, may award reasonable attorneys' fees as part of the costs to the parents or guardians of a handicapped child or youth who is the prevailing party." The Act made it possible for the prevailing party to obtain attorney's fees for the costs of participating in a due process hearing but not for the costs of expert witnesses or the costs of IEP meetings or mediation that preceded the due process hearing.

The provision also refers to the authority of a "court" (not a Hearing Officer) to award attorney's fees. When a parent prevails before a state level Hearing Officer, the parent cannot collect attorney's fees from that officer. He or she must bring a separate action (with a filing fee) in federal district court to obtain attorney's fees if the school district does not agree to resolve the case voluntarily.

Public Law 99–457, also enacted in 1986, reflects one of the most important changes to the EAHCA, because it resulted in the coverage of infants and toddlers. In response to the studies about the importance of early intervention, Congress created Part H, which provides funds for State programs in early intervention services for infants and toddlers with disabilities from birth through two years of age. (Children who are 3–5 years old were already covered under Part B—the school-age provisions for the EAHCA.)

In providing financial assistance to the states serving this population of infants and toddlers, Congress used a much broader and more flexible definition of disability than it had under the EAHCA. For infants and toddlers, it covered all children:

> who need early intervention services because they—(A) are experiencing developmental delays, as measured by appropriate diagnostic instruments and procedures in one or more of the following areas: Cognitive development, physical development, language and speech development, psychosocial development, or self-help skills, or (B) have a diagnosed physical or mental condition which has a high probability of resulting in developmental delay. Such terms may also include, at a State's discretion, individuals from birth to age 2, inclusive, who are at risk of having substantial developmental delays if early intervention services are not provided.

Public Law 99–457, § 672(1).

Unlike the school-age definition for eligibility, this definition allows any child to receive early intervention services merely because the child is experiencing developmental delays (or is at risk of experiencing those delays). Children do not need a diagnosed medical condition and do not need to be put in one of the nine categories (as is the case for school-age children) to be eligible for services.

Nonetheless, the programs made available under the infant and toddler program are not necessarily free of charge. The public law provides that early intervention services "are developmental services which . . . are provided at no cost except where Federal or State law provides for a system of payment by families, including a schedule of sliding fees." "Sliding fees" allow low-income parents to pay less for services than parents with more financial resources. *Id.* at § 672(2)(B).

The programs offered to children under this new provision are also quite different than the programs offered for school-age children. This new provision provides services to the child with a disability as part of a family unit. Instead of an Individualized Educational Plan (IEP), the child receives an Individualized Family Service Plan (IFSP). As the name suggests, services are provided to the family unit, as appropriate.

§ 1.8 1990 AMENDMENTS

The 1990 amendments were both substantive and technical. They amended the definition of disability to include "traumatic brain injury" and "autism." In order to align the special education laws with the recently enacted Americans with Disabilities Act

(ADA), 42 U.S.C. §§ 12101 et seq., the special education law changed all references from "handicap" to "disability." The name of the statute became the "Individuals with Disabilities Education Act" (IDEA). The enactment of the ADA did not directly impact the services required under the IDEA but did mean that individuals with disabilities could expect much more access to programs and services throughout their lives. ADA Title I made it unlawful to discriminate on the basis of disability in employment, ADA Title II made it unlawful for state and local government to discriminate on the basis of disability, and ADA Title III made it unlawful for private entities called "public accommodations," such as restaurants, hotels, and schools to discriminate on the basis of disability. Both ADA Title II and the IDEA would cover public school students but, as will be discussed in *Nutshell* Chapter 4, they would typically have to exhaust their IDEA rights before they could proceed in federal court under ADA Title II.

§ 1.9 1991 AMENDMENTS

The 1991 Amendments revised Part H of the 1986 Amendments, the Infants and Toddlers with Disabilities Program. Under the 1986 Amendments, states were supposed to have plans that would go into effect by July 1, 1991, to deliver services to all infants and toddlers with disabilities, or risk losing their funding for this category of service. Due to budget issues, many states were contemplating dropping out of the Infants and Toddlers with Disabilities Program until their financial picture improved. In response to this sentiment, the 1991 Amendments created a mechanism whereby "States facing serious financial or administrative problems would be allowed to continue to participate in Part H for a limited period of time, even if not in accordance with the timelines in the Act, if the States seeking the extension met certain conditions established by the Congress."

§ 1.10 1994 AMENDMENTS

In 1994, Congress adopted the Improving America's Schools Act, Public Law 103–382. Disability was not a major topic addressed by this statute. Nonetheless, it merged funding for Chapter 1 Handicapped Program with Part B funding under the IDEA. It also gave school districts the discretion to remove children with disabilities to an interim alternative educational setting for up to 45 days when such children bring a weapon to school. This measure was included in a section entitled "local control over violence," but this one provision amended the Individuals with Disabilities Act (section 1415(e)(3)). Congress further amended this provision as part of the broader set of amendments adopted in 1997.

§ 1.11 1997 AMENDMENTS

A. INTRODUCTION

After two years of deliberations, the "Individuals with Disabilities Education Act Amendments of 1997" became law on June 4, 1997, marking the first major revision to the special education laws since 1975. Public Law 105–17. This large overhaul reorganized the IDEA so that, for example, the definitions are alphabetized and Part H became Part C. Eligibility requirements and procedural safeguards were also consolidated. These changes made the statute easier to understand and use. The 1997 Amendments also required states to include nearly all children with disabilities in statewide assessments (with accommodations). The IEP must indicate how assessments will be modified so that the student can fully participate in them. If students cannot participate in regular assessments, then school districts must develop alternative assessments by 2000. Before the 1997 Amendments were passed, school districts often excluded nearly all students with disabilities from their statewide assessments, making it difficult for parents and others to track student progress or hold school districts fully responsible for their educational outcomes.

B. FINDINGS AND PURPOSE

Congress updated the findings to reflect its disappointment with the progress made by children under the IDEA. The 1997 findings state: "the implementation of this chapter has been impeded by low expectations, and an insufficient focus on applying replicable research on proven methods of teaching and learning for children with disabilities."

20 U.S.C. § 1400(c)(4).[2] The findings also provide: "Over 20 years of research and experience has demonstrated that the education of children with disabilities can be made more effective by—(A) having high expectations for such children and ensuring their access in the general curriculum to the *maximum* extent possible . . . (E) supporting high-quality, intensive professional development for all personnel who work with such children in order to ensure that they have the skills and knowledge necessary to enable them—(i) to meet developmental goals and, to the *maximum* extent possible, those challenging expectations that have been established for all children; and (ii) to be prepared to lead productive, independent, adult lives, to the *maximum* extent possible." 20 U.S.C. § 1400(c)(5). In three different places, the findings refer to children receiving programs and services to the "maximum extent possible."

The findings also reflect a concern about educational inequity along both race and class lines. The findings state: "The Federal Government must be responsive to the growing needs of an increasingly more diverse society. A more equitable allocation of resources is essential for the Federal Government to meet its responsibility to provide an equal educational opportunity for all individuals." 20 U.S.C. § 1400(c)(7)(A). The findings also reflect an awareness of the problem of misidentification of

---

[2] Throughout this chapter, citations to the statute refer to the language adopted by Congress at the time of the relevant amendment. In some instances, the language today is slightly or significantly different.

minority children. "(A) Greater efforts are needed to prevent the intensification of problems connected with mislabeling and high dropout rates among minority children with disabilities. (B) More minority children continue to be served in special education than would be expected from the percentage of minority students in the general school population. (C) Poor African-American children are 2.3 times more likely to be identified by their teacher as having mental retardation than their white counterpart." 20 U.S.C. § 1400(c)(8).

As we will see below, Congress sought to attain these enhanced goals by modifying the Child Find provisions as well as the requirements for Individualized Education Programs (IEPs).

C. CHILD FIND

The 1997 Amendments create a new section entitled "Evaluations, eligibility determinations, individualized education programs, and educational placements." 20 U.S.C. § 1414. The first three parts of this section deal with evaluations and eligibility determinations. In contrast with past procedures, schools are required to begin the evaluation process by reviewing existing evaluation data on the child and then, as appropriate, determine what new data is needed. (This change was intended to save school districts some money by avoiding unnecessary evaluations.) The evaluations must meet new, rigorous requirements such as using "technically sound instruments that may assess the relative contribution of cognitive and behavioral factors, in addition to physical or developmental factors." 20 U.S.C. § 1414(d)(2)(C). Additionally, evaluation instruments must be "selected and administered so as not to be discriminatory on a racial and cultural basis." 20 U.S.C. § 1414(d)(3)(A)(i).

The evaluation process was also adjusted so that school districts must allow parents to provide input about their child during the evaluation. (Previously, school districts were not required to give parents that option.) The evaluation process now serves two purposes: (1) determining the child's eligibility for special education and related services *and*, (2) if the child had previously been found eligible for special education, considering what additions or modifications the child will need to his or her special education. Finally, the 1997 Amendments clarify that "a child shall not be determined to be a child with a disability if the determinant factor for such determination is lack of instruction in reading or math or limited English proficiency." 20 U.S.C. § 1414(d)(5). The purpose of this rule was to avoid over identification of students as disabled merely because they are not receiving adequate instruction.

To address the racial inconsistencies noted in the findings, the 1997 Amendments created a mechanism of data collection to track racial disproportionality in disability identification, while refraining from making any structural changes. Hereby, each state is required to "provide for the collection and examination of data to determine if significant disproportionality based on race is occurring in the State with respect to—(A) the identification of children as children with disabilities, including the identification of children as children with disabilities in accordance with a particular impairment described in section 1401(3) of this title; and (B) the placement in particular educational settings of such children." 20 U.S.C. § 1418(c).

D. INDIVIDUALIZED EDUCATION PROGRAMS

The 1997 Amendments add more requirements to the definition of an "individualized education program" which had remained unchanged since its inception as part of the 1975 EAHCA. Reflecting an overarching interest in research-based standards, the Amendments require annual goals to be "measurable" and to include "benchmarks or short-term objectives." 20 U.S.C. § 1414(d)(1)(A). These requirements must align with the mandate that the child is "involved in and progressing in the general curriculum"; however, no definition is given for how much "progress" is enough. 20 U.S.C. § 1414(d)(1)(A). The 1997 Amendments also specify that the child "advance appropriately toward attaining the annual goals" without stating how we determine what is "appropriate." 20 U.S.C. § 1414(d)(1)(B). The purpose of these changes was to encourage school districts to increase the participation of individuals with disabilities in the regular education curriculum. Similarly, the Amendments require an explanation of the extent to which children who qualify for special education will not be participating with nondisabled children in the general education classroom.

The Amendments also expanded the description of who should be a member of the team that writes the IEP. Prior to 1997, the statute required that the following people attend the IEP meeting: a school district representative, the teacher, the parents or guardian, and, when appropriate, the child. The 1997 Act adds to that list of required people in attendance: a special education teacher, "an individual who can interpret the instructional implications of evaluation results," and "other individuals who have knowledge or special expertise regarding the child." 20 U.S.C. § 1414(d)(1)(B). The second requirement was intended to support the research-based requirements of the 1997 Amendments. The Amendments also clarify the parents' right to be involved in placement decisions.

Finally, the Amendments emphasize periodic review of the IEP. Schools must report the progress of students under an IEP as often as it reports progress for nondisabled children (such as quarterly report cards). If it becomes evident that a child is not making progress towards the IEP goals then the team must meet and revise the IEP. The Amendments therefore give parents enhanced opportunities to communicate with school districts about the development and implementation of the IEP.

E. DISCIPLINE

The 1997 Amendments also enhance the ability of school districts to discipline children with disabilities by removing them to an alternative educational setting. Discipline was the most heavily discussed topic at the hearings.

They also provided school districts with greater authority to exclude children with disabilities from regular educational programs if they had inflicted "serious bodily injury," or had engaged in various drugs or weapon offenses. When that kind of conduct occurred, students could be placed in alternative educational settings for up to 45 days.

On the other hand, the 1997 Amendments also enhanced the due process rights of students with disabilities who were excluded from school for more than 10 days and had not engaged in serious bodily injury or various drugs or weapon offenses. If their conduct was found to be disability-related, they could not be forced to change their educational placement.

F. ATTORNEYS/MEDIATION

The 1997 Amendments provide that an attorney can collect their fees from the school district if they attended a meeting that was scheduled as a result of a successful due process hearing. This provision stated: "Attorneys' fees may not be awarded relating to any meeting of the IEP Team unless such meeting is convened as a result of an administrative proceeding or judicial action, or, at the discretion of the State, for a mediation described in subsection (e)." 20 U.S.C. § 1415(i)(3)(D)(ii). For the first time, the IDEA emphasized mediation as a means of resolving disputes, requiring each state to make mediation available and bear the cost of the mediator.

G. PRIVATE SCHOOL EDUCATION

The 1997 Amendments also provide some benefits to parents who send their children to private schools, providing that school districts may offer the special education and related services funded under Part B on the premises of private, including parochial, schools. The Amendments also specify that school districts may be required to reimburse parents for the cost of a private educational placement when the school district has not made a Free Appropriate Public Education available to the child.

§ 1.12 2004 AMENDMENTS

President Bush signed the 2004 Amendments into law on December 3, 2004. Many of the changes aligned the IDEA with No Child Left Behind (NCLB) by requiring special education teachers to meet various standards for "highly qualified teachers."

The racial disproportionality rule was strengthened to require the states to have policies and procedures designed to prevent the inappropriate over identification or disproportionate representation by race and ethnicity of children as children with disabilities.

One of the most important changes made by the 2004 Amendments stipulates that a school district can no longer be required to use the "discrepancy model" in determining whether a child has a specific learning disability. 20 U.S.C. § 1414(b)(6)(A). Under the discrepancy model, a child is learning disabled if there is a significant discrepancy between aptitude and achievement. The 2004 Amendments allow school districts to choose to use a process that determines if the child responds to scientific, research-based intervention as part of the evaluation process. 20 U.S.C. § 1414(b)(6)(B). For example, children who are still behind grade level after research-based intervention can be classified as learning disabled even if there is not a significant discrepancy between their aptitude and achievement.

The notice requirements were also expanded such that within 10 days of receiving a parent's complaint that he or she objects to the school district's evaluation of his or her child or the proposed IEP, the school district must send a response to the parent that states: (1) an explanation of why the agency proposed or refused to take the action raised by the complaint, (2) a description of other options that the IEP team considered and the reasons why those options were rejected, (3) a description of each evaluation procedure, assessment, record, or report the school district used as the basis for the proposed or refused action, and (4) a description of the factors that are relevant to the school district's proposal or refusal. 20 U.S.C. § 1415(c)(1).

Alternative dispute resolution options were further emphasized by the 2004 Amendments, which outlined that prior to an opportunity for a due process hearing, the parties must engage in a resolution session or mediation, unless they agree in writing to waive such a meeting. The school district can only bring an attorney to the resolution session if an attorney also accompanies the parent. A resolution meeting, unlike mediation, does not necessarily involve the presence of a neutral third party and is not voluntary. It is similar to another IEP meeting, although its purpose is to flesh out the issues in the hope of avoiding a due process hearing. 20 U.S.C. § 1415(e) (mediation) & 20 U.S.C. § 1415(f)(1)(B) (resolution session). As will be discussed in *Nutshell* Chapter 9, the parties sometimes request that a mediator attend a resolution session so the difference between a mediation and a resolution meeting is not necessarily stark.

Attorney fee rules were also changed to make them more favorable to school districts in 2004. Courts now had the authority to grant attorney fees to the school district when the plaintiffs' claims were frivolous, without foundation, or brought in bad faith. It also clarified that a parent was not entitled to attorney fees for successfully resolving the matter at a resolution meeting. 20 U.S.C. § 1415(i)(3).

The 2004 Amendments gave school districts more authority to discipline students with disabilities. Whereas the old rules referred to "10 days" or "45 days," the new rules refer to "10 school days" or "45 school days," providing schools with a somewhat longer period from which to exclude students from the classroom without significant due process protections. For students excluded for more than 10 school days (who had not caused serious bodily injury or engaged in weapons or drug-related offenses), the 2004 Amendments limited school district "manifestation determination" committees to two situations where they could conclude that the conduct was a manifestation of the child's disability: (1) when the conduct in question was caused by, or had a *direct and substantial* relationship to the child's disability or (2) the conduct in question was the *direct result* of the school district's failure to implement the IEP. *See* 20 U.S.C. § 1415(k) (placement in alternative educational setting). It was no longer possible to argue that the student engaged in the misconduct because the student had an inadequate IEP.

The 2004 Amendments also gave Hearing Officers more authority to place a child in an alternative educational setting for up to 45 days when a parent challenges a school district's placement decision. Prior language had required the Hearing Officer to consider many factors before placing a student in an alternative educational setting. The 2004 Amendments merely require the Hearing Officer to conclude that, "maintaining the current placement of the child is substantially likely to result in injury to the child or others." *See* 20 U.S.C. § 1415(k)(3)(A).

CHAPTER 2
EARLY CHILDHOOD

§ 2.1 INTRODUCTION

As discussed in *Nutshell* Chapter 1, early intervention services were added to the IDEA in 1986 as Part H in response to evidence that significant brain development occurs in the first three years of life. (The section is now codified as Part C.) The first finding states that "Congress finds [that] there is an urgent and substantial need to enhance the development of infants and toddlers with disabilities, to minimize their potential for developmental delay, and to recognize the significant brain development that occurs during a child's first 3 years of life." 20 U.S.C. § 1431(a)(1).

Unlike Part B of the IDEA, which creates specific categories of covered children, Part C requires a state to cover all children under 3 years of age who need early intervention services because they are experiencing developmental delays or have a high probability of experiencing developmental delays. 20 U.S.C. § 1432(5). In addition, at its own discretion, a state may also include "at-risk infants or toddlers." They are defined as children under 3, "who would be at risk of experiencing a substantial developmental delay if early intervention services were not provided to the individual." 20 U.S.C. § 1432(1).

Part C services are administered by a single lead agency designated or established by the Governor of a state. 20 U.S.C. § 1435(a)(10). A state must also create procedural safeguards and create an interagency coordinating council. 20 U.S.C. § 1435(a)(13) & (15). This coordinating council includes:

- parents,
- service providers,
- a member of the state legislature,
- a person involved in personnel preparation,
- a person from each state agency that provides intervention services,
- a member of the agency for preschool services,
- a member of the state Medicaid agency,
- a member of the Head Start agency,
- a member of a state agency responsible for child care,
- a member of the agency responsible for state regulation of health insurance,
- a member of the office of the coordinator of homeless children and youth,
- a member of the state foster care agency, and
- a member of the state agency responsible for children's mental health.

This council advises and assists the lead agency responsible for determining the Individualized

Family Service Plan services (IFSP). 20 U.S.C. § 1441(e).

In order for states to receive federal funds under Part C, they must establish a comprehensive early intervention system to assist children with disabilities through age 3 (when they transition to Part B). This early intervention system provides assistance to infants *and* their families, unlike Part B, which only provides assistance to the school-aged child. Part C services should be provided within a natural environment, such as the home. The IFSP must include "[a] statement that each early intervention service is provided in the natural environment for that child or service to the maximum extent appropriate." 34 C.F.R. § 303.344(d)(ii)(A). In addition to the many types of services that are often provided to school-age children, IFSP services can include:

- family training,
- counseling,
- home visits,
- health services,
- medical services,
- nursing services, and
- nutrition services.

34 C.F.R. § 303.13(b).

Children are supposed to receive a "smooth and effective" transition from Part C to Part B services by the child's third birthday. 20 U.S.C. § 1412(a)(9). Although Congress phased-in coverage of infants, it required that each state establish a timetable to cover *all* eligible infants and toddlers. *See* 20 U.S.C. § 1435(a).

In addition to following the statutory and regulatory changes to this part of the IDEA, it is important to read relevant guidance from the United States Department of Education. On February 29, 2012, the United States Department of Education issued a "Dear Colleague" letter in which it reiterated that the Least Restrictive Environment (LRE) rule found within the IDEA applies to the placement of preschool children with disabilities *See* Melody Musgrove, *Dear Colleague Letter Preschool Least Restrictive Environment*, U.S. DEP'T OF EDUC. (Feb. 29, 2012) https://www2.ed.gov/policy/speced/guid/idea/memosdcltrs/preschoollre22912.pdf. That letter only applies to preschool and school-age children covered under Part B of the IDEA although it can include preschool children who are only two years of age (and therefore technically covered by Part C) when the state has chosen to place the child in a publicly-funded preschool.

On July 6, 2015, the United States Department of Education issued a "Dear Colleague" letter in which it expressed concern that "a growing number of children with [autism spectrum disorder] may not be receiving needed speech and language services, and that speech-language pathologists and other appropriate professionals may not be included in evaluation and eligibility determinations under the

Individuals with Disabilities Education Act (IDEA), Part B, or in meetings to develop the individualized educational program (IEP) or individualized family service plan (IFSP) under both Parts B and C of IDEA." *See* Melody Musgrove, *Dear Colleague Letter Speech and Language Services for Students with Autism Spectrum Disorder*, U.S. DEP'T OF EDUC. (July 6, 2015). http://www.asha.org/uploadedFiles/US-Dept-Education-ASD-Services-Letter.pdf.

Further, on September 14, 2015, the United States Department of Health and Human Services and the United States Department of Education issued a joint policy statement on the inclusion of children with disabilities in early childhood programs. This guidance addressed the apparent tension between the "natural environment" rule created under Part C and the general rule that children be educated in the "least restrictive environment." https://www2.ed.gov/policy/speced/guid/earlylearning/joint-statement-full-text.pdf. The joint policy stated:

> There may be tensions between the IDEA's requirement that services are identified on an individualized basis and IDEA's natural environments and LRE requirements regarding the service setting. For example, some jurisdictions may interpret IDEA's Part C natural environments provision as only allowing early intervention services to be provided in eligible children's homes, and not fully consider the child's outcomes and how those outcomes may be met in alternative

> settings such as inclusive early childhood programs or other community settings where typically developing children are included. Other jurisdictions may interpret IDEA's free appropriate public education (FAPE) and LRE requirements as only allowing IDEA preschool special education and related services to be delivered in preschool programs operated in a public school building as opposed to non-public school settings, such as child care and Head Start where services can be delivered. In fact, a mixed delivery system of public and private high quality early childhood programs could be important to increasing the availability of inclusive opportunities for children with disabilities.

Id. at 6.

It is therefore no longer appropriate to assume that Part C services need to be delivered in the home; various preschool service providers might also be appropriate. The Third Circuit had previously taken this position in *Andrew M. v. Delaware County Office of Mental Health and Mental Retardation*, 490 F.3d 337, 342 (3rd Cir. 2007) in which it affirmed the determination by the Hearing Officer that the education of twin boys at a preschool met the natural environment test because "it was an environment where typical, non-developmentally-delayed children would be found."

§ 2.2 CHILD FIND

Section 1435 contains extensive requirements that each state must implement to qualify as having an appropriate statewide system of identification and services. These requirements include: (1) a single line of responsibility in a lead agency designated or established by the Governor to carry out the responsibilities (2) a rigorous definition of "developmental delay", (3) a comprehensive Child Find system, (4) a public awareness program focusing on early identification, (5) a central directory of services, resources and experts, and (6) a "timely, comprehensive, multidisciplinary evaluation of the functioning of each infant or toddler with a disability in the State, and a family-directed identification of the needs of each family of such an infant or toddler, to assist appropriately in the development of the infant or toddler." 20 U.S.C. § 1435(a).

Further, section 1437 was amended in 2004 to require the referral for early intervention services for children under the age of 3 who:

> (A) is involved in a substantiated case of child abuse or neglect; or
> (B) is identified as affected by illegal substance abuse, or withdrawal symptoms resulting from prenatal drug exposure

20 U.S.C. § 1437(a)(6).

In order to challenge a state's failure to comply with that regulation, one would need to use the standard due process vehicle provided to challenge noncompliance with the IDEA, as discussed in *Nutshell* § 2.9. One cannot directly bring suit in federal court without first exhausting the state administrative process. *See Henry A. v. Willden*, 678 F.3d 991 (9th Cir. 2012) (dismissing a suit seeking injunctive relief under section 1437(a)(6)(A) because of the failure to exhaust state administrative remedies).

The "Child Find" obligations under the IDEA, with respect to infants and toddlers, have been the subject of extensive litigation. In 1997, the Seventh Circuit allowed a class action lawsuit to go forward under Section 1983 against the state of Illinois for failing to provide services to all eligible infant and toddlers. *See Marie O. v. Edgar,* 131 F.3d 610 (7th Cir. 1997). The state's Auditor General had found that "services were not available in all parts of the state, many eligible children were not being served and were on waiting lists, some federal and state program components were not fully implemented and no tracking or other follow-up was being conducted." *Id.* at 614. The plaintiffs were four children with disabilities who were placed on waiting lists rather than provided with services.

The federal district court had required the state to provide early intervention services to all eligible children with disabilities and required specific steps be taken in the areas of (1) public awareness, (2) procedural safeguards, (3), Child Find, (4) evaluation and assessment, (5) IFSP's, (6) service coordination, (7) elimination of waiting lists, (8) data collection, (9) financial matters, and (10) personnel development. *See Marie O. v. Edgar,* 1996 WL 48515 (N.D. Ill. Feb. 2, 1996). Rather than challenge the district court's decision on the merits, the state sought to argue that the lawsuit was improper for reasons of sovereign immunity. The Seventh Circuit affirmed the district court injunction and ruled against the state on the sovereign immunity issue. The United States Department of Education conducted a review of Illinois' Special Education programs in 2001 and 2002 and found that there remained significant areas in which the state was not meeting its IDEA Part C obligations. *See* Letter from Secretary Linda Renee Baker to Superintendent Robert Schiller (December 31, 2002).

Illinois is not alone in having litigation regarding its failure to meet Part C obligations, especially for a lack of "Child Find." *See e.g., DL v. District of Columbia,* 194 F. Supp.3d 30 (D.D.C. 2016) (finding that the school district failed to ensure that preschool-age children with disabilities were receiving an appropriate public education).

§ 2.3 EVALUATIONS

The IDEA requires that each state have a "timely, comprehensive, multidisciplinary evaluation of the functioning of each infant or toddler with a disability in the State, and a family-directed identification of the needs of each family of such an infant or toddler, to assist appropriately in the development of the infant or toddler." 20 U.S.C.

§ 1435(a)(3). This evaluation and initial assessment must be completed within 45 days, meeting the criteria described below.

Unlike Part B for school-age children, it requires both an evaluation and assessment of the child as well as a *family assessment*. The regulations provide that all evaluations and assessments of the child must:

> be conducted by qualified personnel in order to identify the child's unique strengths and needs and the early intervention services appropriate to meet those needs. The assessment of the child must include the following—(i) A review of the results of the evaluation conducted under paragraph (b) of this section; (ii) Personal observations of the child; and (iii) The identification of the child's needs in each of the developmental areas in § 303.21(a)(1).

34 C.F.R. § 303.321(c).

With respect to the family assessment, the regulations provide that they must be "family-directed" and

> must be conducted by qualified personnel in order to identify the family's resources, priorities, and concerns and the supports and services necessary to enhance the family's capacity to meet the developmental needs of the family's infant or toddler with a disability. The family-directed assessment must—(i) Be voluntary on the part of each family member

> participating in the assessment; (ii) Be based on information obtained through an assessment tool and also through an interview with those family members who elect to participate in the assessment; and (iii) Include the family's description of its resources, priorities, and concerns related to enhancing the child's development.

34 C.F.R. § 303.321(c)(2).

§ 2.4 ELIGIBILITY

Eligibility for an IFSP can be determined by the state's lead agency ensuring that a child receives a "timely, comprehensive, multidisciplinary evaluation," 34 C.F.R. § 303.321(a)(1)(i) or by considering the "child's medical and other records . . . without conducting an evaluation of the child." 34 C.F.R. § 303.321(a)(3)(i). If the child establishes eligibility through their own medical records, the lead agency or service provider "must conduct assessments of the child and family." 34 C.F.R. § 303.321(a)(3)(i). In conducting an evaluation, "no single procedure may be used as the sole criterion for determining a child's eligibility." 34 C.F.R. § 303.321(b).

If the lead agency determines that a child is not eligible for an IFSP, then it must provide written notice to the parents about their right to dispute the eligibility determination through dispute resolution mechanisms. 34 C.F.R. § 303.322.

§ 2.5 INDIVIDUALIZED FAMILY SERVICES PLAN (IFSP)

The IDEA contains five general principles that govern IFSP's: (1) requirements for assessment and program development, (2) requirements for six-month periodic reviews of an annual plan, (3) promptness requirements for the development of a plan, (4) eight requirements for the content of the plan, and (5) requirement for parental written consent before implementation of a plan. 20 U.S.C. § 1436.

The assessment must include: (1) a multidisciplinary assessment of the strengths and needs of the child, (2) a family-directed assessment of the family's resources priorities, concerns, and capacities, and (3) a written individualized plan developed by a multidisciplinary team, which includes a description of appropriate transition services. 20 U.S.C. § 1436(a).

The plan must include the following eight elements in writing:

> (1) a statement of the infant's or toddler's present levels of physical development, cognitive development, communication development, social or emotional development, and adaptive development, based on objective criteria;
>
> (2) a statement of the family's resources, priorities, and concerns relating to enhancing the development of the family's infant or toddler with a disability;

(3) a statement of the measurable results or outcomes expected to be achieved for the infant or toddler and the family, including pre-literacy and language skills, as developmentally appropriate for the child, and the criteria, procedures, and timelines used to determine the degree to which progress toward achieving the results or outcomes is being made and whether modifications or revisions of the results or outcomes or services are necessary;

(4) a statement of specific early intervention services based on peer-reviewed research, to the extent practicable, necessary to meet the unique needs of the infant or toddler and the family, including the frequency, intensity, and method of delivering services;

(5) a statement of the natural environments in which early intervention services will appropriately be provided, including a justification of the extent, if any, to which the services will not be provided in a natural environment;

(6) the projected dates for initiation of services and the anticipated length, duration, and frequency of the services;

(7) the identification of the service coordinator from the profession most immediately relevant to the infant's or toddler's or family's needs (or who is otherwise qualified to carry out all applicable responsibilities under this subchapter) who

> will be responsible for the implementation of the plan and coordination with other agencies and persons, including transition services; and
>
> (8) the steps to be taken to support the transition of the toddler with a disability to preschool or other appropriate services.

20 U.S.C. § 1436(d).

The United States Department of Education has made available this model IFSP form, which would allow a state agency to fulfill the requirements of the IDEA.

Part C INDIVIDUALIZED FAMILY SERVICE

The Individualized Family Service Plan (IFSP) is a written plan that is developed for each eligible infant and toddler with a disability. The Part C regulations specify, at 34 CFR §§ 303.342–303.345, the procedures that State Lead Agencies and early intervention service providers must follow to develop, review, and revise an IFSP for each child. The document below sets out the IFSP content that those regulations require.

Service coordinator: The name of the service coordinator from the profession most immediately relevant to the child's or family's needs (or who is otherwise qualified to carry out all applicable responsibilities under Part C). The service coordinator is responsible for the implementation of the early intervention services identified in the IFSP, including transition services and coordination with other agencies and persons. The service coordinator serves as the single point of contact for carrying out the activities described in 34 CFR § 303.34. [34 CFR §§ 303.34 and 303.344(g)]

Present levels of development: A statement of the child's present levels of physical development (including vision, hearing, and health status), cognitive development, communication development, social or emotional development, and adaptive development based on the information from the child's evaluation and assessments conducted under § 303.321. [34 CFR § 303.344(a)]

Family's resources, priorities, and concerns: With the concurrence of the family, a statement of the family's resources, priorities, and concerns related to enhancing the development of the child as identified through the assessment of the family under 34 CFR § 303.321(c)(2). [34 CFR § 303.344(b)]

Measurable results or measurable outcomes: A statement of the measurable results or measurable outcomes expected to be achieved for the child (including pre-literacy and language skills, as developmentally appropriate for the child) and family, and the criteria, procedures, and timelines used to determine:

- The degree to which progress toward achieving the results or outcomes identified in the IFSP is being made; and
- Whether modifications or revisions of the expected results or outcomes, or early intervention services identified in the ISFP, are necessary. [34 CFR § 303.344(c)]

<table>
<tr><th rowspan="2">Measurable Result or Measurable Outcome (including, as appropriate, pre-literacy and language skills)</th><th colspan="3">For Determining Progress Toward Achieving Measurable Results and Measurable Outcomes, and Whether Modifications or Revisions are</th></tr>
<tr><th>Criteria</th><th>Procedures</th><th>Timelines</th></tr>
<tr><td></td><td></td><td></td><td></td></tr>
<tr><td></td><td></td><td></td><td></td></tr>
</table>

IFSP Team Meeting Date	Measurable Result or Measurable Outcome	Progress	Modifications or Revisions

Early intervention services: A statement of the specific early intervention services (EIS), based on peer-reviewed research (to the extent practicable), that are necessary to meet the unique needs of the child and the family to achieve the results or outcomes identified above, including:

- The beginning date, length, duration, frequency, intensity, method of delivering, and location of the early intervention services. [34 CFR §§ 303.344(d)(1)(i), 303.344(d)(1)(iii), and 303.344(f)];

Early Intervention Service	
Beginning Date	
Length	
Duration	
Frequency	
Intensity	
Method of Delivery	
Location	

<u>Natural environment</u>: A statement that each EIS is provided in the natural environment for that child or service to the maximum extent appropriate, or a justification as to why an early intervention service will not be provided in the natural environment, consistent with 34 CFR §§ 303.13(a)(8), 303.26, and 303.126. [34 CFR §§ 303.344(d)(1)(ii)(A) and (B)]

Early Intervention Service	Is the EIS provided in the natural environment for that child or service to the maximum extent appropriate?	If an EIS is not provided in the natural environment, the justification for that determination, made by the IFSP team, based on the child's outcomes

<u>Educational component</u>: For children who are at least three years of age, a statement of the educational component that promotes school readiness and incorporates pre-literacy, language, and numeracy skills. [34 CFR § 303.344(d)(4)]

Other services: To the extent appropriate, with regard to medical and other services:

- Identification of those services that the child and family needs or is receiving through other sources, but that are neither required nor funded under Part C. [34 CFR § 303.344(e)(1)]

- If those services are not currently being provided, a description of the steps the service coordinator or family may take to assist the child and family in securing those other services. [34 CFR § 303.344(e)(2)]

Payment Arrangements: Payment Arrangements, and identification of potential funding sources. [34 CFR §§ 303.34(b)(9) and 303.344(d)(1)(iv)]

Early Intervention Service	Payment Arrangements (Identify potential funding sources)

TRANSITION FROM PART C SERVICES

Not fewer than 90 days, and, at the discretion of all parties (including the parent), not more than 9 months before the toddler's third birthday, the IFSP must also set out a transition plan, including the steps and services to be taken to support the smooth transition of the toddler with a disability at age three, or as the child exits the program, in accordance with 34 CFR §§ 303.209 and 303.211(b)(6). [34 CFR §§ 303.209(d)(2) and 303.344(h)(1)] The family of the toddler must be included in the development of the transition plan. [34 CFR § 303.209(d)(1)(ii)] The IFSP transition content must include:

- Transition services: Identification of transition services and other activities that the IFSP team determines are necessary to support the transition of the child. [34 CFR §§ 303.209(d)(3)(ii) and 303.344(h)(2)(iv)]

- Transition steps:
    - Discussions with, and training of, parents, as appropriate, regarding future placements and other matters related to the child's transition. [34 CFR § 303.344(h)(2)(i)]

    - Procedures to prepare the child for a change in service delivery, including steps to help the child adjust to, and function in, a new setting, and to exit from the Part C program. [34 CFR §§ 303.209(d)(3)(i) and 303.344(h)(2)(ii)]. Confirmation that child find information about the child has been transmitted to the LEA or other relevant agency, in accordance with 34 CFR § 303.209(b) (and any policy adopted by the State under 34 CFR § 303.401(e)) and, with parental consent if required under 34 CFR § 303.414, transmission of additional information needed by the LEA to ensure continuity of services from the Part C program to the Part B program, including a copy of the most recent evaluation and assessments of the child and the family and most recent IFSP developed in accordance with 34 CFR §§ 303.340 through 303.345. [34 CFR § 303.344(h)(2)(iii)]

- Program options: Review of program options for the toddler with a disability for the period from the toddler's third birthday through the remainder of the school year. [34 CFR § 303.209(d)(1)(i)]

§ 2.6 EARLY INTERVENTION SERVICES

Early intervention services for an eligible child and their family may commence before the completion of the evaluation and assessments if parental consent is obtained, an interim IFSP is developed, and evaluations and assessments are completed within the 45-day timeline. 34 C.F.R. § 303.345.

They are developmental services that (1) are provided under public supervision, (2) are selected in collaboration with the parents, (3) are provided at no cost, except, where federal and state law permit a schedule of sliding fees, (4) are designed to meet the developmental needs of the child and the needs of the family in areas such as physical development, cognitive development, communication development, social or emotional development, or adaptive development, (5) are provided by qualified personnel, and (6) to the maximum extent appropriate, are provided in natural environments. 34 C.F.R. § 303.13(a).

Early intervention services may include (1) assistive technology devices and services, (2) audiology services, (3) family training, counseling and home visits, (4) health services, (5) medical services provided by a licensed physician for diagnostic or evaluation purposes to determine a child's developmental status and need for early intervention services, (6) nursing services, (7) nutrition services, (8) occupational therapy, (9) physical therapy, (10) psychological services, (11) service coordination services, (12) sign language and cued language services, (13) social work services, (14) special instruction, (15) speech-language pathology services, (16) transportation and related costs to enable a child to receive early intervention services, and (17) vision services.

The identification of services must be "based on peer-reviewed research, to the extent practicable, necessary to meet the unique needs of the infant or toddler and the family, including the frequency, intensity, and method of delivering services." 20 U.S.C. § 1436(d)(4).

An issue that can arise in the provision of services is the level of services that the state is obligated to fund. For example, in *Adams v. Oregon*, 195 F.3d 1141 (9th Cir. 1999), the parents and the state disagreed on the amount of services that should be provided to the Adams' son Lucas, who had autism. Lucas' parents wanted their son to be enrolled in a full-time Lovaas program, which is a very intensive, full-day, one-on-one program that breaks tasks down into simple subunits to shape new skills.

The school district argued that Lucas could not tolerate such an intensive program due to his young age, and that 12.5 hours of instruction per week was sufficient. Further, the school district only agreed to provide 7.5 hours per week of services in the summer rather than the 12.5 hours they provided during the school year. Their justification for the reduction was to accommodate staff summer vacation plans. *Id.* at 1144.

The Ninth Circuit said that the legal issue was *not* "whether the IFSP was adequate in light of Lucas' progress" but instead was "whether the IFSP was appropriately designed and implemented so as to convey Lucas with a meaningful benefit." *Id.* at 1149. It also noted that the statute does "not require potential maximizing services." *Id.* at 1150. The Hearing Officer found, and the Ninth Circuit affirmed, that the school-year program met this "meaningful benefit" test given Lucas' age and lack of tolerance for a full-day program. *Id.* at 1150. Nonetheless, the Ninth Circuit found that the summer IFSP plan was not adequate because the reduction in services was "not linked to Lucas' unique developmental needs." *Id.* at 1151. The Ninth Circuit ordered a remand to determine the appropriate level of reimbursement for summer programming.

Although it can be difficult to demonstrate that the services offered under an IFSP are inadequate, it is sometimes possible to argue that the proposed services were pre-determined by the state and did not reflect actual consideration of the child's individual needs. That strategy was successful in *Young v. State,* 2013 WL 146365 (S.D. Ohio Jan. 14, 2013). The plaintiffs bringing suit in the case were parents of a child with moderate to severe autism. The treating professionals recommended that the child, R.Y., receive Applied Behavioral Analysis (ABA) programming. The state allegedly informed the parents that it did not provide ABA therapy because there were no approved providers in their area. *Id.* at *8. The district court granted a temporary restraining order in favor of the plaintiffs, ordering the parties to immediately develop a plan to provide at least 40 hours of ABA services to R.Y. or reimburse the parents for their payments to a provider. *Id.* at *32. Like in *Adam,* the state could not offer an argument that was based on the individualized need of the child.

§ 2.7 PAYMENT FOR EARLY INTERVENTION SERVICES

Early intervention services "are provided at no cost except where Federal or State law provides for a system of payments by families, including a schedule of sliding fees." 20 U.S.C. § 1432(4)(B). Each state sets its eligibility rules for funding subject to this guidance.

For example, the District of Columbia had enacted a sliding fee scale governing payments for certain early intervention services, stating that a family with income of 200 percent above the federal poverty guidelines would be required to pay a percentage of the cost for early intervention services. *See* D.C. Mun. Regs. Tit. 22-B, § 3028.7. For families above the state's cut-off, these expenses can be substantial. Andrew Quinn and Jill Colgan, for example, had a child who required night nursing services. If the cost of those services ($71,430) were deducted from their annual income to determine their eligibility for paid early intervention services, they would have qualified for full payment. But if those monies were not subtracted from their annual income for eligibility purposes, then they were responsible for payment of the full amount. Even though the District initially made a miscalculation and informed them they would be fully reimbursed, the district court affirmed the determination by the Hearing Officer that the District was not responsible for the entire cost of those services. *See Quinn v. District of Columbia,* 740 F. Supp.2d 112 (D.D.C. 2010).

Some families get assistance with early intervention services through the federal Early and Periodic Screening, Diagnosis and Treatment (EPSDT) program as well as the Medicaid Home and Community Based Services (HCBS) Waivers program. *See generally* 42 U.S.C. § 1396d. The EPSDT program provides comprehensive and preventive health care services for children under age 21 who are enrolled in Medicaid. EPSDT services are supposed to cover: screening services, vision services, dental services, hearing services, other necessary health care services, diagnostic services, and treatment. Developmental and behavioral screenings, which include appropriate immunizations, is required for children enrolled in Medicaid as well as children enrolled in the Children's Health Insurance Program (CHIP). (CHIP services are typically available for children whose family earns up to 200 percent of the federal poverty level so it covers some children not covered by EPSDT.) The treatment covered by EPSDT is supposed to apply to all physical and mental illnesses or conditions discovered by any screening and diagnostic procedures. State Medicaid agencies are required to inform all Medicaid-eligible individuals under age 21 that EPSDT services are available and that they cover age-appropriate immunizations; provide or arrange for the provision of screening services for all children; arrange (directly or through referral) for corrective treatment as determined by child health screenings; and report EPSDT performance information annually to the federal government.

Home and community-based services (HCBS) provide opportunities for Medicaid beneficiaries to receive services in their home or community rather than in institutions or other isolated settings. These programs serve a variety of targeted population groups, such as people with intellectual or developmental disabilities, physical disabilities, or mental illness. The Affordable Care Act has also provided states with the flexibility to expand the group of individuals eligible for Medicaid services to include those who earn 133 percent of the federal poverty level. (The continuation of that program is not known at this time.) These programs are administered at the state level so it is important to check a state's website to gather information at the state level on these particular programs.

§ 2.8 PROCEDURAL SAFEGUARDS AND DISPUTE RESOLUTION

Each state must have a comprehensive Child Find system, which includes a system for making referrals to lead agencies or Early Intervention Service (EIS) providers and ensuring rigorous standards to appropriately identify infants and toddlers with disabilities for early intervention services. To facilitate the identification of funding sources and service providers, the regulations require that each state lead agency coordinates its efforts with programs under the Maternal and Child Health Program, EPSDT, the Developmental Disabilities Assistance and Bill of Rights Act of 2000, the Head Start Act, the Supplemental Security Income Program under the Social Security Act, child protection and child welfare programs, childcare programs, the Family Violence Prevention and Services Act, Early Hearing Detection and

Intervention systems, and the Children's Health Insurance Program (CHIP).

Other than situations where there have been exceptional family circumstances, the initial IFSP meeting must be completed within 45 days from the date the lead agency or EIS provider receives the referral of the child. A review of the IFSP must occur every six months, and no single procedure may be used as the sole criterion for determining a child's eligibility. If the lead agency determines that a child is not eligible to receive an IFSP, then the agency must provide the parent with written notice explaining the reasons for the denial, and also provide information about how to dispute the eligibility determination through processes such as mediation, state complaint procedures, or a due process hearing. *See* 34 C.F.R. § 303.430.

Each participating agency must permit parents (or their surrogates) to inspect and review any early intervention records relating to their children that are collected, maintained, or used by the agency. A parent who believes that such records include inaccurate or misleading information or violate the privacy or other rights of the child may request that the participating agency amend the information. If the participating agency refuses to amend the information, then the parent may seek a hearing under 34 C.F.R. § 303.411.

If the lead agency seeks to propose or refuse the identification, evaluation, or placement of a child, then it must give the parent prior written notice within a reasonable time before such an action is taken. The written notice must describe the action being proposed or refused, the reasons for taking the action, and the available procedural safeguards to challenge that action.

Each lead agency must ensure that mediation procedures are available with the state bearing the cost of mediation. 34 C.F.R. § 303.431. The lead agency must select an impartial mediator on a random, rotational, or other impartial basis. If the parties resolve a dispute through mediation, they must execute a legally binding, confidential agreement, which is enforceable in court. When the parties enter into such an agreement, they waive their right to bring a due process complaint about the issue.

The lead agency must also adopt written complaint procedures for an organization or individual to file a signed written complaint, raising issues that occurred no more than a year ago. 34 C.F.R. § 303.432, § 303.434. If there is a failure to provide appropriate services, then a corrective action plan must be put in place and appropriate services must be provided in the future. When a complaint is filed, the lead agency must complete its investigation within 60 days. 34 C.F.R. § 303.433. That investigation can include an on-site investigation, an opportunity for the complainant to provide additional information, and an opportunity for the other entity to respond to the complaint. If a party files a written complaint, which is also the subject of a due process hearing, then the State must set aside any part of the written complaint that is being addressed in the due process hearing until the conclusion of the hearing.

Further, the lead agency must ensure that the parents of a child covered by Part C of the IDEA are afforded the right to participate in a due process hearing. 34 C.F.R. § 303.436. The statute of limitations for a due process hearing is two years (different than the one year statute of limitations for the complaint process). 34 C.F.R. § 303.440.

Within 15 days of receiving notice of the parent's due process complaint, the lead agency must convene a resolution meeting between the parent, a representative of the lead agency, and the relevant members of the IFSP team to discuss the facts that form the basis of the due process complaint *unless*:

(1) the parent and lead agency agree in writing to waive the meeting; or

(2) the parent and lead agency agree to use the mediation process.

The resolution meeting can only be waived or the mediation process used if *both* the parent and the lead agency agree to those modifications. In the absence of those two exceptions, it is expected that a resolution meeting will be held. If the parent refuses to participate in a resolution meeting, the lead agency may request that the Hearing Officer dismiss the parent's due process complaint. If the lead agency fails to hold a resolution meeting, the parent may seek the intervention of a Hearing Officer to begin the due process timeline. 34 C.F.R. § 303.442(b)(5).

In general, a due process hearing should be held within 30 days of a parent filing a due process complaint. A decision should then be rendered no later than 30 or 45 days after the expiration of that 30-day period. 34 C.F.R. § 303.447. Each party has 90 days from the date of the decision of the Hearing Officer to decide to file a civil action in order to appeal the administrative decision.

Due process hearings can be brought on procedural or substantive grounds. When a case is brought on procedural and not substantive grounds, the Hearing Officer can only find that a child was not appropriately identified, evaluated, placed, or provided with early intervention services if the procedural inadequacies:

> (i) Impeded the child's right to identification, evaluation, and placement or provision of early intervention services for the child and that child's family under part C of the Act;
>
> (ii) Significantly impeded the parent's opportunity to participate in the decision-making process regarding identification, evaluation, placement or provision of early intervention services for the child and that child's family under part C of the Act; or
>
> (iii) Caused a deprivation of educational or developmental benefit.

34 C.F.R. § 303.445(a)(2).

A mere procedural error, therefore, does not necessarily entitle the child and their family to relief.

§ 2.9 STAY PUT RULES & TRANSITION TO SCHOOL-AGE RULES

Part C was added to the IDEA in 1986 to provide services for children with disabilities beginning at birth. In 1991, Congress added a provision to the IDEA, which has been subsequently amended, and currently requires the state to provide a "smooth and effective" transition from Part C's early intervention services to Part B's preschool special education programs. 20 U.S.C. § 1412(a)(9). In order for this transition to be seamless, it is supposed to begin no less than 90 days prior to the child's third birthday, include a continuity of services from Part C to Part B, and involve Part B personnel. *See* 34 C.F.R. § 303.209. If the lead agency determines that a child covered under Part C is not eligible for Part B services, then the lead agency must make "reasonable efforts to convene a conference among the lead agency, the family, and providers of other appropriate services for the toddler to discuss appropriate services that the toddler may receive." 34 C.F.R. § 303.209(c).

Part C of the IDEA also has what is called a "stay put" proceeding that governs how services are handled when there is a dispute between the parent and the state agency regarding the provision of services. That rule states:

> During the pendency of any proceeding or action involving a complaint by the parents of an infant or toddler with a disability, unless the State agency and the parents otherwise agree, the infant or toddler shall continue to receive the appropriate early intervention services currently being provided or, if applying for initial services, shall receive the services not in dispute.

20 U.S.C. § 1439(b).

That statutory provision, however, does not explicitly deal with the issue of whether an IFSP stays in effect when there is a dispute as a child transitions from Part C to Part B. On the one hand, the transition is supposed to be "smooth and effective." On the other hand, the services provided under Part B are quite different from the services provided under Part C. Unlike Part B services, Part C services can include services to the family, will typically occur in natural environments (rather than in schools), and will usually involve a service coordinator who coordinates services among multiple agencies. Finally, unlike Part B services, Part C services are not necessarily free. Nonetheless, the IDEA does provide that a state can choose to continue an IFSP (Part C services) after a child's third birthday if it is "consistent with State policy" and "agreed to by the agency and the child's parents." 20 U.S.C. § 1412(a)(9).

The courts were split on whether Part C services continued while parents and school districts disagreed about the content of the Part B plan. In 2005, the Third Circuit ruled that the "stay put" provision should be interpreted to require continuation of Part C services while the parties disputed thc proposed Part B plan. *See Pardini v. Allegheny Intermediate Unit*, 420 F.3d 181 (3rd Cir. 2005). In ruling that the Part C plan should continue during the pendency of the Part B dispute, the court stressed Congress' emphasis on the need for a "seamless" transition from birth to age five. *Id.* at 191. While recognizing that Part B services can be quite different from Part C services, the court found it was consistent with Congress' intent to continue those services merely during the pendency of a transition dispute.

In 2007, the Eleventh Circuit reached the opposite conclusion. *See D.P. v. School Board of Broward County*, 483 F.3d 725 (11th Cir. 2007). The Eleventh Circuit emphasized the stay put provision that exists under Part B of the IDEA, not the stay put provision governing Part C (which was quoted above in *Pardini*). Part B's stay put rule provides:

> Except as provided in subsection (k)(4), during the pendency of any proceedings conducted pursuant to this section, unless the State or local educational agency and the parents otherwise agree, the child shall remain in the then-current educational placement of the child, or, if applying for initial admission to a public school, shall, with the consent of the parents, be placed in the public school program until all such proceedings have been completed.

20 U.S.C. § 1415(j).

The Eleventh Circuit interpreted the "or" clause to mean that a child *should* be placed in the regular public school program if a dispute exists concerning a child's initial IEP. Circuit Judge Rosemary Barkett dissented, finding the majority's conclusion in *D.P.* to be inconsistent with Congress' intentions. Because Congress emphasized the importance of continuity of services, Judge Barkett said that "it would be absurd to apply the 'stay put' provision in a manner that reaches the completely opposite result: the *withdrawal* of existing services to a disabled child when she reaches school age." *D.P.*, 483 F.3d at 732 (Barkett, C.J. dissenting). She also thought it made no sense to allow, as did the majority opinion, the school district merely to comply with the IDEA (when there was a dispute) by placing the children in the regular educational program (with no supports whatsoever.) The plaintiffs in *D.P.* were triplets, who were autistic, and needed an intensive level of intervention services. Judge Barkett thought it was impermissible to allow the school district to satisfy its statutory obligation by merely placing them in a public school classroom.

Although Congress has not amended the IDEA since this split occurred between the Third and Eleventh Circuits, the governing regulations support the view taken by the Eleventh Circuit. Subsection (c) reads:

> If the complaint involves an application for initial services under this part from a child who is transitioning from Part C of the Act to Part B and is no longer eligible for Part C services because the child has turned three, the public agency is not required to provide the Part C services that the child had been receiving. If the child is found eligible for special education and related services under Part B and the parent consents to the initial provision of special education and related services under § 300.300(b), then the public agency must provide those special education and related services that are not in dispute between the parent and the public agency.

34 C.F.R. § 300.518(c).

Other circuits have not considered this issue, but a New York district court has agreed with the Eleventh Circuit, finding that an IFSP is not in effect while a parent contests the child's first IEP under Part B of the IDEA. *See M.M. & H.M. v. New York City Department of Education*, 583 F. Supp.2d 498 (S.D. N.Y. 2008).

Given the Eleventh Circuit decision and the Department of Education regulation, what can a parent do who disagrees with the services provided under an initial IEP? If the parents believe that the IEP proposed by the school district does not provide a Free and Appropriate Public Education (FAPE) as required by Part B of the IDEA, they can choose to reject that IEP and pay for their child to receive what they consider to be appropriate services. They can then seek a due process hearing to determine that the proposed IEP is inappropriate, that their privately-paid services are appropriate, and that they are entitled to reimbursement for their purchase of those services. Although that option is expensive, the Eleventh Circuit recognizes that route is the only viable option for parents who reject an initial IEP and want their child to receive acceptable services during the pendency of their complaint. *See D.P.*, 483 F.3d at 730 n.1.

Further, it is important to recognize that parents cannot expect to have the family-based services provided by an IFSP continue when Part B of the IDEA covers a child. A good example of that rule is the Southern District of New York's decision in *M.M. and H.M. v. New York City Department of Education,* 583 F. Supp.2d 498 (S.D. N.Y. 2008). In this case, a child with autism had received a very supportive IFSP, which included 30 hours per week of 1:1 Applied Behavior Analysis (ABA) therapy, occupational therapy, speech and language therapy, physical therapy and parent training. *Id.* at 501. When the child transitioned to preschool under IDEA Part B, the school district proposed 25 hours per week of instruction in a classroom with 8 students, 1 teacher, and 2 paraprofessionals. The parents rejected this placement and, instead, paid for their child to attend the McCarton School, a private placement, where she would continue to receive 1:1 instruction, using an instructional methodology designed for children with autism. *See* http://mccartonfoundation.org/education (describing the instructional methodology).

In *M.M. and H.M.*, the school district discontinued all IFSP services when the parents chose the private placement even though state law permitted the state to pay for those services for another few months. *Id.* at 513. The parents essentially paid for the continuation of the IFSP services on a private basis while they litigated the adequacy of the IEP proposed by the school district. They argued that, even if they failed to demonstrate that the district's proposed plan did not meet the standards required by Part B of the IDEA, they should be entitled to reimbursement for services during the litigation process as part of the "stay put" rules.

Agreeing with the Eleventh Circuit, the district court in *M.M. and H.M.* refused to provide such reimbursement. Further, because the standard for evaluating the adequacy of an IEP is fairly minimal (as will be discussed later in *Nutshell* Chapter 6), the parents also lost their request for reimbursement for the cost of sending their child to a private placement. Thus, a parent's attempt to maintain IFSP-level services under an IEP can be very expensive and unsuccessful. An advocate therefore should advise parents who are transitioning from an IFSP to an IEP not to expect the same level of services and not to expect the continuation of an IFSP while they challenge the adequacy of an IEP.

An important practice tip when representing a child who is transitioning from an IFSP to an IEP is to check state rules with regard to continuation of an IFSP past a child's third birthday. New York law, for example, provides for an IFSP to continue until September 1st of the calendar year if the child turns three before August 31st, and for an IFSP to continue until January 2nd of the following calendar year if the child turns three after September 1st. While a few months of intensive services under an IFSP may not be what the parents prefer for their child, that option is certainly one of which they should be made aware.

CHAPTER 3
IDEA PART B ELIGIBILITY

§ 3.1 INTRODUCTION

The IDEA is a complicated funding statute under which Congress allocates money to states that, in turn, pass the money on to school districts to educate students with disabilities. The amount of money that a state gets is based on a complicated formula that considers their disability-count in 1997, the growth in the school-age population since 1999, and the percentage of children in poverty. States then develop their own formulas for how to send that money to school districts. The 2004 Amendment to the IDEA allows a school district to use up to 15 percent of its federal IDEA dollars to children who need academic or behavioral support, but have not necessarily been classified as disabled under the IDEA. For an excellent discussion of the eligibility rules, *see* Mark C. Weber, *The IDEA Eligibility Mess*, 57 BUFF. L. REV. 83 (2009).

The bottom line is that Congress has never allocated money to the states to cover even half of the expense of providing special education and related services to children with disabilities. Arguably, school districts have an incentive not to classify a child as "disabled" in order to avoid having to incur the expense of special education and related services. On the other hand, if they want children to be successful, they may want to classify a child as disabled to take advantage of whatever resources are available. Nonetheless, some people argue that school districts are too eager to classify children as "disabled" as an excuse to remove them from the regular classroom and put them in a substandard, segregated, special education classroom or institution. These controversies are worth noting to understand the various dynamics that may underlie a school district's recommendation for a student's disability classification.

In order for a student to be entitled to special education and related services, the student must meet the IDEA's definition of a "child with a disability." That definition provides:

> (A) In general
>
> The term "child with a disability" means a child—
>
> (i) with intellectual disabilities, hearing impairments (including deafness), speech or language impairments, visual impairments (including blindness), serious emotional disturbance (referred to in this chapter as "emotional disturbance"), orthopedic impairments, autism, traumatic brain injury, other health impairments, or specific learning disabilities; and
>
> (ii) who, by reason thereof, needs special education and related services.

20 U.S.C. § 1401(3).

Section 504 and the Americans with Disabilities Act have a different definition of disability that will be discussed in *Nutshell* Chapter 4.

§ 3.2 "NEEDS" SPECIAL EDUCATION AND RELATED SERVICES

Notice that the statute requires that a child *also* must need special education and related services to qualify as disabled. It is not sufficient to just be in one of the disability categories. The courts are not clear what it means to "need" special education and related services but that rule is part of the statutory definition of a "child with a disability." Some courts have made it clear that it is important to look at the entire academic setting to determine whether the "need" rule can be met. A child with an autism spectrum disorder, for example, may be performing at an average level in core academic courses but have a disability that is affecting his or her social functioning during the school day. *See Mr. I v. Maine School Administrative Dist. 55*, 416 F. Supp.2d 147 (D. Maine 2006). Nonetheless, the Second Circuit ruled that it is appropriate not to consider a child with an emotional-behavior disability as covered by the IDEA when the child had superior intellectual aptitude and performed at or above grade level. While recognizing that the child had "difficulty with interpersonal relationships and negative feelings," the court found that the parents had not demonstrated an adverse educational effect, which is necessary for IDEA eligibility. *J.D. ex rel. J.D. v. Pawlet School Dist.*, 224 F.3d 60, 68 (2nd Cir. 2000).

A recent case that does a good job explaining the meaning of the "need" requirement is *L.J. v. Pittsburg Unified School District*, 850 F.3d 996 (9th

Cir. 2017). In this case, a child with a number of disabilities, including emotional disturbance, was consistently not classified as disabled and not found to "need" special education and related services because he managed to perform at grade level while in school. The school district argued that his emotional disturbance did not have a negative impact on his academic work because his suicide attempts were outside of the school. The Ninth Circuit said:

> That he attempted suicide outside the school environment is immaterial. His emotional disturbance adversely affected his attendance and his teachers all reported that L.J.'s classroom absences, due to psychiatric hospitalizations, hurt his academic performance. To distinguish between where a student attempted suicide—between home and school—misses the point. The point being that whether having a suicidal ideation and attempting suicide interfered with L.J.'s education.

Id. at 1006.

Further, the school district argued that he did not "need" special education and related services because he was being academically successful in a regular classroom environment. The school had provided the student with mental health counseling, a one-on-one paraeducator, and a behavior service plan even though he wasn't on an IEP. The parent had argued that she was entitled to have such services put in writing on a permanent basis through an IEP rather than rely on the school district's voluntary offerings of such services that are not typically provided to general education students. The Ninth Circuit agreed with the parent. It found that it was incorrect to say that the child was learning adequately without special education and related services when the student was, in fact, receiving services that are typically limited to students with disabilities. The Ninth Circuit, also, did not even acknowledge that mere average performance, without specialized instruction, precludes a child from being classified as disabled under the IDEA. It said: "L.J. has shown himself to be an intelligent child, so his academic performance could have been even more improved with the appropriate specially designed instruction." *Id.* at 1006.

The question of whether a child "needs" special education and related services, and is therefore entitled to an IEP is different than the question of whether the IEP, itself, meets the requirements of providing the child with an "appropriate" Individualized Education Program. That issue will be discussed in Nutshell Chapter 6.

§ 3.3 PART (A) REGULATORY DEFINITIONS: OVERVIEW

For each of the ten disability categories mentioned in Part (A), the regulations provide a more specific definition. In some cases, it divides one of the categories mentioned in Part (A) into subcategories.

This table reflects a snapshot of the use of the most common disability categories over time:

Table 1: Percentage of Children in Disability Category Per Year

Type of Disability	Autism	Emotional Disturbance	Intellectual Disability	Other Health Impairments	Specific Learning Disability	Speech or Language Impairment
1976–77	—	7.7	26.0	3.8	21.5	35.2
1980–81	—	8.4	20.0	2.4	35.3	28.2
1990–91	—	8.3	11.3	1.2	45.2	20.9
2000–01	1.5	7.6	9.9	4.8	45.4	22.0
2005–06	3.3	7.1	8.3	8.5	40.8	21.8
2007–08	4.5	6.7	7.6	9.7	38.9	22.0
2010–11	6.5	6.1	7.0	11.1	36.7	21.7
2012–13	7.8	5.6	6.7	12.1	35.4	21.1
2013–14	8.3	5.5	6.6	12.6	35	20.6

At the present time, the most commonly used disability classifications are specific learning disability, speech or language impairment, and other health impairment. The autism category has shown a significant increase in classification over time, while the intellectual category has shown a significant decrease in classification over time.

§ 3.4 DISABILITY CATEGORIES

A. AUTISM

(i) Autism means a developmental disability significantly affecting verbal and nonverbal communication and social interaction, generally evident before age three, that

> adversely affects a child's educational performance. Other characteristics often associated with autism are engagement in repetitive activities and stereotyped movements, resistance to environmental change or change in daily routines, and unusual responses to sensory experiences.
>
> (ii) Autism does not apply if a child's educational performance is adversely affected primarily because the child has an emotional disturbance, as defined in paragraph (c)(4) of this section.
>
> (iii) A child who manifests the characteristics of autism after age three could be identified as having autism if the criteria listed in paragraph (c)(1)(i) of this section are satisfied.

34 C.F.R. § 300.8(c)(1).

The AMERICAN PSYCHIATRIC ASSOCIATION DIAGNOSTIC AND STATISTICAL MANUAL OF MENTAL DISORDERS, FIFTH EDITION (2013) [DSM-5] now defines autism as "autism spectrum disorder." The term "Asperger's" is no longer used to describe people who have autism and are high functioning. Instead, the DSM-5 suggests that they would be listed as being on the autism spectrum. The DSM-5 also cautions that, "individuals who have marked deficits in social communication, but whose symptoms do not otherwise meet criteria for autism spectrum disorder, should be evaluated for social (pragmatic) communication disorder." DSM-5 at 51.

According to the DSM-5, the two essential features of autism spectrum disorder are:

> (1) Persistent deficits in social communication and social interaction across multiple contexts, as manifested by [deficits in]:
>
> (a) social-emotional reciprocity,
>
> (b) nonverbal communicative behaviors,
>
> (c) developing, maintaining, and understanding relationships, and
>
> (2) Restricted, repetitive patterns of behavior, interests, or activities, as manifested by deficits in:
>
> (a) stereotyped or repetitive motor movements, use of objects, or speech
>
> (b) insistence on sameness, inflexible adherence to routines, or ritualized patterns of verbal or nonverbal behavior
>
> (c) highly restricted, fixated interests that are abnormal in intensity or focus
>
> (d) hyper- or hyporeactivity to sensory input or unusual interests in sensory aspects of the environment.

See DSM-5 at 50–51.

It is also expected that symptoms of autism spectrum disorder are present in the early developmental period and cause clinically significant impairment in social, occupational, or other important areas of functioning.

B. DEVELOPMENTAL DELAY

Congress amended the IDEA in 1997 to provide states with flexibility to use the "developmental delay" category (defined below) in order to include children through the age of 9 under IDEA Part B.

> Child aged 3 through 9
>
> The term "child with a disability" for a child aged 3 through 9 (or any subset of that age range, including ages 3 through 5), may, at the discretion of the State and the local educational agency, include a child—
>
> (i) experiencing developmental delays, as defined by the State and as measured by appropriate diagnostic instruments and procedures, in 1 or more of the following areas: physical development; cognitive development; communication development; social or emotional development; or adaptive development; and
>
> (ii) who, by reason thereof, needs special education and related services.

20 U.S.C. § 1401(3)(B).

Thus, all students between the ages of 3 and 21 can qualify for special education and related services under the IDEA if they meet the definition set forth in 20 U.S.C. § 1401(3)(A). Further, states have the discretion to qualify students for special education and related services from ages 3 to 9 by meeting a broader definition of disability under 20 U.S.C. § 1401(3)(B). Most states take advantage of this opportunity for students between the age of 3 and 5 but, once they enter kindergarten, they are usually required to meet the more stringent definition of disability under 20 U.S.C. § 1401(3)(A) to receive special education and related services.

At the present time, approximately 30 states extend the age range for developmental delay beyond age 5 with 15 states extending the age range to age 9 (MS, AZ, GA, ID, IL, KS, MD, MA, NH, ND, SC, TN, IA, and WY) and 10 states extending the age range to age 8 (NE, AL, AK, DE, HI, KY, LA, OK, RI, and WA). Those rules, however, are fluid and should be confirmed at the state level. For an excellent discussion of state rules, *see* Joan Danaher, *nectac Notes no. 27, Eligibility policies and practices for young children under Part B of IDEA,* January 2011 (The National Early Childhood Technical Assistance Center).

Even if states use this flexibility, there is the important question of how they define "developmental delay." Most states use some kind of quantitative criteria for determining whether there is a "developmental delay" in one of the following developmental measures: physical development; cognitive development; communication development; social or emotional development; or adaptive development. The most common rule is one in which the child is at least 2.0 standard deviations below the mean on one developmental measure or at least 1.5 standard deviations below the mean in at least two developmental measures.

When states permit quantitative criteria, they sometimes also allow professional judgment to be used in lieu of quantitative criteria. For example, Connecticut allows a child to be classified as having a "developmental delay" if there is a 2 standard deviation discrepancy in one area, a 1.5 standard deviation discrepancy in two areas *or* "informed clinical opinion of multidisciplinary team, with written documentation when standardized instrument is not appropriate and/or child requires significant adaptation to perform on a standardized instrument." Similarly, Colorado provides that classification in the "developmental delay" category can occur if the child has a 1.5 standard deviation discrepancy in one area *or* "[h]as identifiable condition known through empirical data to be associated with significant delays in development or [i]nformed opinion of assessment team including the parent(s) with documentation of the rationale for the inability to obtain a standardized score." *Id.* at 9. It can be quite difficult to run norm-referenced tests on young children, especially if they are not verbal for example.

The "developmental delay" category is typically used only for preschool children; thus, it is important for parents and others to understand that the rules will become tighter when the child ages out of that category. The policy behind the developmental delay category is that it is sometimes hard to have a diagnosis for why, for example, a young child may not be verbal. Is there a hearing impairment, language impairment, autism, or a mental health impairment, which is causing the child not to speak? The developmental delay category allows the school district and parent to have flexibility until the reason for the delay can be understood. By age 9, however, in all states, there needs to be a more refined classification in order for the child to continue to be classified as disabled for IDEA purposes.

C. EMOTIONAL DISTURBANCE

> (i) Emotional disturbance means a condition exhibiting one or more of the following characteristics over a long period of time and to a marked degree that adversely affects a child's educational performance:
>
> (A) An inability to learn that cannot be explained by intellectual, sensory, or health factors.
>
> (B) An inability to build or maintain satisfactory interpersonal relationships with peers and teachers.
>
> (C) Inappropriate types of behavior or feelings under normal circumstances.
>
> (D) A general pervasive mood of unhappiness or depression.
>
> (E) A tendency to develop physical symptoms or fears associated with personal or school problems.
>
> (ii) Emotional disturbance includes schizophrenia. The term does not apply to children who are socially maladjusted, unless it is determined that they have an emotional

> disturbance under paragraph (c)(4)(i) of this section.

34 C.F.R. § 300.8(c)(4).

The term "emotional disorder" is an umbrella category for many different kinds of disorders. The DSM-5, for example, includes various disorders such as bipolar disorders, depressive disorders, anxiety disorders, obsessive-compulsive disorders, trauma and stressor-related disorders, dissociative disorders, somatic symptom and related disorders, feeding and eating disorders, elimination disorders, and sleep-wake disorders. This is an example where the IDEA uses a term that is not a genuine diagnostic category.

One confusing aspect of this definition is the exclusion for children who are "socially maladjusted." On the one hand, the regulation says a child can have an emotional disorder when the child engages in "inappropriate types of behaviors" yet it also says a child cannot be classified as having an emotional disorder merely because they are "socially maladjusted." In determining whether that rule applies, courts have often looked at whether the child engaged in inappropriate behavior such as drug use or truancy. There is no consistency with how courts apply the "socially maladjusted" rule so it is difficult to predict its application. The Eighth Circuit concluded that the "socially maladjusted" rule did not apply to a case involving a girl who used alcohol and drugs, *see Independent School District No. 284 v. A.C.*, 258 F.3d 769 (8th Cir. 2001) but the Fourth Circuit found the socially maladjusted rule did apply on similar facts. *See Springer v. Fairfax County School Board*, 134 F.3d 659 (4th Cir. 1998).

The example of Tiffiney Johnson can reflect how difficult it can be for school districts, Hearing Officers, and courts to distinguish between a child who is "socially maladjusted" and one who is "emotionally disturbed." Tiffiney's parents requested that the local school district classify her as disabled after she was expelled from a private school in eighth grade. *See Johnson v. Metro Davidson County School System*, 108 F. Supp.2d 906 (M.D. Tenn. 2000). She had numerous evaluations and there was some evidence she had ADHD and oppositional-defiance disorder as well as what was called a "parent/child" problem. One expert said that Tiffiney was likely a sociopath. During the course of the time period while the school district evaluated Tiffiney, she was expelled from a second private school. The dispute among the experts seemed to revolve around how much to blame the parents or Tiffiney for her inappropriate behavior. One expert said that she "did not think that Tiffiney's problems were the result of a dysfunctional family or inadequate parenting; rather the family's problems resulted from Tiffiney's problems." *Id.* at 911. Another expert insisted that Tiffiney's problems stemmed from "social maladjustment" rather than an "emotional disorder." *Id.* at 917. Both the school district and Hearing Officer concluded that Tiffiney did not meet the IDEA's definition of disability and was therefore not entitled to special education and related services.

The district court reversed the Hearing Officer's determination. The judge found that the preponderance of the evidence did indicate that Tiffiney had an underlying "emotional disorder." Moreover, despite the evidence of satisfactory progress when she attended school, her record of expulsion also indicated that "Tiffiney's needs were not accommodated within the regular education system." *Id.* at 918–19. He therefore found that she qualified as a child with a disability and ordered the school district to reimburse the parents for the cost of private education, when they refused to send her to public school in a regular classroom setting with no additional support. By the time the district court ruled on the case, Tiffiney had been admitted to a substance abuse treatment center where she was diagnosed with polysubstance abuse, ADHD, and anxiety disorder, reinforcing the parent's argument that she was a student with a disability. *Id.* at 912.

D. HEARING IMPAIRMENTS

> (3) Deafness means a hearing impairment that is so severe that the child is impaired in processing linguistic information through hearing, with or without amplification, that adversely affects a child's educational performance.
>
> (5) Hearing impairments means an impairment in hearing, whether permanent or

> fluctuating, that adversely affects a child's educational performance but that is not included under the definition of deafness in this section.

34 C.F.R. § 300.8(c).

A hearing disorder that does not fit easily within the "hearing impairment" category is a central auditory processing disorder (CAPD or APD). Children with APD typically have normal levels of hearing but a neurological condition is adversely affecting their ability to process or interpret information. They often have trouble separating language sounds from background noise so it can especially affect them in noisy environments (such as a classroom where there is a lot of background noise). For example, a teacher may say, "tell me how a chair and a couch are alike" and the student with APD may hear, "tell me how a cow and a hair are alike." Audiologists sometimes say that a child with APD may hear a classroom conversation as if he or she is in a car on a highway with the window open and where the announcer is speaking with a strong accent. The student may be able to concentrate and follow a conversation, but he or she may tire easily and likely make many mistakes in his or her listening comprehension.

Although APD may adversely affect a child's classroom performance, school districts sometimes have difficulty knowing how to classify that child's disability for the purpose of the IDEA. Sometimes, such children are classified as having Attention

Deficit Disorder although their underlying challenge is one of listening rather than concentration. Other times, they are classified as having a learning disability because some students with APD have difficulty with reading or language skills. Some school districts will even say the child has a learning disability in "listening" even though that kind of learning disability is not one listed in the DSM-5.

Alternatively, some school districts will label this disorder as a type of hearing impairment because the child fails to hear or comprehend speech in a classroom environment in a way that is comparable to a child who has a hearing loss. Moreover, some school districts may classify the child as having an "other health impairment," (OHI) because of a lack of alertness due to difficulties in hearing. Finally, some school districts will label a child with APD as having a disability for the purposes of Section 504 of the Rehabilitation Act (and provide the child with an auxiliary aid to assist with classroom communication) but not label the child as disabled for the purposes of the IDEA.

This discussion by audiologist Teri James Bellis can be helpful in understanding the difference between APD and other disorders:

> In its very broadest sense, APD refers to how the central nervous system (CNS) uses auditory information. However, the CNS is vast and also is responsible for functions such as memory, attention, and language, among others. To avoid confusing APD with other disorders that

can affect a person's ability to attend, understand, and remember, it is important to emphasize that APD is an auditory deficit that is not the result of other higher-order cognitive, language, or related disorder.

There are many disorders that can affect a person's ability to understand auditory information. For example, individuals with Attention Deficit/Hyperactivity Disorder (ADHD) may well be poor listeners and have difficulty understanding or remembering verbal information; however, their actual neural processing of auditory input in the CNS is intact. Instead, it is the attention deficit that is impeding their ability to access or use the auditory information that is coming in. Similarly, children with autism may have great difficulty with spoken language comprehension. However, it is the higher-order, global deficit known as autism that is the cause of their difficulties, not a specific auditory dysfunction. Finally, although the terms language processing and auditory processing sometimes are used interchangeably, it is critical to understand that they are not the same thing at all.

For many children and adults with these disorders and others—including intellectual disabilities and sensory integration dysfunction—the listening and comprehension difficulties we often see are due to the higher-order, more global or all-encompassing disorder

> and not to any specific deficit in the neural processing of auditory stimuli per se. As such, it is not correct to apply the label APD to these individuals, even if many of their behaviors appear very similar to those associated with APD. In some cases, however, APD may co-exist with ADHD or other disorders. In those cases, only careful and accurate diagnosis can assist in disentangling the relative effects of each.

Teri James Bellis, *Understanding Auditory Processing Disorders in Children,* available at http://www.asha.org/public/hearing/disorders/understand-apd-child.htm.

There is very little case law on auditory processing disorders as a covered disability category, but there was one recent Ninth Circuit case on this issue. *See E.M. v. Pajaro Valley Unified School District Office of Administrative Hearings*, 758 F.3d 1162 (9th Cir. 2014). In that case, the Ninth Circuit concluded that APD could meet the definition of "other health impairment" if there is evidence that the APD could have limited the child's "alertness." *Id.* at 1177. Because of the lack of evidence of that factor in the record, the Ninth Circuit affirmed the lower court holding that the child did not qualify as disabled on that basis. The Ninth Circuit said it was permissible for APD to be covered under the specific learning disability or other health impairment categories. In the Ninth Circuit's view, the fact that the child did not meet the criteria for learning disability did not preclude the school district from being required to consider whether the child was disabled under the OHI category. Thus, the Ninth Circuit's treatment of APD is not entirely consistent with the views of many professionals within the audiology community who think that APD is sometimes confused with ADHD.

E. INTELLECTUAL DISABILITIES

> Intellectual disabilities (or what used to be called "mental retardation") means significantly subaverage general intellectual functioning, existing concurrently with deficits in adaptive behavior and manifested during the developmental period, that adversely affects a child's educational performance.

34 C.F.R. § 300.8(c)(6).

Notice that the IQ score is not the sole determinant of whether a child has an intellectual disability. An IQ under 70 is often considered to be an indicator of an intellectual disability but the American Psychiatric Association notes that "a person with an IQ score above 70 may have such severe adaptive behavior problems in social judgment, social understanding, and other areas of adaptive functioning that the person's actual functioning is comparable to that of individuals with a lower IQ score." DSM-5 at 8.

There must also be evidence of deficits in adaptive behavior in order for a person to have an intellectual disability. The DSM-5 defines deficits in adaptive functioning as including deficits in "communication, social participation, and independent living, across multiple environments, such as home, school, work, and community." *Id.* at 33.

F. MULTIPLE DISABILITIES

> Multiple disabilities means concomitant impairments (such as mental retardation-blindness or mental retardation-orthopedic impairment), the combination of which causes such severe educational needs that they cannot be accommodated in special education programs solely for one of the impairments. Multiple disabilities does not include deaf-blindness.

34 C.F.R. § 300.8(c)(7).

Children in this category could have qualified under one of the other categories, but this category is used as a way to make sure that a broad range of services are provided to the child, rather than a limited provision of services under one disability category. In theory, school districts can list more than one disability category on an IEP, but in practice, school districts often require one primary disability category that is used for eligibility purposes. In that situation, the multiple disabilities category can be a way of signaling that the child has more than one impairment. This category, however, is also limited to students with "severe" disabilities so it may not be the appropriate choice for a child, for example, who has ADHD and a speech/language impairment. In that case, it might make more sense to list the two disability categories individually.

G. OTHER HEALTH IMPAIRMENT

> Other health impairment means having limited strength, vitality, or alertness, including a heightened alertness to environmental stimuli, that results in limited alertness with respect to the educational environment, that—
>
> (i) Is due to chronic or acute health problems such as asthma, attention deficit disorder or attention deficit hyperactivity disorder, diabetes, epilepsy, a heart condition, hemophilia, lead poisoning, leukemia, nephritis, rheumatic fever, sickle cell anemia, and Tourette syndrome; and
>
> (ii) Adversely affects a child's educational performance.

34 C.F.R. § 300.8(c)(9).

The "other health impairment" (OHI) classification is quite broad and can include attention-deficit/hyperactivity disorder (ADHD), diabetes, epilepsy, heart conditions, hemophilia, lead poisoning, leukemia, nephritis, rheumatic fever, sickle cell anemia and Tourette Syndrome. *See* http://www.parentcenterhub.org/repository/specific-disabilities/. Of all of the impairments under OHI, the most common impairment is ADHD.

The DSM-5 lists two types of ADHD: (1) inattention and (2) hyperactivity and impulsivity. A child need not have hyperactivity in order to have Attention-Deficit Disorder. Although it is awkward, that is why the DSM-5 places a slash between Attention-Deficit and Hyperactivity Disorder. One can have an attention-deficit disorder that does not include hyperactivity. Nonetheless, the DSM-5 uses the term "ADHD" to include both kinds of disorders (rather than have a separate term "ADD" for those individuals without hyperactivity).

H. SPECIFIC LEARNING DISABILITY

1. General Considerations

> (i) General. Specific learning disability means a disorder in one or more of the basic psychological processes involved in understanding or in using language, spoken or written, that may manifest itself in the imperfect ability to listen, think, speak, read, write, spell, or to do mathematical calculations, including conditions such as perceptual disabilities, brain injury, minimal brain dysfunction, dyslexia, and developmental aphasia.
>
> (ii) Disorders not included. Specific learning disability does not include learning problems that are primarily the result of visual, hearing, or motor disabilities, of intellectual disability, of emotional disturbance, or of environmental, cultural, or economic disadvantage.

34 C.F.R. § 300.8(c)(10).

The DSM-5 calls this disability a "Specific Learning Disorder" (SLD). One controversial aspect of the DSM-5's definition is that it does not have a separate definition for "dyslexia" although it recognizes that: "*Dyslexia* is an alternative term used to refer to a pattern of learning difficulties characterized by problems with accurate or fluent word recognition, poor decoding, and poor spelling abilities." DSM-5, at 67. Similarly, there was controversy about the DSM-5's failure to list "dyscalculia" as an impairment. As with dyslexia, the DSM-5 notes: "*Dyscalculia* is an alternative term used to refer to a pattern of learning difficulties characterized by problems processing numerical information, learning arithmetic facts, and performing accurate or fluent calculations." DSM-5, at 67.

In response to criticisms that the DSM-5 did not specifically mention the terms dyslexia, dyscalculia, and dysgraphia, the United States Department of Education issued a letter on October 23, 2015 indicating that "there is nothing in the IDEA that would prohibit the use of the terms dyslexia, dyscalculia, and dysgraphia in IDEA evaluation, eligibility determinations, or IEP documents." *See* Michael K. Yudin, *Dear Colleague Guidance on Dyslexia,* U.S. DEP'T OF EDUC. (Oct. 23, 2015) https://www2.ed.gov/policy/speced/guid/idea/memosdcltrs/guidance-on-dyslexia-10-2015.pdf. Rather than use the terms dyslexia, dyscalculia, or dysgraphia, the DSM-5 provides that an individual should be diagnosed with an impairment in reading, written expression, or mathematics.

One controversy with the SLD category is whether a child with high intellectual aptitude can also have a specific learning disability, especially when the student performs overall at or above grade level. Such individuals are sometimes called "gifted-disabled" or "twice-exceptional." The First Circuit recently decided that question in the affirmative in a case involving a girl with a significant impairment in reading fluency who also had strong reading comprehension and very strong overall grades. *See Doe v. Cape Elizabeth School District*, 832 F.3d 69 (1st Cir. 2016). The First Circuit emphasized that the regulations use the word "or" between the various domains in which a student could have a learning disability: (i) Oral expression, (ii) Listening comprehension, (iii) Written expression, (iv) Basic reading skill, (v) Reading fluency skills, (vi) Reading comprehension, (vii) Mathematics calculation, or (viii) Mathematics problem solving. *See* 34 C.F.R. § 300.309(a)(1). A child can have an impairment in reading fluency but not have an impairment in basic reading skills or reading comprehension and be considered to have a learning disability. How a school district should *measure* whether a child has an impairment, like a reading fluency impairment, will be discussed in *Nutshell* Chapter 5.

Further, if a school would conclude that a student, like the child in the *Doe* case, has a fluency impairment, the school district still needs to conclude if the child "needs" special education and related services to be covered by the IDEA. In *Doe*, the "need" question was remanded for further consideration. As discussed in *Nutshell* § 3.2, to be covered by the IDEA a child with a listed disability must also *need* special education and related services to be covered by the IDEA. As the First Circuit noted in *Doe*, "a child who needs only accommodations or services that are not part of special education to fulfill the objective of the need inquiry does not 'need' special education." *Id.* at 85. Instead, that student might have a Section 504 plan as will be discussed in *Nutshell* Chapter 4.

2. Discrepancy Model

The specific learning disability category is the most common disability classification under the IDEA and the one that has spawned the most criticism. Congress has tried to improve this classification category by adding the "response to intervention" (RTI) rule but some people would argue that such a change has only made the category more subject to criticism.

Controversy about the learning disability category existed from the date of the creation of special education laws. When Congress enacted the Education for All Handicapped Children Act (EAHCA) in 1975 and mandated the education of all children with disabilities, a key supporter of the bill noted that "[n]o one really knows what a learning disability is." 121 Cong. Rec. 25,531 (daily ed. July 29, 1975)(statement of Rep. Bill Lehman). Although Congress instructed the Commissioner of Education to study the term, the IDEA retains the same definition of learning disability from 1975.

Nonetheless, in response to criticism of exclusive reliance on the "discrepancy model," Congress amended the IDEA in 2004 to allow states to develop other mechanisms to determine if a child has a learning disability. Specifically, a school district can determine if a "child does not make sufficient progress to meet age or State-approved grade-level standards in one or more of the areas identified in paragraph (a)(1) of this section when using a process based on the child's response to scientific, research-based intervention." 34 C.F.R. § 300.309(a)(2)(i). This model is often called the "Response to Intervention" model or RTI model. In order to understand the RTI model, it is helpful to understand the discrepancy model.

The Fourth Edition of the DSM reflects a commonly-used definition of learning disability under the discrepancy model:

> Learning Disorders are diagnosed when the individual's achievement on individually administered, standardized tests in reading, mathematics, or written expression is substantially below that expected for age, schooling, and level of intelligence. The learning problems significantly interfere with academic achievement or activities of daily living that require reading, mathematical, or writing skills. A variety of statistical approaches can be used to establish that a discrepancy is significant. Substantially below

is usually defined as a discrepancy of more than 2 standard deviations between achievement and IQ.

AMERICAN PSYCHIATRIC ASSOCIATION, DIAGNOSTIC AND STATISTICAL MANUAL OF MENTAL DISORDERS 46 (4th ed. 1994)

In practice, the discrepancy model creates a comparison between a child's aptitude and a child's achievement on a norm-referenced measure. On such measures, 100 is usually the mean, with 70 (2nd percentile) being 2 SD's below the mean, 85 (16th percentile) being 1 SD below the mean, 115 (84th percentile) being 1 SD above the mean, and 130 (98th percentile) being 2 SD's above the mean. Some examples can help explain the criticism of this model.

Table 2: Discrepancy Model Outcomes for Learning Disabilities

Aptitude Score	Achievement Score	Difference between Aptitude and Achievement	Qualifies as LD?
70 (2 SD's below mean)	70 (2 SD's below mean)	0 SD's	Not disabled
85 (1 SD below mean)	70 (2 SD's below mean)	1 SD	Not disabled

100 (mean)	70 (2 SD's below mean)	2 SD's	Disabled
115 (1 SD above mean)	100 (mean)	1 SD	Not disabled
115 (1 SD above mean)	85 (1 SD below mean)	2 SD's	Disabled
130 (2 SD's above mean)	100 (mean)	2 SD's	Disabled

As this chart reflects, a child with an IQ of 130 (98th percentile) and achievement scores of 100 (average) can qualify as disabled, yet a child with an IQ of 85 (16th percentile) and an achievement score of 70 (2nd percentile) might not qualify as disabled. From a resource allocation perspective, some people thought it made no sense to devote extra educational resources to the child with a 130 IQ and average reading abilities as compared to the child with an 85 IQ and a very weak reading score of 70 (2nd percentile).

The following graphic may help the reader better understand the data in Table 2. As the chart reflects, 100 is an average IQ score. Every 15 points above or below 100 reflects 1 SD. As a child moves from average (100) to 2 SD's below the mean, the child's percentage declines dramatically to the 2nd percentile at an IQ score of 70. Thus, for a child with an average IQ to be performing 2 SD below the mean, the child has to be performing at or below the 2nd percentile. By contrast, if a child has an IQ of 115 (1 SD above the mean), the child would merely need to have an achievement score of 85 to have a 2 SD discrepancy between aptitude and achievement. Rather than performing better than only 2 percent of the population, the child could perform better than 16 percent of the population and qualify for special education instruction.

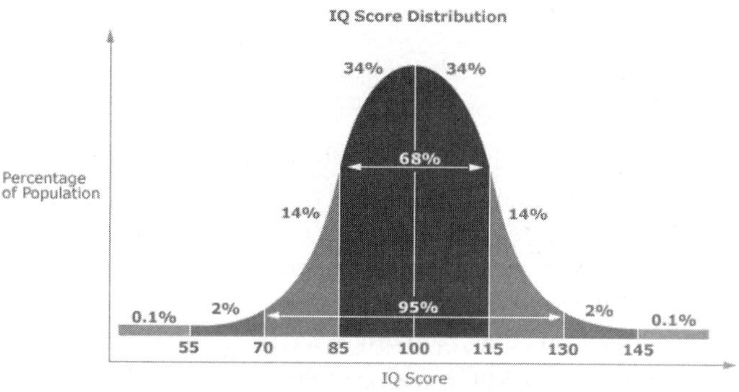

Some people argued that the IDEA discrepancy model worked well for middle-class children who tended to have higher IQ's and did not work as well for poor, urban children who tended to have lower IQ scores. *See* MARK KELMAN & GILLIAN LESTER, JUMPING THE QUEUE: AN INQUIRY INTO THE LEGAL TREATMENT OF STUDENTS WITH LEARNING DISABILITIES (1998). For example, a student with an IQ of 85 would not be considered intellectually disabled because the student does not have an IQ around 70, as required for that classification. An IQ of 85, nonetheless, is one standard deviation below the mean for IQ's, so one could imagine a student struggling in school with an 85 IQ. To be classified as learning disabled, however, the student would have to have achievement scores 2 SD's below an 85—at or about a 55 on the above chart. An achievement score of 55 would place the student at the 2nd percentile in terms of achievement, which is extraordinarily low, so that, functionally, it is nearly impossible for a student with an IQ of 85 to be classified as learning disabled even though the student might need extra assistance to grasp grade-level materials.

Because there is a correlation between IQ and economic class, the discrepancy model makes it, in practice, very difficult for low-income children to qualify as learning disabled even when their academic performance is quite weak. Professors Kelman and Lester argued that the discrepancy model disproportionately worked to the benefit of high-income students who were more likely to have high IQ's along with low achievement scores, and that "discrepancy" might allow them to get extra educational resources or testing accommodations in comparison to low-income students with comparable achievement profiles (but lower IQ's).

3. Development of RTI Model

In response to complaints about exclusive reliance on the discrepancy model, Congress amended the

IDEA in 2004 to provide that a school district "shall not be required to take into consideration whether a child has a severe discrepancy between achievement and intellectual ability in oral expression, listening comprehension, written expression, basic reading skill, reading comprehension, mathematical calculation, or mathematical reasoning." 20 U.S.C. § 1414(b)(6)(A). Instead, a school district "may use a process that determines if the child responds to scientific, research-based intervention as part of the evaluation procedures described in paragraphs (2) and (3)." *Id.* at 1414(b)(6)(B).

The purpose behind this movement towards RTI was to allow school districts to spend special education dollars to try to help children attain grade-level proficiency even if those children did not meet the 2 standard deviation discrepancy model for a learning disability. In fact, the RTI model was added to the IDEA after Congress enacted the No Child Left Behind Act (NCLB) in 2002 and endorsed the RTI model in that statute to help children achieve grade-level expectations. Rather than spend a significant amount of money on eligibility evaluations for IDEA purposes, it was hoped that more resources could be devoted to closing the gap between a child's performance and grade-level expectations by improving instruction based on "scientific, research-based intervention." *See* 70 Fed. Reg. 35,782, 35,802 (June 21, 2005).

The development of RTI has sometimes been challenging to coordinate with the requirements of the IDEA. States that have adopted the RTI model have typically created a tiered system of intervention for children performing below grade level. As the child moves up the tiers of intervention, the intervention becomes more intensive. When several increasingly intensive tiers of intervention have not resulted in the child performing at grade level then the school district will refer the child to special education under the theory that the educational deficit is due to an underlying impairment rather than merely poor instruction.

The tiered model looks something like the triangle below:

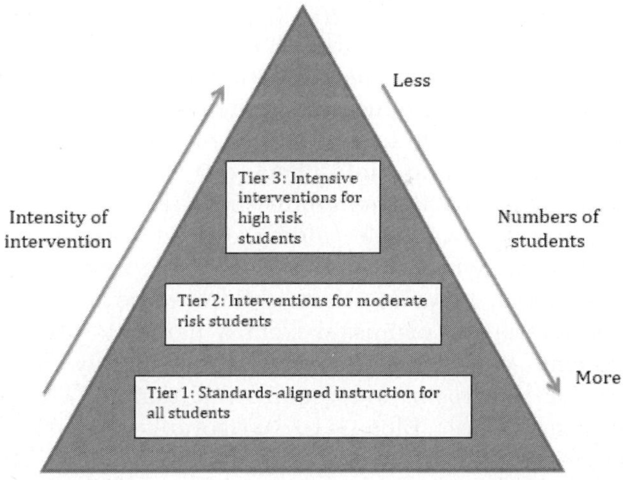

As intervention services move to the top of the triangle, the intensity of the interventions increase and the percentage of students served typically decreases. Depending on the school system, children who are in Tier 3 would also have been referred to special education services so that an IEP could be developed for that child. The Tier 3 interventions, while intensive, may not satisfy the IDEA's requirement that they be "individualized," because a school may offer one type of instruction for all students in the Tier 3 category. If a child has an IEP then the instruction is supposed to be individualized for that child. An IEP might indicate that a child needs a different instructional strategy than the one being offered in the Tier 3 setting.

For some children, the RTI model may be successful at moving them to grade-level performance with short-term, intensive teaching strategies and then placing them back in Tier 1 like the other general-education students. They received help, did not have to face the stigma of a disability classification, and the school district avoided an expensive disability-eligibility evaluation process and, instead, was able to devote these resources to intensive, short-term instruction. Some researchers have noted, however, that "children who once met the criteria for dismissal from a particular tier of tutoring can again perform inadequately in a regular classroom and require additional RTI and tutoring." *See* Elena L. Grigorenko, *Dynamic Assessment and Response to Intervention: Two Sides of One Coin,* 42 J. Learn. Disabil. 111 (2009), available at https://www.ncbi.nlm.nih.gov/pmc/articles/PMC3575109/#R22.

4. Criticisms of the RTI Model

The primary criticism of RTI is that it may delay the development of an IEP for a child who clearly needs an individualized educational program. The following "Dear Colleague" letter from the United States Department of Education reflects important guidance on the inappropriateness of having delays occur as a result of the use of the RTI process:

UNITED STATES DEPARTMENT OF EDUCATION

OFFICE OF SPECIAL EDUCATION AND REHABILITATIVE SERVICES

January 21, 2011

MEMORANDUM

TO: State Directors of Special Education

FROM: Melody Musgrove, Ed.D.
Director
Office of Special Education Programs

SUBJECT: A Response to Intervention (RTI) Process Cannot Be Used to Delay-Deny an Evaluation for Eligibility under the Individuals with Disabilities Education Act (IDEA)

The provisions related to child find in section 612(a)(3) of the Individuals with Disabilities Education Act (IDEA), require that a State have in effect policies and procedures to ensure that the State identifies, locates and evaluates all children with disabilities residing in the State, including children with disabilities who are homeless or are wards of the State, and children with disabilities attending private schools, regardless of the severity of their disability, and who are in need of special education and related services. It is critical that this identification occur in a timely manner and that no procedures or practices result in delaying or denying this identification. It has come to the attention of the Office of Special Education Programs (OSEP) that, in some instances, local educational agencies (LEAs) may be using Response to Intervention (RTI) strategies to delay or deny a timely initial evaluation for children suspected of having a disability. States and LEAs have an obligation to ensure that evaluations of children suspected of having a disability are not delayed or denied because of implementation of an RTI strategy.

A multi-tiered instructional framework, often referred to as RTI, is a schoolwide approach that addresses the needs of all students, including struggling learners and students with disabilities, and integrates assessment and intervention within a multi-level instructional and behavioral system to maximize student achievement and reduce problem behaviors. With a multi-tiered instructional framework, schools identify students at-risk for poor learning outcomes, monitor student progress, provide evidence-based interventions, and adjust the intensity and nature of those interventions depending on a student's responsiveness.

While the Department of Education does not subscribe to a particular RTI framework, the core characteristics that underpin all RTI models are: (1) students receive high quality research-based instruction in their general education setting; (2) continuous monitoring of student performance; (3) all students are screened for academic and behavioral problems; and (4) multiple levels (tiers) of instruction that are progressively more intense, based on the student's response to instruction. OSEP supports State and local implementation of RTI strategies to ensure that children who are struggling academically and behaviorally are identified early and provided needed interventions in a timely and effective manner. Many LEAs have implemented successful RTI strategies, thus ensuring that children who do not respond to interventions and are potentially eligible for special education and related services are referred for evaluation; and those children who simply need intense short-term interventions are provided those interventions.

The regulations implementing the 2004 Amendments to the IDEA include a provision mandating that States allow, as part of their criteria for determining whether a child has a specific learning disability (SLD), the use of a process based on the child's response to scientific, research-based intervention[1]. See 34 CFR

[1] The Department has provided guidance regarding the use of RTI in the identification of specific learning disabilities in its letters to: Zirkel—3-6-07, 8-15-07, 4-8-08, and 12-11-08; Clarke—5-28-08; and Copenhaver—10-19-07. Guidance related to the use of RTI for children ages 3 through 5 was provided in the letter to

§ 300.307(a)(2). OSEP continues to receive questions regarding the relationship of RTI to the evaluation provisions of the regulations. In particular, OSEP has heard that some LEAs may be using RTI to delay or deny a timely initial evaluation to determine if a child is a child with a disability and, therefore, eligible for special education and related services pursuant to an individualized education program.

Under 34 CFR § 300.307, a State must adopt, consistent with 34 CFR § 300.309, criteria for determining whether a child has a specific learning disability as defined in 34 CFR § 300.8(c)(10). In addition, the criteria adopted by the State: (1) must not require the use of a severe discrepancy between intellectual ability and achievement for determining whether a child has an SLD; (2) must permit the use of a process based on the child's response to scientific, research-based intervention; and (3) may permit the use of other alternative research-based procedures for determining whether a child has an SLD. Although the regulations specifically address using the process based on the child's response to scientific, research-based interventions (i.e., RTI) for determining if a child has an SLD, information obtained through RTI strategies may also be used as a component of evaluations for children suspected of having other

---

Brekken—6-2-10. These letters can be found at http://www2.ed.gov/policy/speced/guid/idea/index.html.

disabilities, if appropriate.

The regulations at 34 CFR § 300.301(b) allow a parent to request an initial evaluation at any time to determine if a child is a child with a disability. The use of RTI strategies cannot be used to delay or deny the provision of a full and individual evaluation, pursuant to 34 CFR §§ 300.304–300.311, to a child suspected of having a disability under 34 CFR § 300.8. If the LEA agrees with a parent who refers their child for evaluation that the child may be a child who is eligible for special education and related services, the LEA must evaluate the child. The LEA must provide the parent with notice under 34 CFR §§ 300.503 and 300.504 and obtain informed parental consent, consistent with 34 CFR § 300.9, before conducting the evaluation. Although the IDEA and its implementing regulations do not prescribe a specific timeframe from referral for evaluation to parental consent, it has been the Department's longstanding policy that the LEA must seek parental consent within a reasonable period of time after the referral for evaluation, if the LEA agrees that an initial evaluation is needed. See Assistance to States for the Education of Children with Disabilities and Preschool Grants for Children with Disabilities, Final Rule, 71 Fed. Reg., 46540, 46637 (August 14, 2006). An LEA must conduct the initial evaluation within 60 days of receiving parental consent for the evaluation or, if the State establishes a timeframe within which the evaluation must be conducted, within that timeframe. 34 CFR § 300.301(c).

> If, however, the LEA does not suspect that the child has a disability, and denies the request for an initial evaluation, the LEA must provide written notice to parents explaining why the public agency refuses to conduct an initial evaluation and the information that was used as the basis for this decision. 34 CFR § 300.503(a) and (b). The parent can challenge this decision by requesting a due process hearing under 34 CFR § 300.507 or filing a State complaint under 34 CFR § 300.153 to resolve the dispute regarding the child's need for an evaluation. It would be inconsistent with the evaluation provisions at 34 CFR §§ 300.301 through 300.111 for an LEA to reject a referral and delay provision of an initial evaluation on the basis that a child has not participated in an RTI framework.
>
> We hope this information is helpful in clarifying the relationship between RTI and evaluations pursuant to the IDEA. Please examine the procedures and practices in your State to ensure that any LEA implementing RTI strategies is appropriately using RTI, and that the use of RTI is not delaying or denying timely initial evaluations to children suspected of having a disability. If you have further questions, please do not hesitate to contact me or Ruth Ryder at 202-245-7513.

As will be discussed in *Nutshell* Chapter 5, the IDEA has strict time limits concerning evaluations of children once there is reason to suspect the child has a disability. Further, if a school district does *not* suspect that a child has a disability and is therefore not even entitled to an evaluation, then the school district must explain their rationale, as discussed in *Nutshell* Chapter 5.

Finally, a new area of controversy has developed—whether to use RTI for impairments *other* than a learning disability. The 2004 IDEA Amendments only refer to the possible use of RTI to assist with the diagnosis of a learning disability. The 2004 Amendments do not refer to the use of RTI for any other disability category. The empirical literature justifying the use of RTI is only in the context of learning disabilities, mostly focused on delays in learning to read, and not in other areas such as speech and language impairments or autism.

I. SPEECH OR LANGUAGE IMPAIRMENT

> Speech or language impairment means a communication disorder, such as stuttering, impaired articulation, a language impairment, or a voice impairment, that adversely affects a child's educational performance.

34 C.F.R. § 300.8(c)(11).

This is the second most common disability category. The DSM-5 separates this category into language disorders, speech sound fluency (i.e., stuttering) disorders, and social (pragmatic) communication disorders.

Language disorders: Children with language disorders have reduced vocabulary, limited sentence structure, and impairments in discourse, but those difficulties are not attributable to hearing or other sensory impairments, a neurological condition, an intellectual disability, or a global developmental delay. A child can have an impairment in *expressive* ability (i.e., the production of vocal, gesture, or verbal signals) while not having an impairment in *receptive* ability (i.e., receiving and comprehending language) or vice versa. "Children with receptive language impairments have a poorer prognosis than those with predominantly expressive impairments." DSM-5 at 43. While children with an intellectual disability will typically have language delays, they should not be classified as having a language impairment unless "the language deficits are clearly in excess of the intellectual limitations." DSM-5, at 43.

Speech-sound Disorders: Children with speech-sound disorders "may experience difficulty with phonological knowledge of speech sounds or the ability to coordinate movements for speech in varying degrees." DSM-5, at 44. A speech and language pathologist makes the diagnosis by comparing a child's speech and language with what one would expect for that child's age and developmental stage. For example, one would only expect a two-year-old to have speech that is 50 percent understandable but one would expect a four-year-old to have speech that is overall intelligible. By age 7, children should be producing speech sounds clearly and pronouncing most words correctly although certain sounds may be misarticulated until age 8 (i.e., *l, r, s, z, th, ch, dzh, and zh*). The deficits should not be the result of a "physical, structural, neurological, or hearing impairment."

Fluency Disorders: Children with fluency disorders (stuttering) usually develop their disorder by age 6, with the onset ranging from ages 2 to 7. This disturbance is characterized by frequent repetitions or prolongations of sounds or syllables and by other types of speech dysfluencies, including broken words (e.g., pauses within a word), audible or silent blocking (i.e., filled or unfilled pauses in speech), circumlocutions (i.e., word substitutions to avoid problematic words), words produced with an excess of physical tension, and monosyllabic whole-word repetitions (e.g., "I-I-I-I see him"). DSM-5 at 46.

Disturbances in fluency can interfere with academic achievement, but studies also show that 65 percent to 85 percent of children do not have a lifelong disturbance in fluency.

Social (pragmatic) communication disorders: Children with pragmatic speech disorders have difficulty understanding and following social rules of verbal and nonverbal communication. Because this disorder requires an adequate developmental progression in speech and language, a diagnosis is not appropriate in children younger than four years old. Children presenting with symptoms of this disorder may actually have autism spectrum disorder, attention-deficit/hyperactivity disorder, social anxiety disorder, or an intellectual disability.

J. LESS COMMON DISABILITIES

1. Deaf-Blindness

> Deaf-blindness means concomitant hearing and visual impairments, the combination of which causes such severe communication and other developmental and educational needs that they cannot be accommodated in special education programs solely for children with deafness or children with blindness.

34 C.F.R. § 300.8(c)(2).

A school district could classify a child with this impairment as hearing impaired or visually impaired. Classifying the child in this combination category may, in some instances, provide the school district with access to additional resources.

2. Orthopedic Impairment

> Orthopedic impairment means a severe orthopedic impairment that adversely affects a child's educational performance. The term includes impairments caused by a congenital anomaly, impairments caused by disease (e.g., poliomyelitis, bone tuberculosis), and impairments from other causes (e.g., cerebral palsy, amputations, and fractures or burns that cause contractures).

34 C.F.R. § 300.8(c)(8).

The term "orthopedic impairment" is also an umbrella term for various conditions that affect a child's use of his or her limbs. A child could be born with a congenital anomaly, become paralyzed as the result of a car accident, or have a condition like cerebral palsy which can affect the use of various limbs. While an orthopedic impairment does not necessarily limit a child's educational performance, lack of accessibility in a school building can have a major impact on a child's education. Even if the building is accessible, a child may need training to learn how to navigate around the classroom or building. A teacher may also have to consider a student's navigational needs when placing the desks or tables and chairs within the classroom.

A child with an orthopedic impairment may have a Section 504 plan because the child merely needs an accessible building, rather than special education and related services. For example, a district court judge found that a high school senior with an orthopedic impairment who needed accommodations, like an elevator key, could bring a claim under Section 504 but not the IDEA. *See D.R. v. Antelope Valley Union High School*, 746 F. Supp.2d 1132 (C.D. Cal. 2010). The tardiness and disruptions that resulted from the inaccessible building did not cause her to need any specialized instruction. She merely needed an elevator key rather than the school's ineffective "mobility plan" which required her to seek the assistance of a mobility liaison to open the elevator doors. As will be discussed in *Nutshell* Chapter 4, this kind of accommodation is ideal for a Section 504 plan rather than an IEP under the IDEA.

3. Traumatic Brain Injury

> Traumatic brain injury means an acquired injury to the brain caused by an external physical force, resulting in total or partial functional disability or psychosocial impairment, or both, that adversely affects a child's educational performance. Traumatic brain injury applies to open or closed head injuries resulting in impairments in one or more areas, such as cognition; language; memory; attention; reasoning; abstract thinking; judgment; problem-solving; sensory, perceptual, and motor abilities; psychosocial behavior; physical functions; information processing; and speech. Traumatic brain injury does not apply to brain injuries that are congenital or degenerative, or to brain injuries induced by birth trauma.

34 C.F.R. § 300.8(c)(12).

Typically, children develop a traumatic brain injury (TBI) as a result of an accident or from being shaken violently. The manifestations of TBI can be quite varied, ranging from impairments in walking or other physical activities to impairments in thinking and reasoning.

4. Visual Impairment

> Visual impairment including blindness means an impairment in vision that, even with correction, adversely affects a child's educational performance. The term includes both partial sight and blindness.

34 C.F.R. § 300.8(c)(13).

While visual impairments typically involve near-sightedness and far-sightedness, they can also include:

- *strabismus*, where the eyes look in different directions and do not focus simultaneously on a single point;
- *congenital cataracts*, where the lens of the eye is cloudy;
- *retinopathy of prematurity*, which may occur in premature babies when the light-sensitive retina hasn't developed sufficiently before birth;
- *retinitis pigmentosa*, a rare inherited disease that slowly destroys the retina;
- *coloboma*, where a portion of the structure of the eye is missing;
- *optic nerve hypoplasia*, which is caused by underdeveloped fibers in the optic nerve and which affects depth perception, sensitivity to light, and acuity of vision; and

- *cortical visual impairment* (CVI), which is caused by damage to the part of the brain related to vision, not to the eyes themselves.

See Visual Impairment, Including Blindness (March 31, 2017), http://www.parentcenterhub.org/repository/visualimpairment/.

Typically, if a child's vision is correctable to 20/20 with the use of corrective lenses then the child will not be classified as disabled under the IDEA or Section 504. In some cases, parents need to be informed about local resources to acquire free or low-cost corrective lenses for their child.

§ 3.5 CONCLUSION

The question of whether a student is a "child with a disability" can be a confusing question, in part, because there is not strong alignment between the IDEA and the DSM-5. Psychologists tend to be familiar with the DSM categories and use that terminology. By contrast, an IDEA category, like "serious emotional disturbance," is not a DSM-5 category. Psychologists also tend to use words like "may" or "possibly" when school district officials applying the IDEA could be seeking a firm diagnosis. Finally, a psychologist who only sees a child in a clinical setting may not have much information about how the disability affects a child's academic functioning on a day-to-day basis in the classroom. It is often not realistic to expect psychologists who are performing evaluations to observe a child in a school setting or even review schoolwork. People who act as advocates for children with disabilities sometimes need to educate psychologists on the way their terminology may be interpreted by school district professionals.

CHAPTER 4

SECTION 504/ADA ELIGIBILITY

§ 4.1 INTRODUCTION

Section 504 of the Rehabilitation Act of 1973, 29 U.S.C. §§ 701 et seq. provides that:

> No otherwise qualified individual with a disability in the United States . . . shall, solely be reason of her or his disability, be excluded from the participation in, be denied the benefits of, or be subjected to discrimination under any program or activity receiving Federal financial assistance. . . .

29 U.S.C. § 794.

The definition of disability under Section 504 cross-references the definition of disability found in the Americans with Disabilities Act (ADA), 42 U.S.C. §§ 12101 et seq. Thus, this chapter refers to ADA/Section 504 plans as identical concepts.

> (1) Disability
>
> The term "disability" means, with respect to an individual—
>
> (A) a physical or mental impairment that substantially limits one or more major life activities of such individual;
>
> (B) a record of such an impairment; or
>
> (C) being regarded as having such an impairment (as described in paragraph (3)).

(2) Major life activities

(A) In general

For purposes of paragraph (1), major life activities include, but are not limited to, caring for oneself, performing manual tasks, seeing, hearing, eating, sleeping, walking, standing, lifting, bending, speaking, breathing, learning, reading, concentrating, thinking, communicating, and working.

(B) Major bodily functions

For purposes of paragraph (1), a major life activity also includes the operation of a major bodily function, including but not limited to, functions of the immune system, normal cell growth, digestive, bowel, bladder, neurological, brain, respiratory, circulatory, endocrine, and reproductive functions.

(3) Regarded as having such an impairment

For purposes of paragraph (1)(C):

(A) An individual meets the requirement of "being regarded as having such an impairment" if the individual establishes that he or she has been subjected to an action prohibited under this chapter because of an actual or perceived physical or mental impairment whether or not the impairment limits or is perceived to limit a major life activity.

(B) Paragraph (1)(C) shall not apply to impairments that are transitory and minor. A transitory impairment is an impairment with an actual or expected duration of 6 months or less.

(4) Rules of construction regarding the definition of disability

The definition of "disability" in paragraph (1) shall be construed in accordance with the following:

(A) The definition of disability in this chapter shall be construed in favor of broad coverage of individuals under this chapter, to the maximum extent permitted by the terms of this chapter.

(B) The term "substantially limits" shall be interpreted consistently with the findings and purposes of the ADA Amendments Act of 2008.

(C) An impairment that substantially limits one major life activity need not limit other major life activities in order to be considered a disability.

(D) An impairment that is episodic or in remission is a disability if it would substantially limit a major life activity when active.

(E)

(i) The determination of whether an impairment substantially limits a major life activity shall be made without regard to the ameliorative effects of mitigating measures such a—

(I) medication, medical supplies, equipment, or appliances, low-vision devices (which do not include ordinary eyeglasses or contact lenses), prosthetics including limbs and devices, hearing aids

> and cochlear implants or other implantable hearing devices, mobility devices, or oxygen therapy equipment and supplies;
>
> (II) use of assistive technology;
>
> (III) reasonable accommodations or auxiliary aids or services; or
>
> (IV) learned behavioral or adaptive neurological modifications.
>
> (ii) The ameliorative effects of the mitigating measures of ordinary eyeglasses or contact lenses shall be considered in determining whether an impairment substantially limits a major life activity.
>
> (iii) As used in this subparagraph—
>
> (I) the term "ordinary eyeglasses or contact lenses" means lenses that are intended to fully correct visual acuity or eliminate refractive error; and
>
> (II) the term "low-vision devices" means devices that magnify, enhance, or otherwise augment a visual image.

42 U.S.C. § 12102.

Although this definition of disability is rather long and complicated, most education cases involving children in grades K–12 only involve prong (A)—actually disabled. Further, the rule of construction found in section (4)—that the definition of disability "should be construed in favor of broad coverage"—allows for a fairly broad scope of coverage in the education context. It is hard to imagine a situation in which a child who is covered by the IDEA's definition of disability would not be covered by the ADA/Section 504 definition of disability. There are many situations, however, where a child may be "disabled" for ADA/Section 504 purposes but not be disabled under the IDEA because they need "accommodations" but not "special education and related services." The interplay between the two statutes is complicated and requires special attention. It will be discussed below.

§ 4.2 IDEA EXHAUSTION RULE

The IDEA has a specific rule regarding the relationship between enforcement under the IDEA, Section 504, and the ADA.

> Nothing in this chapter shall be construed to restrict or limit the rights, procedures, and remedies available under the Constitution, [the ADA, Section 504], or other Federal laws protecting the rights of children with disabilities, except that before the filing of a civil action under such laws seeking relief that is also available under this subchapter, the procedures under subsections (f) and (g) shall be exhausted to the same extent as would be required had the action been brought under this subchapter.

20 U.S.C. § 1415(*l*).

As that provision states, one must file an action under the IDEA, and exhaust those remedies before pursuing relief under the ADA or Section 504. The IDEA's administrative procedures for seeking relief will be discussed in *Nutshell* Chapter 9. But, briefly, the IDEA requires a parent who believes their child is not receiving a Free and Appropriate Public Education (FAPE), as required by the IDEA, to seek relief in front of a state-level Hearing Officer before filing a complaint in a state or federal court. Further, the relief available under the IDEA does not include compensatory damages for pain and suffering.

There are essentially two types of cases in which a party may sue directly under the ADA or Section 504 and would not be subject to the IDEA's exhaustion requirement. The first is one in which the complaining party is not someone who is defined as a "child with a disability under the IDEA." The second is where the complaining party is a "child with a disability" as defined by the IDEA, but the child is seeking relief that is available under the ADA or Section 504 outside the educational context.

A. NOT A CHILD WITH A DISABILITY UNDER THE IDEA

There are two types of cases where the complaining party is not a "child with a disability" as defined by the IDEA and thus, can proceed directly under the ADA or Section 504: (1) where the parent, not the child, is the person with a disability and (2) where the child is not covered by the IDEA because the child does not need special education and related services, even though the child may have a disability.

Courts have long understood that parents can proceed directly under Section 504 or the ADA when the school district is not providing equal program access to the parents of a child, even when the child is not disabled. For example, in *Rothschild v. Grottenthaler,* 907 F.2d 286 (2nd Cir. 1990), the Second Circuit found that a school district violated Section 504 when it failed to provide sign language interpreting services at the school district's expense, to parents for school-initiated activities related to their children's education. Similarly, one could use Section 504 or the ADA to require a school to make its facility physically accessible so that parents could attend school functions even if no child at the school was affected by the lack of physical accessibility.

The second category is a bit more complicated. As covered in *Nutshell* Chapter 3, a student is only covered by the IDEA if the student "needs special education and related services." Not all children with a disability have that particular need. Some children may only "need" what we call a reasonable accommodation such as the use of an auxiliary aid, extended time on testing, preferential seating, or additional breaks during testing. These accommodations can be provided without any specialized instruction.

It can be very difficult to determine if a student needs special education and related services, or only needs accommodations that can be provided under

Section 504. Thus, a school district will often first determine if a student is a child with a disability, and only when that answer is in the negative, consider whether the student might qualify for accommodations under Section 504/ADA as an individual with a disability. On the other hand, school districts sometimes suggest that a child start with a Section 504 plan and only transition to an IEP if the Section 504 plan is inadequate. It is not uncommon for students to move back and forth between a Section 504 plan and an IEP.

In a recent publication, the United States Department of Education provides examples of children who might be covered by Section 504 but not the IDEA. *See* United States Department of Education, Parent and Educator Resource Guide to Section 504 in Public Elementary and Secondary Schools (December, 2016), available at https://www2.ed.gov/about/offices/list/ocr/docs/504-resource-guide-201612.pdf. Some of these examples include:

1. Rosita is earning B's and C's in school and has trouble concentrating during class lessons. She takes longer than most students to complete in-class assignments. The classroom teacher does not think Rosita needs special education services but thinks she may have ADHD and could use, as an accommodation, extra time to complete assignments and assistance to stay on task during class. Depending on the effectiveness of a Section 504 plan, a parent may want to request an IEP if it appears that Rosita does need special education

and related services to benefit from her education.

2. Robert is falling asleep in class even though he is getting a good night of sleep. Staff should seek an evaluation to determine whether Robert has a physical impairment, like narcolepsy, that may be interfering with his ability to stay awake in school. After getting an appropriate evaluation, the group can determine if Robert needs any specialized instruction under the IDEA or other kinds of accommodations that could be provided under Section 504.

3. Omar has a history of cancer, which is currently in remission. Because of his record of disability, Omar qualifies as an individual with a disability under Section 504. If he is experiencing bullying or harassment because of his record of a disability, the school staff may want to suggest a Section 504 plan.

4. Maya is a very strong student who has gastroesophagael reflux disease (GERD). Her disease causes frequent vomiting and absences from school due to her inability to digest food normally. It may make sense to provide a Section 504 plan for Maya because she may need an accommodation for her frequent absences from school. She also may need protections from bullying and harassment.

The problem for parents if their child appears to be in any of these categories is that they may have trouble knowing, in advance, whether the school district takes the view that their child is covered under the IDEA rather than only under ADA/Section 504.

- School districts often consider children with ADHD to be eligible for services under the IDEA. Even if Rosita does not need special education and related services in the early primary grades, she may need additional assistance in middle school or high school.
- Even if Robert's or Maya's diagnoses are a physical impairment, it is possible that their physical impairment is causing them to miss instructional material.
- Even though Omar's cancer is in remission, he may have anxiety that affects his ability to concentrate or may have frequent medical appointments that cause him to miss classes. Either of those results may cause him to need specialized assistance even if his cancer is in remission.

B. SEEKING RELIEF ALSO AVAILABLE UNDER THE IDEA

1. The *Fry* Decision

The Supreme Court decided a case in 2017 that provides guidance when a parent can seek relief directly under Section 504 rather than exhaust remedies under the IDEA. *See Fry v. Napoleon Community Schools,* 137 S. Ct. 743 (2017).

Ehlena Fry has cerebral palsy. When she entered kindergarten, the school district provided her with an IEP, which included one-on-one support throughout the day. The parties conceded that she received a Free Appropriate Public Education as required under the IDEA through the various educational services provided under her IEP. *Id.* at 751.

The dispute between the Frys and the school district centered on whether Ehlena could bring a trained service dog, a goldendoodle named Wonder, to school with her. Wonder was trained to do the following work:

> retrieving dropped items, helping her balance when she uses her walker, opening and closing doors, turning on and off lights, helping her take off her coat, and helping her transfer to and from the toilet.

Id. at 751.

When this dispute first occurred, the school district agreed to allow Wonder to accompany Ehlena to school on a 30-day trial basis but, at the end of the trial period, informed the Frys that Wonder was not welcome at the school anymore. The Frys filed a complaint with the United States Department of Education's Office for Civil Rights (OCR) under the ADA and Section 504. OCR rendered a decision in favor of the Frys but the Frys decided to transfer Ehlena to a new school in a different district because they were concerned that the school administration would "resent" Ehlena and "make her return to school difficult." *Id.* at 751. The Frys, however, persisted in their complaint under the ADA and Section 504. They filed a lawsuit in federal court in which they sought a declaration that the school district had violated the ADA and Section 504, along with a request for monetary damages to compensate for Ehlena's injuries. Her injuries were alleged to include: emotional distress and pain, embarrassment, and mental anguish. *Id.* at 752.

The district court dismissed the case based on the pleadings, ruling that exhaustion was required. *See E.F. ex rel. Fry v. Napoleon Community Schools,* 2014 WL 106624 (E.D. Mich. Jan. 10, 2014). The Sixth Circuit affirmed, concluding that the IDEA procedures would have been useful. "Either they would have prevailed and effectively resolved their dispute without litigation, making it possible for [Ehlena] to attend school with Wonder, or else they have failed but in the process generated an administrative record that would have aided the district court in evaluating their complaint." *Fry v. Napoleon Community Schools,* 788 F.3d 622, 629 (6th Cir. 2015). The focus of the Sixth Circuit's analysis was whether the Frys could demonstrate that Wonder's presence would enhance Ehlena's education by, for example, making her "feel more comfortable and confident." *Id.* at 629.

Reversing the Sixth Circuit, the Supreme Court said the proper test is whether "the gravamen of a complaint against a school concerns the denial of a FAPE, or instead addresses disability-based discrimination." 137 S. Ct. at 756. To answer that question, the Court says one should ask "a pair of hypothetical questions":

- "First, could the plaintiff have brought essentially the same claim if the alleged conduct had occurred at a public facility that was *not* a school—say, a public theater or library?"
- "And second, could an *adult* at the school—say, an employee or visitor—have pressed essentially the same grievance?"

Id. at 756.

The Court then provides two contrasting examples to show how those rules would be implemented. First, a child uses a wheelchair and the school building lacks any ramps. Because the child could sue a municipal library or theatre for failing to have a ramp under Section 504 or the ADA, then she could also sue the school district under Section 504 or the ADA without exhausting her IDEA remedies. Second, a child with a learning disability sues a school district to obtain remedial tutoring in math. Because one could not obtain that kind of relief against a public theater or library, the student would have to exhaust IDEA remedies.

Further, to determine the "gravamen" of a suit, the Court says one might look at whether the parent ever sought to invoke the IDEA's procedures before switching to the Section 504/ADA remedies. "A plaintiff's initial choice to pursue that process may suggest that she is indeed seeking relief for the denial of a FAPE—with the shift to judicial proceedings prior to full exhaustion reflecting only strategic calculations about how to maximize the prospects of such a remedy." *Id.* at 757.

Although it was clear that the Frys were seeking a remedy that could be obtained against a public theatre or a library if they denied a person the right to use a service animal, the Court remanded the case back to the lower courts to determine if the Frys had sought Ehlena's ability to use a service dog in school under the IDEA. "Accordingly, on remand, the court below should establish whether (or to what extent) the Frys invoked the IDEA's dispute resolution process before bringing this suit. And if the Frys started down that road, the court should decide whether their actions reveal that the gravamen of their complaint is indeed the denial of a FAPE, thus necessitating further exhaustion." *Id.* at 758–59.

2. Application of the *Fry* Decision

Unlike the plaintiffs discussed in *Nutshell* § 4.2(A), the plaintiffs covered by the *Fry* non-exhaustion rule will often be children who do have a disability covered under the IDEA. Ehlena Fry had an IEP and, in fact, received assistance from a one-on-one aide in the classroom. Further, the right that such plaintiffs are seeking is one that they could also seek against non-educational entities like a public theatre or library. Such rights are not limited to students.

This rule does not readily follow from the exhaustion language used under the IDEA, which asks whether one is "seeking relief that is also available under [the IDEA]." *Id.* at 746. The Court never asks, for example, whether the Frys *could* have argued that Ehlena's IEP provides that she be permitted to bring her service dog to school even though schools typically do not permit dogs in their buildings. As the Sixth Circuit noted, it is common for IEPs to not be limited to a list of special education and related services that a child might need; they often also list accommodations that must be made such as extended time on exams, or special testing settings, or permission to bring a service dog into a classroom.

Because one goal of the IDEA is to help students "be prepared to lead productive and independent adult lives," one can imagine that learning how to use a service dog could be a part of that educational progression *See* 20 U.S.C. § 1400(c)(5)(A)(ii). Further, because we tend to think of education broadly under the IDEA—to include elements such as socialization—one could imagine that the use of a service dog is considered a part of one's education, broadly speaking. As the Sixth Circuit noted: "an IEP should take into account any potential accommodations that will make a disabled child feel more comfortable in the school environment, since such accommodations will help the child participate actively in school activities." *Id.* at 629. Nonetheless, the proceedings in the *Fry* litigation suggest that her parents did not seek to argue that she was entitled to use a service dog under the IDEA due to its classroom educational benefits. They emphasized that the use of the service dog was important for

Ehlena to have Wonder at school so she could "form a bond" with the dog, which would make it a more effective service animal "outside of school." *Id.* at 628.

The Supreme Court opinion, however, did not ask whether the Frys might have prevailed under the IDEA—whether the relief was available under the IDEA. Instead, the *Fry* test appears to flip the statutory language by asking *what relief is available under the ADA or Section 504,* not by asking what relief is available under the IDEA. So what would this ruling mean on the ground as parents and school districts develop ADA/Section 504 plans or IEPs?

Arguably, parents might want to ask school districts to draft Section 504 plans for those accommodations that are available independently of the IDEA, such as an accessible building, permission to bring a service dog in a school building, or even sign language interpreter services at all activities. A district court decision in *Kimble v. Douglas County School District,* 925 F. Supp.2d 1176 (D. Col. 2013) suggests that a parent can choose to drop all IDEA-required services and merely ask the school district to provide the services available under Section 504/ADA. In that case, the parents asked the school district to implement a Section 504 plan "which may designate assistive technologies and additional curriculum augmentations." *Id.* at 1179. After *Fry,* it may be the situation that the parent could pursue accommodations that are allowed generally—in a non-educational setting—through a Section 504 Plan and use the courts to challenge such a plan if a school district does not develop an appropriate one. But, it is unlikely that a parent could circumvent the IDEA entirely in such a situation. As with Ehlena, the parents would still likely want to pursue an IEP under the IDEA for various special education services that are not available in a non-educational setting. After *Fry,* parents or their children can likely only litigate (without IDEA exhaustion) those aspects of the plan that would also be developed in a non-educational context, like effective communication.

One advantage of the pure Section 504/ADA strategy is that some accommodations, like using a service animal or having an accessible entrance, are clearly guaranteed by ADA/Section 504 without demonstrating that they are educational in nature. Further, such a strategy would allow a parent to sue directly in court, without exhausting IDEA remedies, if the school district failed to offer those accommodations. A disadvantage of this strategy is that some parents *prefer* an IEP to an ADA/Section 504 plan because they like the annual meetings required with IEPs and even may desire the complaint and due process avenues for relief available under the IDEA. For the Frys, there was no benefit in pursuing an IDEA remedy because their daughter was already enrolled in another school and they wanted compensatory damages (which are not available under the IDEA).

The *Fry* decision might be especially helpful for parents who are seeking accommodations that are clearly permitted under ADA/Section 504 but are more controversial under the IDEA. This is especially true in the area of communication.

The ADA Title II effective communication regulations provide:

> A public entity shall take appropriate steps to ensure that communications with applicants, participants, members of the public, and companions with disabilities are as effective as communications with others.

28 C.F.R. § 35.160(a)(1).

Although the IDEA does not require the school district to compare a student's access to communication with access provided to nondisabled students, the ADA/Section 504 standard clearly does. The rule specifically asks if communication is "as effective as communications with others," which makes it a nondiscrimination standard rather than an access to education standard.

This emphasis on what kind of communication could be required under ADA/Section 504 would arguably reach a different result in one of the most important Supreme Court cases brought under the IDEA—*Board of Education v. Rowley*, 458 U.S. 176 (1982). Amy Rowley's parents asked the school district to provide a sign language interpreter for Amy when she was in grade school, but the school district refused, arguing that Amy could obtain a

Free and Appropriate Public Education without the use of an interpreter because she was advancing successfully from grade to grade without one. The Supreme Court agreed with the school district, concluding that the IDEA does *not* create an equal educational opportunity standard. The IDEA "generates no additional requirement that the services so provided be sufficient to maximize each child's potential 'commensurate with the opportunity provided other children.'" *Id.* at 198. Instead, the Court concluded that a school district merely has to provide "personalized instruction with sufficient support services to permit the child to benefit educationally from that instruction." *Id.* at 203. In Amy's case, she was found to benefit educationally without a sign language interpreter.

But, if this case would proceed under the *Fry* standard, Amy Rowley would be entitled to a sign language interpreter were she to attend a lecture at a museum or public library under the effective communication regulation. As the Title II Section by Section analysis explains: "Sign language or oral interpreters, for example, may be required when the information being communicated in a transaction with a deaf individual is complex, or is exchanged for a lengthy period of time." 28 C.F.R. § 35.160(a)(1) App. The school day, like a public lecture, easily satisfies this rule. Under the ADA/Section 504, Amy Rowley is entitled to an interpreter during the school day—even if she could benefit educationally without one—because she is entitled to have access to oral communication on the same basis as nondisabled students. The record in the *Rowley* case clearly established that Amy Rowley missed a great deal of oral communication by relying on lip reading. Although her parents unsuccessfully argued that the equal opportunity standard should bc incorporated into the IDEA, the *Fry* case seems to import that standard into educational cases in which the student is seeking an accommodation they could receive outside the educational context.

Even before *Fry* was decided, the Ninth Circuit had applied the effective communication standard to a school-age child who wanted Communication Access Realtime Translation (CART) services under the ADA even though the Hearing Officer had ruled that the child was not entitled this service. *See K.M. ex rel. Bright v. Tustin Unified School District,* 725 F.3d 1088 (9th Cir. 2013). This was not an exhaustion case since the parents first filed the IDEA action before pursuing the Section 504 lawsuit. The Ninth Circuit ruled that the school district's compliance with the IDEA standard did not preclude the parents from pursuing a claim under the ADA Title II's effective communication regulation. After *Fry,* a parent could theoretically always pursue this matter under the ADA effective communication regulation rather than waste time pursuing it under the IDEA's more limited rules with regard to FAPE. Following the decision by the Ninth Circuit, the parties reached a settlement agreement in the amount of $197,500. *See K.M. ex rel. Bright v. Tustin Unified School District,* 78 F. Supp.3d 1289, 1295 (C.D. Cal. 2015).

3. Post-*Fry* Decisions

The courts have been divided on how to apply the *Fry* decision. Judge Mark W. Bennett, N.D. of Iowa, on March 23, 2017, decided one instructive case. *See K.G. v. Sergeant Bluff-Luton Community School District,* 2017 WL 1098829 (N.D. Iowa March 23, 2017). This case involved a fairly straightforward application of *Fry* in a context where a school district allegedly engaged in conduct that resulted in physical and emotional injuries to a seven-year-old child who was autistic. He was allegedly dragged across a classroom floor causing serious carpet burns and serious psychological and behavioral issues, including PTSD. *Id.* at *3. The parents sought to bring their claims under the Fourth and Fourteenth Amendments, as well as Section 504, rather than the IDEA. The district court allowed the case to proceed (without exhausting the IDEA remedy) because the gravamen of the complaint was "unlawful and unreasonable use of physical force against KG." *Id.* at *12. Although the complaint did allege that the use of force was inconsistent with the IEP, the judge found that those facts were "an indication of the *unreasonableness* of the use of force, not as the *gravemen* of the wrongfulness of the conduct." *Id.* at *12 (emphasis in the original). Further, the IEP violations were "not the central allegations of the wrongfulness of the conduct." *Id.* at *12. The judge was careful to offer caution at the end of the opinion that the plaintiffs might not ultimately prevail, but he thought the allegations were strong enough to defeat a motion for summary judgment and avoid exhaustion under the IDEA.

This Iowa case is only a district court decision that conceivably could be reversed on appeal. The judge, nonetheless, was careful to read the *Fry* decision closely and try to determine what was the "gravamen" of the lawsuit. Because a nondisabled child could allege inappropriate physical mistreatment, this case did not hinge on the existence of an IEP. It is the case, however, that plaintiffs alleged that the teacher acted inconsistently with the existing IEP and behavior management plan. Had the student stayed at the school, the parents could have sought closer adherence to the existing plans under the IDEA. However, since the student had transferred to a new school district, there was really little relief that would be available under the IDEA. As in *Fry*, monetary damages were the only appropriate remedy for the student and parents.

In a case with somewhat similar facts, the district court required exhaustion of the IDEA remedies before proceeding under Section 504. *See N.S. v. Tennessee Department of Education*, 2017 WL 1347753 (M.D. Tenn. April 12, 2017). In this case, the plaintiffs also alleged that they suffered injuries. Rather than being dragged across a carpet, they alleged they were subject to isolation and restraint. In dismissing the case for a failure to exhaust IDEA remedies, Judge Aleta Trauger said:

> The discipline of students is primarily educational in nature and isolations and restraints are considerations for the classroom environment, where students need to have

> their behavior managed in order to learn effectively. . . . Isolation and restraint techniques are not implemented on adult employees or visitors of the Knox County schools, nor are they implemented on minors such as the plaintiffs in other public institutions. . . . the instant action that is primarily about the alleged denial of a FAPE.

Id. at *11.

One could imagine that Judge Trauger would have similarly viewed the Iowa case as being merely about behavior management under an IEP and found that exhaustion was required. An important difference between these cases, however, might be that the student in the Iowa case was no longer attending the school at the time the district court case was brought.

In a factually different case, the court found that the plaintiff could proceed on his claim alleging peer-harassment. Because the harassment included being called names such as "stupid," "fat," "weak," "fag," "pussy," "shit stain," and "bubble butt," he alleged discrimination under the ADA, Section 504, and Title IX. *See Bowe v. Eau Claire Area School District,* 2017 WL 1458822 (W.D. Wisc. April 24, 2017). While it was true that the plaintiff had autism, the court found that a student who did not have an IEP could have brought these bullying allegations. The plaintiff sought a "harassment-free environment" rather than a FAPE. *Id.* at *5. Presumably, the court would have allowed the case to go forward even if the epithets had been exclusively disability-related because a harassment-free environment is a right more suited to an ADA claim than an IDEA claim.

In cases involving somewhat different facts, other courts have ordered IDEA exhaustion post-*Fry*. For example, in a procedurally complicated case, the grandparents of J.D. tried to use the federal courts to order the school district to continue to pay for their grandchild's residential placement after his parents (and their eight other children) moved to Nicaragua. *See J.D. v. Graham Local School District Board of Education,* 2017 WL 1807626 (S.D. Ohio May 5, 2017). The dispute between the school district and grandparents appeared to be over the validity of the power of attorney. Those documents were relevant to the issue of whether the child lived in the grandparents' school district. The grandparents had initiated the action under the IDEA's due process procedures. Although the State Level Review Officer ruled that "stay put" did apply to this case, she had no jurisdiction in the matter to enter a final order until the juvenile court resolved the issue regarding the power of attorney, so the grandparents sought a temporary restraining order in federal court. *See In the Matter of the Appeal of the Due Process Hearing on behalf of J.D. and Graham Local Schools,* Case No. SE 3421–2017 (Monica R. Bohlen April 26, 2017). Nonetheless, the court did not dismiss the claim, pending further briefing on the jurisdictional issue, seemingly recognizing that the state administrative process might prove futile.

Similarly, in *L.D. v. Los Angeles Unified School District,* 2017 WL 1520417 (C.D. Cal. April 26, 2017), the court ruled that the plaintiffs needed to exhaust their IDEA claim before appearing in federal court. In this case, the plaintiffs complained that the school district had failed to abide by a settlement agreement that had been reached under the IDEA after they had filed for due process. Because the gravemen of their complaint was the adequacy of the IEP, and they had previously sought to vindicate those rights under the IDEA, the court required them to exhaust their IDEA remedies. The case was dismissed without prejudice, allowing the plaintiffs to re-file once exhaustion had occurred.

The post-*Fry* cases may reflect that the rule announced in *Fry* will be challenging for lower court judges to apply. If there is an ongoing administrative complaint in process, it seems unlikely that lower court judges will allow parties to circumvent those processes by bringing a federal district court claim. If the plaintiff can demonstrate that a nondisabled student or a disabled adult (who is not covered by the IDEA) could seek similar relief, then it appears the court will allow the plaintiffs to go forward without exhausting IDEA remedies. It also may help if the plaintiff is no longer attending school in the district so that a new IEP would not be an effective remedy. Yet, it may take further consideration for the courts to create a consistent application of the *Fry* test.

§ 4.3 VOUCHERS

The use of vouchers for students with disabilities has become an increasingly common practice and may spawn future litigation. States sometimes offer parents vouchers from state funds to help pay for their child to attend a private school, often a private school that exclusively serves students with certain disabilities such as autism. The parent typically signs a waiver stating that they understand their child is no longer attending a public school and is no longer covered by the IDEA (since the IDEA does not directly apply to private education.) Because these vouchers have historically been taken from *state* funds, they do not necessarily trigger Section 504 coverage, because Section 504 coverage is dependent on the receipt of *federal* financial assistance. Nonetheless, the ADA Title III covers private schools.

It is possible that the federal government will someday make available vouchers that go directly to parents or private schools to help pay for some disability-related education. The schools covered by those vouchers might still *not* be covered by the IDEA; however, the flow of federal financial assistance should make them covered by Section 504.

In thinking about *vouchers,* it is important to distinguish them from what are often called "charter schools." Charter schools are typically *public schools*—wholly funded with state tax dollars. As public schools, they are fully covered by the IDEA.

§ 4.4 SAMPLE SECTION 504 PLAN

The development of a Section 504 plan is similar to the development of an IEP as will be discussed in *Nutshell* Chapter 6. The school district will have an educational evaluation of the student and a team will develop a Section 504 plan. Unlike an IEP, however, there will typically not be specialized instruction under a Section 504 plan. There will be accommodations such as extra time or preferential seating. Below is an example of an evaluation followed by a Section 504 plan.

BELINDA[1]

1. Evaluation

Summary of Evaluation

STUDENT: Belinda	CHRONOLOGICAL AGE: 12–2
DATE OF EVALUATION: November 2012	GRADE: 7th

Background and School History:

Belinda was born after an uncomplicated pregnancy. Developmental milestones were reported within normal limits. She was a colicky baby for the first 3 months, and became clingy after 4 months of age. She had trouble separating from her mother during her toddler years. She had minor surgery at age 2, and was burned in an accident at 3 years of age. At age 8 she had a concussion and spent

1 Thank you to Dr. Nicole Ofiesh for giving me permission to share this example.

several nights in the hospital. Otherwise, she has been a healthy child. As a preschool student, she only talked in whispers and wanted her mother with her. Currently, she is socially active and successful.

All report cards through 5th grade indicate grade-level skills. Nevertheless, there were reports of difficulties with lower than expected STAR testing, writing skills, math concepts, and reading in 3rd and 4th grade. Belinda was evaluated in 4th grade, and findings indicated age appropriate cognitive skills, but a weakness in executive function skills, particularly working memory and integration of novel information. Belinda was given a diagnosis of **Learning Disability Not Otherwise Specified**. Her low standardized test scores were attributed to anxiety in a timed test situation. In 5th grade, a psychologist did a school observation to look more closely at attention difficulties. Though Belinda's attention appeared to waiver somewhat, schoolwork was completed and it was decided not to pursue further testing.

Entrance tests scores for middle school indicate Verbal Reasoning at the 25th percentile, reading comprehension at the 19th percentile and 25th percentile for math achievement. After allowing her to be independent for first semester of 6th grade, her mother inquired about her progress, finding out that Belinda often sloppily did her homework, did not follow directions, and left parts incomplete. For second half, Belinda worked with another teacher on a regular basis after school and work was done more carefully. Belinda played the lead in the school play, and did quite well. Socially, she had a successful year.

Belinda took the ERB's Comprehensive Testing Program 4 assessment at the end of 6th grade. She earned mostly average scores by national norms. Her quantitative reasoning score was in the average range and her reading comprehension score was at the 2nd percentile, according to these norms.

A school observation in 7th grade indicates that Belinda was often off-task and tended to blurt out incorrect answers. The teacher expressed concerns over Belinda's ability to process information in a timely manner, her difficulty remembering what she learned, and her low vocabulary.

Teacher/Parent Comments:

Teacher comments at the end of 6th grade include the following:

- Computer science: less engaged, off task, disruptive during work time, developed a good website
- Humanities: improved work habits and effort, needs to spend more time in prewriting, submits assignments on time, approaches expectations
- Math: shows energy and persistence, difficulty staying on task, off topic conversations
- Science: approached course expectations in vocabulary and concepts. Inconsistent

classwork and homework completing, struggled to use time wisely, trouble staying focused.

Comments from Belinda's mother include

- Reading is a huge issue for Belinda. She does not read anything that is not required for school.
- It took all summer with the help of a tutor to read one of summer reading books. The other one she only read the summary outline
- Spelling is fair and "she is good at writing narrative stories". On essays her writing is very simple
- She has difficulty with word problems in math, sometimes misreading
- She has become a good self advocate, talking with teachers and asking for help

Behavior During Testing:

Belinda was cooperative during the 2 sessions of testing, but did not engage with the examiner and made little eye contact. In a one-to-one situation, attention was adequate. She seemed to know more than she was able to express. She was motivated to do her best, but sometimes gave up easily. Test results are considered to be valid.

Test Results:

CLUSTER/Test	Standard Score	Percentile Rank
Wechsler Intelligence Scale for Children (WISC)		
VERBAL COMPREHENSION	106	66
PERCEPTUAL REASONING	108	70
WORKING MEMORY	97	42
PROCESSING SPEED	91	27
Woodcock-Johnson III (Cognitive)		
Visual Matching	91	27
Decision Speed	128	97
Retrieval Fluency	89	24
Rapid Picture Naming	107	67
(Cluster Scores not meaningful considering discrepancy of scores)		
Wide Range Assessment of Memory and Learning, 2nd Edition		
VERBAL MEMORY INDEX	105	63

VERBAL RECOGNITION INDEX	102	55
VISUAL MEMORY INDEX	97	42
VISUAL RECOGNITION INDEX	90	25
ATTENTION/ CONCENTRATION	94	34
Wechsler Individual Achievement Test—III		
LISTENING COMPREHENSION	80	09
Word Reading	101	53
Reading Comprehension	66	02
ESSAY COMPOSITION	95	37
Spelling	101	53
Word Count	92	30
SENTENCE COMPOSITION	114	82
MATH PROBLEM SOLVING	115	84
NUMERICAL OPERATIONS	105	63

Rating Scale Results:

BASC: Clinically significant areas from more than one rater include attention, hyperactivity, functional communication, and anger control.

Conners' Rating Scales: Clinically significant areas from more than one rater include inattention, hyperactivity/impulsivity, learning problems, and executive function skills.

BRIEF: Clinically significant areas from more than one rater include ability to inhibit and shift focus, working memory, ability to plan, organize, and self-monitor.

Strengths and Areas of Concern From Testing:

Strengths include verbal comprehension and reasoning, writing at the sentence level, and ability to solve math word problems.

Areas of Concern include working memory, attention, focus, executive functioning, hyperactivity and impulsivity. Academic areas of concern include reading and listening comprehension, as well as essay and report writing.

Diagnoses:

- ADHD, Primarily Inattentive
- Adjustment Disorder with Anxiety
- Mixed Receptive and Expressive Language Disorder
- Developmental Reading Disorder

Recommended Accommodations and Strategies for class and tests:

- Extended time on tests
- Availability of sample products for assignments
- Preferential seating
- Summary statements for new material given in class
- Use of highlighter for reading directions
- Check understanding of oral and written instructions
- Provide step-by-step written instructions for all tasks
- Allow all written work to be done on a computer
- No penalization for mechanical or spelling errors

Recommended Strategies for Study Skills and Educational Therapy:

- Preloading of vocabulary used in topics coming up in class
- Reading summaries before reading a book
- SQ3R for reading textbooks
- Use of graphic organizers for study and writing assignments

- Becoming proficient in word processing
- Learn Active Reading strategies
- Work with an educational specialist to focus on reading comprehension strategies, essay writing steps, following directions and note taking

Recommended Strategies for ADHD:

- Provide sources of motivation with a ratio of 5–1 positive
- Provide strategies for efficient completion of tasks
- Develop a behavioral management plan to address difficulties with initiation, attention, staying on task, and completing tasks in a timely manner
- Learn external supports for herself, such as lists, goals, self-rewards, breaking up tasks into steps, using a timer, etc.
- Break long tasks into small chunks with deadlines
- Provide breaks between tasks
- Encourage routine physical exercise

2. Section 504 Plan

SECTION 504 ELIGIBILITY DETERMINATION

504 Meeting Participants: Section 504 requires that "a group of persons, including persons knowledgeable about the child, the meaning of evaluation data, and placement recommendations" make eligibility and accommodation or placement/services decisions for students.

Section 504 Eligibility Inquiry: "Does the student have a physical or mental impairment that substantially limits one or more major life activities?" The 504 team needs to answer the following two questions.

1. **Mental or Physical Impairment:** (Document discussion here, including the reasoning and the sources of information that were considered. Attach extra sheets of paper as needed.) Describe the nature (or possible diagnosis) of the suspected mental or physical impairment and the source of information.

Student had outside psychoeducational evaluation. She has been diagnosed with Attention Deficit Disorder, Primarily Inattentive and Adjustment Disorder with Anxiety. Also, she was diagnosed with Developmental Reading Disorder. Student had independent Speech/Language Assessment. She was diagnosed with Mixed Receptive and Expressive Language Disorder.

Does the student have a mental or physical impairment (including behavioral issues that significantly impede the student from accessing education)?

Team Conclusion: X Yes □ No (skip #2, student is not eligible)

2. **Major Life Activity and Substantial Limitation.** (Document discussion here, including reasoning and what sources of information were considered. Attach extra sheets of paper as needed.) State what major life activities are thought to be substantially limited.

Attention and focus in school; Working memory and language processing; Reading and taking exams

Describe how the suspected impairment may substantially limit the above major life activity/-ies.

- *Difficulties with focus and concentration in class;*
- *Test taking impacted by reading and attention disorders*
- *Anxiety may further limit memory skills*
- *Difficulty following complex oral directions and/or lectures*
- *Reading Comprehension impacted by reading and attention disorder*

Does the impairment(s) substantially limit one or more major life activities?

Team Conclusion: X Yes □ No

The 504 Team analysis of the eligibility question indicate: (Check one)

□ The student is eligible under Section 504 and will receive a 504 Plan. The 504 Team should continue to develop the 504 Plan appropriate for the student, or schedule a subsequent meeting for this purpose.

□ The student is not eligible for services/accommodations under Section 504 as the impairment does not meet the above criteria.

□ The student is eligible under Section 504 but does not require accommodations/services at this time.

X (Re-Evaluation) The student remains eligible under Section 504 and will receive an updated 504 Plan.

SECTION 504 ELIGIBILITY DETERMINATION (504–4)

Accommodations:

Specific Need: *Attention and executive skills deficit*	Accommodations/Services *Extra Time on tests in school and standardized tests* Who will implement the accommodation: Classroom teacher	Start Date *8/16*	End Date *5/17*
Specific Need: *Attention*	Accommodations/Services *Access to the testing center* Who will implement the	Start Date *8/16*	End Date *5/17*

and executive skills deficit	accommodations: Guidance Counselor		
Specific Need *Attention and executive skills deficit*	Accommodations/Services *Preferential seating, away from distractions* Who will implement the accommodations: Classroom teacher	Start Date *8/16*	End Date *5/17*
Specific Need *Receptive and expressive language deficit*	Accommodations/Services *Segmenting exams to one page at a time* Who will implement the accommodations: Classroom teacher	Start Date *8/16*	End Date *5/17*
Specific Need *Attention and executive skills deficit*	Accommodations/ Services *Segmenting of long term assignments* Who will implement the accommodations: Classroom teacher	Start Date *8/16*	End Date *5/17*
Specific Need *Receptive and expressive language deficit*	Accommodations/Services *Note cards for formulas as approved with teacher* Who will implement the accommodations: Math Teacher	Start Date *8/16*	End Date *5/17*

Specific Need *Receptive and expressive language deficit*	Accommodations/Services *Spanish—for audio or verbal assessments allow for repeat of information for student clarity* Who will implement the accommodation: Spanish Teacher	Start Date *8/16*	End Date *5/17*
Specific Need *Attention and executive skills deficit*	Accommodation/Services *Spanish—list of irregular verbs and sample template of conjugation for common verb tenses* Who will implement the accommodation: Spanish Teacher	Start Date *8/16*	End Date *5/17*

3. Analysis

Belinda has a classic profile for ADHD although she also has weak reading skills. Because the primary recommendations were accommodations rather than specialized instruction, her school district decided to put her on a Section 504 plan instead of an IEP. It appears that her parents were willing to work with an educational specialist outside of the school day to improve her reading comprehension and merely seek accommodations in the classroom. Since Belinda is already in seventh grade, her school is probably no longer offering reading instruction during English class. With this profile, some parents would insist on specialized instruction in reading during the school day, while other parents might prefer for their child to remain in the regular English class and receive specialized instruction at their own cost outside of the school day. With a verbal aptitude score in the 66th percentile and a reading comprehension score in the 2nd percentile, Belinda's parents could have had a strong argument for specialized reading instruction.

By agreeing to a Section 504 plan, Belinda is getting strong support in the classroom. The team considered her needs in math, English, and Spanish classes, and apparently thinks she will have stronger reading comprehension if she reads one page at a time. If this approach is not successful and Belinda continues to struggle in reading comprehension, the team could convert her Section 504 plan into an IEP. In this kind of situation, a parent has to decide whether to contest the school district's reluctance to create an IEP or accept the Section 504 plan and see how it works out. The parent would also have to consider whether the child *wants* specialized reading instruction during the school day. Many children feel stigmatized by such specialized instruction. As we will see in *Nutshell* Chapter 5, some children convert from a Section 504 plan to an IEP when the accommodations under a Section 504 plan prove insufficient.

CHAPTER 5
EVALUATIONS

§ 5.1 CHILD FIND

The IDEA has extensive rules about evaluations and eligibility determinations. The beginning of this process involves what is called "Child Find." *See* 20 U.S.C. § 1412(a)(3). This provision requires states to have a program in place to identify, locate, and evaluate all children to determine if they have disabilities "including children with disabilities who are homeless children or are wards of the State and children with disabilities attending private schools, regardless of the severity of their disabilities." The regulations clarify that each state must have in place "a practical method . . . to determine which children are currently receiving needed special education and related services." 34 C.F.R. § 300.111. These rules include "[h]ighly mobile children, including migrant children." 34 C.F.R. § 300.111(c).

As soon as a child is identified as a potential candidate for services under the IDEA, the school district has a duty to locate that child and complete the evaluation process. Failure to locate and evaluate a potentially disabled child constitutes a violation of the IDEA. *See* 20 U.S.C. § 1412(a)(3). Lawsuits against the District of Columbia have created much of the case law in the Child Find area. In 2001, the United States Office of Special Education Programs (OSEP) entered into a Compliance Agreement with the District of Columbia Public Schools (DCPS) to ensure that the district provided timely evaluations of children potentially considered disabled but OSEP repeatedly found DCPS not to be in compliance with that Agreement. *See e.g., DL v. District of Columbia*, 730 F. Supp.2d 84, 97 (D.D.C. 2010). In a case brought by private parties in 2010, the plaintiffs argued that one would expect at least 6 percent of the preschool population in the District of Columbia to qualify as disabled under the IDEA, yet D.C. only served 2.94 percent of its 3–5 year-olds under the IDEA, "which was the lowest rate in the country." *Id.* at 95. The district court relied on the following conclusions, as well as OSEP's annual determination that DCPS was not in compliance with its Agreement, to grant summary judgment to the plaintiffs on the Child Find allegation:

- "defendants' public awareness and outreach efforts were unlikely to result in a substantial increase in the number of referrals to preschool special education;"
- "defendants' refusal to accept and act on referrals made by primary referral sources was impeding identification of children eligible for pre-school special education;" and
- only "62.02% of all children ages 3 through 5 received an eligibility determination within 120 days of referral.

Despite the successful litigation against D.C. and the entry of various consent decrees, litigation continues regarding DCPS' Child Find obligations. *See D.L. v. District of Columbia*, 194 F. Supp.3d 30

(D.D.C. 2016), for an appeal filed June 27, 2016 (decision pending; oral argument held before Judges Tatel, Griffith, and Millett on March 31, 2017).

The D.C. litigation is highly unusual because it is a class action lawsuit. More typically, parents bring actions against a school district under the Child Find obligation because they fail to properly evaluate an individual child. The Child Find obligation is violated when no evaluation is completed, despite a plausible suspicion of disability status.

A good example of a Child Find obligation can be found in a recent case brought against the Greenwich Board of Education. *See Greenwich Board of Education v. G.M. and J.M.,* 2016 WL 3512120 (June 22, 2016). The Child Find violation occurred when K.M. was in kindergarten and first grade at Riverside Elementary School in Greenwich, Connecticut. During kindergarten, K.M.'s parents brought to her teacher's attention that K.M.'s family had a history of learning disabilities. In November of kindergarten, K.M. was assigned to a Response to Intervention (RTI) team where she began to receive some specialized instruction. K.M.'s parents began supplementing the school district's assistance with a private reading tutor, and they also hired a private psychologist, Dr. Jill Greenberg, in first grade who determined that K.M. had a specific reading disorder, ADHD, and generalized anxiety. *Id.* at *3. Based on Dr. Greenberg's evaluation, the parents then sent the principal a request for a referral to determine eligibility for special education and related services. Rather than conduct an evaluation, the school district convened a team, which met and concluded that K.M. was "ineligible for special education and related services because she 'has responded to the current level of interaction.' " [sic—probably meant "intervention"] *Id.* at *4.

K.M.'s parents brought a due process hearing against the school district challenging the school's summary denial of the parents' request for K.M. to be evaluated. At the due process hearing, the school district did not contest that it failed to evaluate K.M. Its justification for the failure to evaluate was that K.M. was making sufficient progress through the RTI program. *Id.* at *10. Emphasizing that the IDEA requires a school district to conduct an evaluation when there are merely "signs" of disability, the district court noted these "signs" included:

- Dr. Greenberg's report
- K.M.'s reading level dropping from grade level to below grade level while she was receiving intervention services
- Even school district personnel acknowledging that they wanted to continue to monitor K.M. during second grade because they "didn't know" if K.M. was eligible under IDEA

Id. at *11.

In affirming the Hearing Officer's Child Find violation, the district court judge emphasized the difference between *knowing* that a child is disabled under the IDEA and *suspecting* that a child may be disabled, thereby triggering the evaluation requirement. Further, the district court judge emphasized a letter to Dr. Perry A. Zirkel in which the Department of Education said: "An RTI process does not replace the need for a comprehensive evaluation." *Id.* at *13. In this case, the court found that the school district "prematurely and improperly cut-off the disability review process," causing a denial of FAPE. *Id.* at *13. While not all procedural violations of the IDEA constitute a substantive denial of FAPE, the court found that this procedural violation did meet that threshold by foreclosing the parents entirely from accessing the IDEA decision-making process. *Id.* at *13. The rules that apply to determining whether a procedural violation is "substantive" will be discussed in *Nutshell* Chapter 9.

Because courts frequently refer to the Zirkel letter, it is copied below for important reference.

UNITED STATES DEPARTMENT OF EDUCATION

OFFICE OF SPECIAL EDUCATION AND REHABILITATIVE SERVICES

MARCH 6, 2007

Dr. Perry A. Zirkel
Lehigh University
Department of Education and Human Services
College of Education
Mountaintop Campus 111 Research Drive

Bethlehem, Pennsylvania 18015-4794

Dear Dr. Zirkel:

Thank you for your recent correspondence to Mr. John Hager, Assistant Secretary for the Office of Special Education and Rehabilitative Services, U.S. Department of Education regarding issues related to identifying children and youth with specific learning disabilities. Your letter was referred to the Office of Special Education Programs (OSEP), for response.

You requested guidance from OSEP relating to procedures for identifying children with specific learning disabilities, as required by 34 CFR § 300.307(a). Specifically, you inquired if a State may: (1) prohibit local educational agencies (LEAs) from using severe discrepancy and require them to use response to intervention (RTI); (2) permit severe discrepancy, RTI, and a third research-based model, thereby leaving the choice among the three options to each LEA; and (3) prohibit or permit the use of a successive combination of RTI and severe discrepancy (i.e., RTI as the initial steps and severe discrepancy as part of the culminating determination).

The regulations at 34 CFR § 300.307(a) provide that a State must adopt criteria for determining whether a child has a specific learning disability, and LEAs must use the criteria adopted by the State educational agency (SEA). The criteria adopted by the States cannot require LEAs to use a severe discrepancy between intellectual ability and achievement to determine whether a child has a specific learning disability. 34 CFR § 300.307(a)(*l*). Moreover, the Analysis of Comments and Changes section of the final Part B Regulations to the Individuals with Disabilities Education Act of 2004 (IDEA 2004) indicates that States may prohibit the use of a discrepancy model. 71 Fed. Reg. 46646 (August 14, 2006). Accordingly, while a State cannot require the use of a severe discrepancy model, a State may prohibit, or make optional, the use of a severe discrepancy model.

As required in 34 CFR § 300.304(b)(*l*) and (2), consistent with section 614(b)(2) of the Act, an evaluation of a child suspected of having a disability, including a specific learning disability, must include a variety of assessment tools and strategies and cannot rely on any single procedure as the sole criterion for determining eligibility for special education and related services. With respect to a child suspected of having a specific learning disability, in accordance with 34 CFR § 300.307(a)(2) and (3), State criteria must permit the use of a process based on the child's response to scientific, research-based intervention, and may permit the use of other alternative research-based procedures (emphasis added). An RTI process does not replace the need for a comprehensive evaluation, and the results of an RTI process may be one component of the information reviewed as part of the evaluation procedures required under 34 CFR §§ 300.304 and 330.305. Finally, the manner in which the State chooses to use RTI as one component of a comprehensive evaluation is left up to the States.

Based on section 607(e) of the IDEA, we are informing you that our response is provided as informal guidance and is not legally binding, but represents an interpretation by the U.S. Department of Education of the IDEA in the context of the specific facts presented.

If you have any further questions, please do not hesitate to contact us.

Alexa Posny, Ph.D. Director
Office of Special Education Programs

One of the important points in the letter is that school districts cannot rely on a "sole criterion" for determining eligibility. RTI cannot be the sole criterion for determining that there is not even a suspicion of disability to trigger the evaluation requirement.

Further, it is important to remember that the requirement to evaluate students who are suspected of being disabled does not only cover students suspected of a learning disability. For example, it also covers children suspected of having an "emotional disturbance." As will be discussed below, school districts sometimes fail to engage in proper evaluations when students have serious behavior problems or even are attempting suicide.

§ 5.2 EVALUATION PROCEDURES

The IDEA requires that, in conducting an evaluation to determine IDEA eligibility, the school district shall:

> (A) use a variety of assessment tools and strategies to gather relevant functional, developmental, and academic information, including information provided by the parent, that may assist in determining—(i) whether the child is a child with a disability; and (ii) the content of the child's individualized education program, including information related to enabling the child to be involved in and progress in the general curriculum, or, for preschool children, to participate in appropriate activities;
>
> (B) not use any single measure or assessment as the sole criterion for determining whether a child is a child with a disability or determining an appropriate educational program for the child; and
>
> (C) use technically sound instruments that may assess the relative contribution of cognitive and behavioral factors, in addition to physical or developmental factors.

20 U.S.C. § 1414(b)(2).

The rules also provide that the child must be "assessed in all areas of suspected disability." 20 U.S.C. § 1414(b)(3)(B). The assessments must also be "administered by trained and knowledgeable personnel." 20 U.S.C. § 1414(b)(3)(A)(iv). "A group of qualified professionals and the parent of the child" must make the determination of whether a child has a covered disability. 34 C.F.R. § 300.306(a)(1).

The obligation to assess the child in all areas of suspected disability is that of the school district, not the parent. The Ninth Circuit explains the nature of that obligation well in *N.B. and C.B. v. Hellgate Elementary School District*, 541 F.3d 1202 (9th Cir. 2008). In this case, like other cases cited by the Ninth Circuit, the school district acknowledged the child needed to be assessed to determine if he was disabled under the IDEA but expected the parent, rather than the school district, to obtain the evaluation. While parents are permitted to supplement the record with evaluations that the school district should consider, the school district cannot justify their incomplete evaluation information by blaming the parent for a failure to provide information. Nonetheless, in this case, the parents initially lost before the administrative law judge and the district court; the Ninth Circuit reversed those earlier decisions in ruling that the school district failed to meet its obligation to evaluate the child in all areas of suspected disability.

Similarly, in *Union School District v. B. Smith,* 15 F.3d 1519, 1523 (9th Cir. 1994), the Ninth Circuit held that the "failure of the [parents] to turn over portions of a specialist's report cannot excuse the District's failure to procure the same information for itself." It is the school district's responsibility to ensure that the appropriate evaluations are conducted, not the parent's. In this case, the parents prevailed at all stages of the litigation—Hearing Officer, district court, and court of appeals.

When there is reason to suspect a child is disabled, the school district needs to complete a full, proper evaluation rather than allow informal observations to be the basis of concluding a child is not disabled. A good example of that rule can be found in *Timothy O. v. Paso Robles Unified School District,* 822 F.3d 1105 (9th Cir. 2016). Like in many cases discussed in this *Nutshell*, the parents lost before the Hearing Officer when they first challenged the school district's conduct, as well as in the district court, but eventually attained relief in the court of appeals. In the *Timothy O.* case, the student, Luke, had been diagnosed as autistic when he was quite young and had received special services most likely under an IFSP. When he was turning three, his parents approached the school district about developing an IEP. Their request triggered the school district's obligation to have him evaluated. That evaluation became a source of litigation.

The school district's assessment included an evaluation by a district resource specialist and a speech and language therapist. Luke was to be evaluated for academic/pre-academic achievement, sensory-motor development, communication development, and health issues. He was *not* to be evaluated for "social/adaptive behavior" even though autism was the most likely diagnostic category.

These two professionals, however, were not able to administer standard assessment tools because of "compliance" issues. *Id.* at 1114. In other words, they could not get Luke to cooperate with the testing professionals. Luke's parents were present during this attempt to assess Luke.

The school psychologist was also present at the evaluation even though he had not been listed on the notice to the parents describing the evaluation that would take place. The psychologist did not administer any standard assessment instruments. He merely observed Luke, and based on these informal observations, the school district concluded that Luke had an expressive language impairment but not autism.

Luke's parents supplemented the record with a private evaluation that offered a provisional diagnosis that Luke was on the autism spectrum. The school district, however, did not reconsider its decision not to evaluate Luke for autism because the school psychologist took the position that his "earlier observation of Luke had dispelled any suspicion that Luke had such a disorder and because [the private] 'provisional' diagnosis was not conclusive." *Id.* at 1115. The school district seemed to conflate "knowing" that Luke had autism with the legal requirement that they assess for autism if there was reason to "suspect" the impairment. The Ninth Circuit found that the failure to conduct an appropriate violation for Luke precluded the IEP team from creating a proper educational plan for him. Thus, the evaluation errors resulted in a denial of his right to a Free and Appropriate Public Education.

§ 5.3 INDEPENDENT EDUCATIONAL EVALUATIONS

A. INTRODUCTION

When a school district does not do a proper evaluation of a child in all of the areas of suspected disability, the parent can request that the school district pay for their independent evaluation. The following regulation applies to this situation:

> (1) A parent has the right to an independent educational evaluation at public expense if the parent disagrees with an evaluation obtained by the public agency, subject to the conditions in paragraphs (b)(2) through (4) of this section.
>
> (2) If a parent requests an independent educational evaluation at public expense, the public agency must, without unnecessary delay, either—
>
> (i) File a due process complaint to request a hearing to show that its evaluation is appropriate; or
>
> (ii) Ensure that an independent educational evaluation is provided at public expense, unless the agency demonstrates in a hearing pursuant to §§ 300.507 through 300.513 that the evaluation obtained by the parent did not meet agency criteria.
>
> (3) If the public agency files a due process complaint notice to request a hearing and the

> final decision is that the agency's evaluation is appropriate, the parent still has the right to an independent educational evaluation, but not at public expense.
>
> (4) If a parent requests an independent educational evaluation, the public agency may ask for the parent's reason why he or she objects to the public evaluation. However, the public agency may not require the parent to provide an explanation and may not unreasonably delay either providing the independent educational evaluation at public expense or filing a due process complaint to request a due process hearing to defend the public evaluation.
>
> (5) A parent is entitled to only one independent educational evaluation at public expense each time the public agency conducts an evaluation with which the parent disagrees.

34 C.F.R. § 300.502(b).

B. PARENTS' BASES FOR OBJECTION

1. Introduction

It is important to understand each step of the way this rule works. As discussed in *Nutshell* § 5.2, the school district has a responsibility to conduct an evaluation in all areas of suspected disability. That evaluation needs to conform to professional standards, using appropriate diagnostic instruments. If parents "disagree" with that evaluation then they can request that the school district pay for an independent evaluation.

Parents should put their disagreement in writing and give the school district an opportunity to respond by agreeing to pay for an independent evaluation or by filing for due process. Federal law does not specify an amount of time in which a school district must respond. Some states specify a time frame, ranging from 5 days (Massachusetts) to 30 days (Maine).

Although the regulatory language merely says that the parent must "disagree" with the school district's evaluation, that opinion is rarely enough, in practice, to force the school district to pay for the independent evaluation. When a parent requests that the school district pay for an independent evaluation, the school district can object by filing a due process complaint to demonstrate that the evaluation they already conducted was "appropriate." An "appropriate" evaluation is generally considered to be one that used professionals to evaluate the child in all areas of suspected disability. It's not enough for a parent merely to want what we might call a "second opinion." There needs to be some flaw in the school district's evaluation process in order for the parent to prevail at the due process hearing if the school district takes the matter to due process.

If the school fails to contest the parent's right to have a publicly-funded, independent educational evaluation by filing for due process, then the school district is supposed to make certain that the evaluation takes place. Typically, the school district expects the parent to schedule the IEE from professionals who meet school district professional criteria and seek reimbursement. If a parent cannot afford to make payment and seek reimbursement, then the school district should agree to pay the provider directly. Disputes sometimes occur about the rates charged by a private evaluator so it is important for the parent to communicate with the school district before choosing a private evaluator for an IEE. The IEE is supposed to be "independent"; thus, a school district cannot overly restrict the list of potential evaluators.

Despite the clear regulatory language regarding IEE's, school districts do not always follow these rules, and Hearing Officers do not always protect parents' rights in this context. A recent decision by the D.C. District Court reflects the persistence a parent may need in order to use this rule.

The school district first evaluated R.P. when he was five or six years old in November 2013. More than 15 disciplinary events occurred after November 2013. In January 2014, Potomac Preparatory School concluded that R.P. was not eligible to receive services under the IDEA. In March 2014, R.P. attempted to commit suicide by jumping out of a school window because "he wanted to die." *Horne v. Potomac Preparatory P.C.S.*, 209 F. Supp.3d 146 (D.D.C. 2016).

As early as March 31, 2014, R.P.'s mother, Deidre Horne, requested that R.P. be re-evaluated based on ongoing behavioral problems and declining grades.

Although she did not use the phrase "independent educational evaluation" (IEE) in her March 31st letter, she did use that term in a May 7, 2014 email. The school held a meeting with Horne on May 16, 2014 and declined to fund an IEE. It requested that she withdraw her request for an IEE, suggesting that it was aware she had made an IEE request by that date. Horne renewed her request for an IEE on May 20, 2014. Because the school district had still not authorized the IEE or filed for due process to contest her right to an IEE, Horne notified the school on August 1, 2014 that she was going to have her son evaluated by an independent examiner and would be seeking reimbursement from the school. Horne filed for due process on August 5, 2014, requesting reimbursement for an IEE. On August 15, 2014, the school district filed a response and counterclaim arguing that its 2013 evaluation was appropriate; therefore, Horne was not entitled to an IEE at the public's expense. The Hearing Officer ruled in favor of the school district finding that its delay was not an "unnecessary delay" and that the school's 2013 evaluation was appropriate.

2. Unnecessary Delay

Horne appealed the Hearing Officer's decision, arguing that the delay by the school district constituted an "unnecessary delay" and that the events that occurred between November 2013 and March 2014's suicide attempt demonstrated that the school's evaluation was not "appropriate." The rationale for concluding that the delay was not "unnecessary" was that the school continued to have conversations with Horne during the summer of 2014 about her son's educational plan (but not about whether it would fund an IEE). However, as the district court found, the "IDEA does not require a parent to do more than request an IEE." *Id.* at 155. Although Horne had requested an IEE, the school district had indicated that it would not fund the IEE. The school district then needed to promptly file for due process if it planned not to fund the IEE. The district court cited two other cases where courts had found unnecessary delays—*Pajaro Valley Unified School District v. J.S.*, 2006 WL 3734289 (N.D. Cal Dec. 15, 2006) (three month delay) and *M.M. v. Lafayette School District*, 2012 WL 3257662 (N.D. Cal. Aug. 8, 2012) (74 day delay). It also distinguished two cases where the delay occurred because the parties were having ongoing discussions about funding the IEE—*J.P. ex rel. E.P. v. Ripon Unified School District,* 2009 WL 1034993 (E.D. Cal. 2009) (3 weeks after final impasse) and *L.S. ex rel. K.S. v. Abington School District,* 2007 WL 2851268 (E.D. Pa. 2007) (6 weeks while efforts to resolve dispute continued).

3. Appropriateness of the School District's Evaluation

The second significant issue in the case was whether the district's evaluation of R.P. was "appropriate." The district argued that the only relevant factor was whether its 2013 evaluation used appropriate methodology. Horne's lawyer successfully argued that the events that occurred between November 2013 and May 2014 triggered a new obligation to evaluate R.P. under the IDEA's Child Find rules. The school district's failure to comply with its Child Find obligation made its evaluation inappropriate, not the methodology used in the evaluation itself.

The *Horne* case is unusual in that the court used evidence that occurred after the initial evaluation to conclude that an IEE was necessary. The court may have been influenced by some unusual facts in the case. The public charter school that R.P. had been attending had been closed by the District of Columbia because it fell below the school district's academic benchmarks. *Id.* at 157. R.P. was enrolling in a new public school and the court may have considered it essential for him to be classified as disabled in order to receive an appropriate IEP. Moreover, it made no sense to remand for further discussions with the now-closed public school.

A more typical consideration of a request for an Independent Educational Evaluation can be found in *Seattle School District, No. 1 v. B.S.*, 82 F.3d 1493 (9th Cir. 1996). In this case, A.S.'s mother requested an evaluation when her daughter was eight years old, in April 1990. At that time, the school district completed an evaluation and concluded that A.S. was not disabled. After a three-month hospitalization following verbally and physical assaultive behavior, the school district re-evaluated A.S. in May 1993. After this second evaluation, the school district concluded A.S. was disabled and recommended that she attend a day program within the district. A.S.'s mother was not satisfied with this evaluation because she believed A.S. needed to be in a residential program. She sought to have the district pay for A.S. to have an evaluation by a child psychiatrist. The school district denied this request and filed for due process before an ALJ arguing that their evaluation had been appropriate, and they should not be required to pay for an IEE.

Both the ALJ and the district court concluded that the school district's evaluation was not appropriate because the school district "failed to include on the assessment team anyone with knowledge in the disorders known to be the cause of A.S.'s problems." *Id.* at 1499. That statement from the Ninth Circuit was based on an updated regulation. As the Ninth Circuit recognized in a more recent decision, the regulations no longer require an "expert" in the diagnostic category to be present at the evaluation meeting. *See R.P. ex rel. C.P. v. Prescott Unified School District,* 631 F.3d 1117, 1122 (9th Cir. 2011). Nonetheless, the *Seattle School District* case is sometimes cited for the proposition that there must be "at least one teacher or specialist with knowledge in the suspected area of disability." *S.B. ex rel. Dilip B. v. Pomona Unified School District,* 2008 WL 1766953, at * 6 (C.D. Cal. April 15, 2008).

While it is not clear that a court today would conclude the school district's evaluation was inappropriate merely because there was no one present who was an expert in the child's alleged disability, it is still the case that most situations would follow that process—the parent requests an

IEE, the school district files for due process, and a Hearing Officer determines if the parent was entitled to an IEE because the school district's evaluation was not "appropriate." The rules that today govern whether a school district evaluation is "appropriate" will be discussed in *Nutshell* § 5.4

4. Who Initiates the Hearing

Interpretations of the IEE requirement vary significantly from circuit to circuit with some circuits not requiring the school district to initiate a hearing to contest the parents' request for an IEE. The Fifth and Sixth Circuits have ruled that the school district can object to the appropriateness of the IEE by defending its evaluation at a due process hearing initiated by the parents. *See P.R. v. Woodmore Local School District,* 256 Fed. Appx. 751, 755 (6th Cir. 2007); *Seth B. v. Orleans Parish School Board,* 810 F.3d 961, 970 (5th Cir. 2016).

By contrast, the Seventh, Eighth, and Eleventh Circuits have ruled that the school district must initiate a hearing to challenge the parents' request for an IEE if they are not willing to pay for it. *See Evans v. District No. 17,* 841 F.2d 824, 830 (8th Cir. 1988); *Board of Education v. Illinois State Board of Education,* 41 F.3d 1162, 1169 (7th Cir. 1994); *Jefferson County Board of Education v. Lolita S.,* 581 Fed. Appx. 760, 765–66 (11th Cir. 2014). The ambiguity stems from the language in § 300.502(b)(ii) excusing a school district from paying for an IEE if it "demonstrates in a hearing . . . that the evaluation obtained by the parent did not meet agency criteria." By contrast, § 300.502(b)(i) provides that the school district must "file" a complaint and "request" a hearing. The regulation is ambiguous about *who* must initiate the hearing. Does (b)(ii)'s reference to a hearing implicitly reference a school district initiated hearing? The Fifth and Sixth Circuits say no; the Seventh, Eighth, and Eleventh Circuits say yes.

§ 5.4 ELIGIBILITY EVALUATIONS

A. STATUTORY AND REGULATORY LANGUAGE

The general principles that apply to eligibility evaluations are described at 20 U.S.C. § 1414(a) & (b). The regulatory language repeats and amplifies the statutory requirements.

These are the regulations that apply to a school district's evaluation procedures when it seeks to determine if a child is covered by the IDEA. We will look at each part of these regulations below.

> Evaluation procedures.
>
> (a) Notice. The public agency must provide notice to the parents of a child with a disability, in accordance with § 300.503, that describes any evaluation procedures the agency proposes to conduct.
>
> (b) Conduct of evaluation. In conducting the evaluation, the public agency must—
>
> (1) Use a variety of assessment tools and strategies to gather relevant functional,

developmental, and academic information about the child, including information provided by the parent, that may assist in determining—

(i) Whether the child is a child with a disability under § 300.8; and

(ii) The content of the child's IEP, including information related to enabling the child to be involved in and progress in the general education curriculum (or for a preschool child, to participate in appropriate activities);

(2) Not use any single measure or assessment as the sole criterion for determining whether a child is a child with a disability and for determining an appropriate educational program for the child; and

(3) Use technically sound instruments that may assess the relative contribution of cognitive and behavioral factors, in addition to physical or developmental factors.

(c) Other evaluation procedures. Each public agency must ensure that –

(1) Assessments and other evaluation materials used to assess a child under this part—

(i) Are selected and administered so as not to be discriminatory on a racial or cultural basis;

(ii) Are provided and administered in the child's native language or other mode of communication and in the form most likely to yield accurate information on what the child knows and can do academically, developmentally, and functionally, unless it is clearly not feasible to so provide or administer;

(iii) Are used for the purposes for which the assessments or measures are valid and reliable;

(iv) Are administered by trained and knowledgeable personnel; and

(v) Are administered in accordance with any instructions provided by the producer of the assessments.

(2) Assessments and other evaluation materials include those tailored to assess specific areas of educational need and not merely those that are designed to provide a single general intelligence quotient.

(3) Assessments are selected and administered so as best to ensure that if an assessment is administered to a child with impaired sensory, manual, or speaking skills, the assessment results accurately reflect the child's aptitude or achievement level or whatever other factors the test purports to measure, rather than reflecting the child's impaired sensory, manual, or speaking skills (unless those skills are the factors that the test purports to measure).

(4) The child is assessed in all areas related to the suspected disability, including, if appropriate, health, vision, hearing, social and

emotional status, general intelligence, academic performance, communicative status, and motor abilities;

(5) Assessments of children with disabilities who transfer from one public agency to another public agency in the same school year are coordinated with those children's prior and subsequent schools, as necessary and as expeditiously as possible, consistent with § 300.301(d)(2) and (e), to ensure prompt completion of full evaluations.

(6) In evaluating each child with a disability under §§ 300.304 through 300.306, the evaluation is sufficiently comprehensive to identify all of the child's special education and related services needs, whether or not commonly linked to the disability category in which the child has been classified.

(7) Assessment tools and strategies that provide relevant information that directly assists persons in determining the educational needs of the child are provided.

34 C.F.R. § 300.304.

B. NOTICE AND CONSENT

The first rule, § 300.304(a), specifies that the school district will give notice to the parent before conducting an evaluation. Most states have a form that a school district would use to provide such notice and request permission for an evaluation. Below is the form used by North Carolina to provide notice and obtain parent/guardian consent for an evaluation:

PARENT/GUARDIAN/STUDENT AT AGE OF MAJORITY CONSENT FOR EVALUATION/REEVALUATION

Check Purpose: □ Initial Evaluation
□ Reevaluation

Student: Student Name Grade: Grade School: School Name

Dear ____:

The IEP Team has recognized the need for gathering more information about your child. The proposed screening(s) and evaluation(s) administered by qualified personnel will include the use of assessment instruments in the areas checked below to help identify strengths, areas of concern and to determine the existence of a disability. Each LEA must conduct a full and individualized initial evaluation before the initial provision of special education and related services to a child with a disability.

AREA	**INFORMATION**
□ Physical Health	Vision, hearing, medical screening/evaluation.
□ Educational	A variety of assessments measuring academic achievement and special abilities.
□ Psychological	A battery of tests and testing procedures measuring mental ability, skills, perceptual

	development, and processing development. behavioral/emotional
□ Intellectual Assessment	An intellectual assessment may or may not yield an intellectual quotient (IQ) score.
□ Social Appraisal	Developmental history, social, personal, and behavioral.
□ Speech/Language	Understanding and using spoken language or using other modes of communication screening/evaluation.
□ Motor	Visual motor integration, eye/hand coordination, fine and gross motor.
□ Adaptive Behavior	Functional behavior that is needed to meet the natural and social demands in one's environment, including daily living and self-help skills.
□ Vocational Evaluation	A comprehensive process involving an interdisciplinary team approach in assessing an individual's vocational potential, training, and work placement needs.
□ Other	____

PARENT/GUARDIAN CONSENT

The results of these evaluations will be shared with you. You are entitled to a copy of the evaluation report(s).

Please sign A or B and return to:

Name: _____

A. **YES, I give my permission** for my child to receive evaluation or reevaluation services. I have received the Handbook on Parents' Rights that explains due process procedures.

Signature: ______________________

B. **NO, I do not give my permission** for my child to receive evaluation or reevaluation services. I have received the Handbook on Parents' Rights that explains due process procedures.

Signature: ______________________

This is the final action (decision) of the local education agency. If you disagree, you, as the parent or adult student, are entitled to the due process rights that are described in your Handbook on Parents' Rights (https://ec.ncpublicschools.gov/parent-resources/parents-rights-handbook). The deadline for filing a petition for a due process hearing is one year (1 year) from receipt of this notice.

If you do not have a copy of the Handbook on Parents' Rights or would like another one, please contact your school principal or call the local director of Exceptional Children Programs. The principal or director can also help you understand your rights if you have any questions, or you can call the Exceptional Children's Assistance Center, 1-800-962-6817. Please save this notice for your records.

Typically, if the parent does not consent to an evaluation, then the school district will not conduct one. However, the school district can file for due process to obtain permission to evaluate a child who it suspects is disabled.

The North Carolina form also states the types of evaluations that the school district will conduct. The school is supposed to evaluate the child in all areas of suspected disability. If the completion of this, or a comparable form, suggests that the school district is overlooking an important area of disability, the parent can object to the scope of the evaluation. The failure to evaluate a child in all areas of suspected disability would be a factor in a parent seeking a publicly-funded IEE, as discussed in *Nutshell* § 5.3.

Once a school district receives the parent's consent for an initial evaluation, the initial evaluation must be conducted within 60 days unless a different time frame has been established by the state. 34 C.F.R. § 300.301(c)(1). This time frame does not apply if the parent of a child "repeatedly fails or refuses to produce the child for the evaluation." 34 C.F.R. § 300.301(d)(1).

§ 5.5 SPECIFIC LEARNING DISABILITIES

A. DISCREPANCY MODEL

Because of criticism of the "discrepancy model" for determining learning disabilities, Congress amended the IDEA to provide for alternative methods of assessing a learning disability. While a state may still permit the use of the discrepancy model, it also must allow other methods to be used to determine the presence of a learning disability. This general rule is provided in the statute at 20 U.S.C. § 1414(b)(6). The regulations amplify these rules:

> Specific learning disabilities.
>
> (a) General. A State must adopt, consistent with § 300.309, criteria for determining whether a child has a specific learning disability as defined in § 300.8(c)(10). In addition, the criteria adopted by the State—
>
> (1) Must not require the use of a severe discrepancy between intellectual ability and achievement for determining whether a child has a specific learning disability, as defined in § 300.8(c)(10);
>
> (2) Must permit the use of a process based on the child's response to scientific, research-based intervention; and
>
> (3) May permit the use of other alternative research-based procedures for determining whether a child has a specific learning disability, as defined in § 300.8(c)(10).
>
> (b) Consistency with State criteria. A public agency must use the State criteria adopted pursuant to paragraph (a) of this section in determining whether a child has a specific learning disability.

34 C.F.R. § 300.307.

There is not one consistent approach because each state has implemented regulations to comply with the learning disability rules.

When the discrepancy model is used to determine if a student has a learning disability then the school district typically administers an aptitude test and an achievement test to the student. The discrepancy model is discussed in *Nutshell* § 3.4. If there is a discrepancy between the achievement test score one would expect based on the aptitude score, then the student can be classified as having a learning disability in that particular subject (e.g., reading, writing, math). States typically require the discrepancy between aptitude and achievement to be more than 1.5 or 2.0 standard deviations. Thus, if a student has an aptitude of 100, then a score of 70 on an achievement test would be 2 standard deviations lower than what one would expect based on the student's aptitude. In order to make a determination based on the discrepancy model, the student needs an aptitude (i.e., IQ) score. In California, however, most school districts no longer conduct IQ tests because of the Ninth Circuit decision in *Larry P. v. Riles,* 793 F.2d 969 (9th Cir. 1984), where the court concluded that IQ tests were impermissibly used to place African-American children in classes for the "educable mentally retarded." Those classes were segregated from the regular classroom and characterized as "dead-end classes" that carried significant stigma. *Id.* at 973.

The following regulation governs the use of the discrepancy model to determine if a student has a learning disability.

> Determining the existence of a specific learning disability.
>
> (a) The group described in § 300.306 may determine that a child has a specific learning disability, as defined in § 300.8(c)(10), if—
>
> (1) The child does not achieve adequately for the child's age or to meet State-approved grade-level standards in one or more of the following areas, when provided with learning experiences and instruction appropriate for the child's age or State-approved grade-level standards:
>
> (i) Oral expression.
>
> (ii) Listening comprehension.
>
> (iii) Written expression.
>
> (iv) Basic reading skill.
>
> (v) Reading fluency skills.
>
> (vi) Reading comprehension.
>
> (vii) Mathematics calculation.
>
> (viii) Mathematics problem solving.

34 C.F.R. § 300.309.

The critical language in this regulation is the reference to standards "in one or more of the following areas." A student with a specific learning disability in reading fluency, for example, might have overall good grades but may score very poorly on a test of reading fluency especially if the student has a high aptitude.

A good example of a close reading of this regulation can be found in *Doe v. Cape Elizabeth School District,* 832 F.3d 69 (1st Cir. 2016). When Jane Doe was in second grade, the IEP team concluded that she was a student with a specific learning disability in reading fluency and was eligible to receive specialized instruction to improve her reading fluency skills. *Id.* at 74–75. When Jane was in eighth grade, the school district concluded that she was no longer eligible for classification as a student with a learning disability because of her strong scores on various tests including state standardized tests. Based on results from private testing, Jane's parents argued that Jane should still be classified as having a learning disability due to low scores on various tests of reading fluency.

Jane's parents brought a due process claim to challenge the school district's findings. After the Hearing Officer ruled in favor of the school district, Jane's parents filed suit in federal court. While recognizing that the Hearing Officer gave "scant consideration" to various reading fluency scores, the district court affirmed the Hearing Officer's decision. *Id.* at 76.

The First Circuit vacated and remanded the district court decision. Quoting 34 C.F.R. § 300.309(a)(1), the court noted that "the consideration of a child's academic measures under the first prong requires consideration of the nexus between those academic measures and the area of the child's deficiency." *Id.* at 79. Thus, the IEP team could only consider Jane's high grades and standardized test scores "insofar as they are indicative of her fluency skills." *Id.* at 79. Further, the court noted that "reading fluency was added to the [regulatory] list of disabilities in part to identify students who, like Jane, excel academically but may have a SLD based on a fluency deficit." *Id.* at 80. The inclusion of "reading fluency" on the list of disabilities would make "it more likely that a child who is gifted and has an SLD would be identified." *Id.* at 80 (quoting U.S. Department of Education letter). Thus, the First Circuit concluded that "the district court erred in relying on Jane's overall academic achievements without assessing the relevance of such achievements to her reading fluency skills." *Id.* at 81. The First Circuit provided the following instructions to the district court on remand:

> [T]he court should first determine whether Jane's generalized academic measures, such as school grades and NECAP and NWEA scores, may serve as fair proxies of her reading fluency ability. If the court answers that question in the affirmative, it should then weigh all relevant factors and decide whether those components of Jane's performance that reflect her reading fluency skills could counteract the (relatively) negative results of specific reading fluency assessments.

Id. at 81.

While not insisting that Jane be considered to have a specific learning disability, the First Circuit did instruct the lower court to give less weight to generalized academic assessments. Further, the First Circuit emphasized that Jane's parents would have to demonstrate that Jane "needs" specialized instruction (as discussed in *Nutshell* § 5.5 C, below) even if she is found to have a specific learning disability.

B. RTI OR RESEARCH-BASED APPROACH

Rather than using the discrepancy model, states can adopt the response to intervention (RTI) or alternative research-based approach. The RTI method was described in *Nutshell* § 3.4.

The "alternative research-based" method is an approach used in some states to allow a student to be classified as having a specific learning disability based on a pattern of strengths and weaknesses in performance, achievement or both, relative to age, state-approved grade-level standards or intellectual development. *See* 34 C.F.R. § 300.309(a)(2)(ii). When this approach is used, it is typical for the team to identify specific areas of cognitive processes that interfere with learning. For example, a student could be identified as having difficulty with math because of deficits in working memory or processing speed. *See Edward K. Schultz & Tammy L. Stephens,* SLD Identification: An Analysis of State Policies, Advocacy Institute, available at https://www.advocacyinstitute.org/resources/SLD.Identification.State.Policy.shtml (date unknown).

C. "NEEDS" SPECIAL EDUCATION SERVICES

For students with specific learning disabilities, like all disabilities, it is not enough for the student to have a disability. The impairment must negatively affect the student's ability to benefit from classroom instruction so that the student "need[s] special education and related services" "by reason [of]" his or her disability. 20 U.S.C. § 1401(3)(A)(ii). To "need" special education and relate services, the student typically needs "specialized instruction" in order to attain educational benefit. There is no accepted definition of what it means to "need" specialized instruction and this issue is often disputed when a child has a high intellectual aptitude and performs overall at grade level despite having a specific learning disability. Sometimes, students in this situation will have an educational plan under Section 504 rather than the IDEA. That possibility is discussed in *Nutshell* Chapter 4. But many parents are not satisfied with a Section 504 plan if their child has a learning disability in reading (e.g., dyslexia) because they want specialized reading instruction for their child. In that case, it is often possible to argue that the child's reading fluency is below grade level even if the child manages to achieve average academic achievement overall. "Reading fluency skills" are specifically listed in the IDEA regulations as an area of potential weakness that can result in a learning disability classification. *See* 34 C.F.R. § 300.309(a)(1)(v).

§ 5.6 SAMPLE EVALUATION FORM

This is a modified version of the evaluation team report form used in Ohio. Most states make these forms available on their special education websites. School districts often have a dynamic version of these forms available and information can be entered on them during the ETR meeting. Sometimes there is a projector available so the team members can see the information being typed as the meeting progresses.

The form below is only a part of what a state ETR form would contain but it can provide a sense of how a form is completed.

INDIVIDUAL EVALUATOR'S ASSESSMENT

Section to be completed by each individual evaluator

EVALUATOR: ______________________

NAME: ____________________________

POSITION: _________________________

AREAS OF ASSESSMENT:

Indicate the area(s) that were assessed by the evaluator in accordance with the evaluation plan.

EVALUATION METHODS AND STRATEGIES

Indicate the types of assessment strategies used to gather information about the child's performance

□ Observations

- □ Scientific, Research-Based Interventions
- □ Norm-Referenced Assessments
- □ Interview
- □ Curriculum-Based Assessments
- □ Classroom-Based Assessments
- □ Review of Records and Relevant Trend Data
- □ Other

ASSESSMENT INFORMATION

Provide a summary of the information obtained from the assessment results per the evaluation plan including the child's strengths, areas of need and baseline data

SUMMARY OF ASSESSMENT RESULTS:

DESCRIPTION OF EDUCATIONAL NEEDS:

IMPLICATIONS FOR INSTRUCTION AND PROGRESS MONITORING:

TEAM SUMMARY

Combine all Part 1's Individual Evaluator's Assessment from all evaluators into team summary

INTERVENTIONS SUMMARY

Provide a summary of all interventions done prior to the child's referral for an evaluation or done as part of the initial evaluation. For all reevaluations provide a summary of interventions routinely provided to this child.

REASON(S) FOR EVALUATION:

SUMMARY OF INFORMATION PROVIDED BY PARENTS OF THE CHILD:

SUMMARY OF OBSERVATIONS: (only required for preschool and SLD)

MEDICAL INFORMATION:

SUMMARY OF ASSESSMENT RESULTS:

DESCRIPTION OF EDUCATIONAL NEEDS:

IMPLICATIONS FOR INSTRUCTION AND PROGRESS MONITORING:

DOCUMENTATION FOR DETERMINING THE EXISTENCE OF A SPECIFIC LEARNING DISABILITY

REQUIRED NOTIFICATION

If the child has participated in a **process that assesses the child's response to scientific, research based intervention,** indicate if the parents were notified about the following prior to the evaluation:

The state's policies regarding the amount and nature of student performance data that would be collected and the general services that would be provided.	Yes	No
Strategies for increasing the child's rate of learning	Yes	No
The parents' right to request an evaluation	Yes	No

Section A must be completed. Either Section B or Section C must be completed.

A. IDENTIFIED AREAS

Identify one or more of the following areas in which the team has determined that the child is not achieving adequately for the child's age or state-approved grade-level standards when provided with learning experiences and instruction appropriate for the child's age or state-approved grade-level standards.

- ☐ Oral Expression
- ☐ Listening Comprehension
- ☐ Reading Fluency Skills
- ☐ Reading Comprehension
- ☐ Written Expression
- ☐ Basic Reading Skill
- ☐ Mathematics Calculation

- ☐ Mathematics Problem Solving

B. RESPONSE TO SCIENTIFIC, RESEARCH-BASED INTERVENTION

Assessment information should be summarized in this section if the evaluation team used a process based on a child's response to scientific, research-based interventions to determine whether the child has a specific learning disability in one or more of the areas identified in Section A.

C. PATTERNS OF STRENGTHS AND WEAKNESSES

Assessment information should be summarized in this section, if the evaluation team used alternative research-based procedures to determine if the child exhibited a pattern of strengths and weaknesses in performance, achievement or both, relative to age, state-approved grade-level standards or intellectual development that the team determined to be relevant to the identification of a specific learning disability in one or more of the areas identified in Section A.

D. EXCLUSIONARY FACTORS

The evaluation team has determined that its findings are NOT primarily the result of:

- ☐ A Visual, Hearing, or Motor Disability

- □ Limited English Proficiency
- □ Mental Retardation
- □ Environmental or Economic Disadvantage
- □ Emotional Disturbance
- □ Cultural Factors

E. DOCUMENTATION-UNDERACHIEVEMENT NOT DUE TO A LACK OF APPROPRIATE INSTRUCTION

Regardless of the process used to identify a child as having a specific learning disability, the team must ensure that the child's underachievement is not due to a lack of appropriate instruction in reading or math by considering the following information:

1. Data that demonstrate that prior to, or as part of the referral process, the child was provided appropriate instruction in general education settings, delivered by qualified personnel.

Summarize the data used by the team to document this requirement:

2. Data-based documentation of repeated assessments of achievement at reasonable intervals, reflecting formal assessment of student progress during instruction, that was provided to the child's parent.

Summarize the data-based documentation used by the team to document this requirement:

E. OBSERVATION

Summarize the child's academic performance and behavior in the areas of difficulty as observed in the child's learning environment including the regular classroom setting.

F. MEDICAL FINDINGS

Describe the educationally relevant medical findings, if any:

ELIGIBILITY DETERMINATION

It is the determination of the team that:

Yes	No	The determining factor for the child's poor performance is not due to a lack of appropriate instruction in reading or math or the child's limited English proficiency. For the preschool-age child the determining factor for the child's poor performance is not due to a lack of preschool pre-academics.
Yes	No	The child meets the state criteria for having a disability (or continuing to have a disability) based on the data provided in this document.
Yes	No	The child demonstrates an educational need that requires specially designed instruction

If the response is **NO** to any question, then the child is **NOT** eligible for special education. If the response to all three questions is **YES**, then the child **IS** eligible for special education.

The child is eligible for special education and related services in the category of:

____

BASIS FOR ELIGIBILITY DETERMINATION:
(or Continued Eligibility)

Provide a justification for the eligibility determination decision, describing how the student meets or does not meet the eligibility criteria as defined in OAC 3301–51–01 (B)(10) (Definitions) and OAC 3301–51–06 (Evaluations). Include how the disability affects the child's progress in the general education curriculum.

This sample evaluation form attempts to track the legal requirements for evaluations. There is a different cover page for school-age evaluations and preschool evaluations because Ohio, like most other states, allows the team to use the category of "developmental delay" for a preschool evaluation. Further, the preschool evaluation has fewer elements than the school-age evaluation because there is no need to consider transition services towards a career and academic progress at the preschool age. Once one gets past the initial information, the forms for both school-age children and preschool children are the same. Each evaluator would complete the form entitled "Individual

Evaluator's Assessment." Thus, there might be several versions of that form.

If the student is identified as having a "specific learning disability" then Ohio, like most states, requires additional documentation to reflect how the student responded to interventions or exhibited a pattern of strengths or weaknesses to reflect a specific learning disability. In other words, Ohio allows a student to be classified as learning disabled based on the RTI process *or* the alternative research-based approach.

The form also reflects various factors that have to be *excluded* before a student can be identified as having a specific learning disability so the team can conclude that the student's underachievement wasn't due to a lack of appropriate instruction. The purpose of this documentation is to avoid over-identification of specific learning disabilities. These questions are dictated, in part, by 34 C.F.R. § 300.306(b), which requires school districts to rule out a lack of appropriate instruction or limited English proficiency as the reason for a child's poor academic performance rather than a disability.

At the end of the form, each team member indicates whether they agree with the conclusion. One team member is the school district's official representative so that person's view is the team's recommendation. If the parent disagrees with the team's recommendation then various procedural safeguards are triggered. The Ohio form gives the parent an opportunity to state why he or she disagrees with the team's recommendation.

Procedural safeguards will be discussed in *Nutshell* Chapter 9.

Each state has its own form for eligibility evaluations. Some states have different forms for different categories of disabilities. For example, North Carolina has a general form and a more specific worksheet for each disability category. *See* http://ec.ncpublicschools.gov/policies/forms/statewide-forms. Many states do not have their forms on a publicly available website. In that situation, it is a good idea to ask the school district to provide you with a copy of the forms they use in advance so you can know what to anticipate with respect to documentation.

§ 5.7 SOME EXAMPLES

A. INITIAL EVALUATION

Jimmy is an eight-year-old boy who was in first grade when the school district administered a battery of tests. His parents delayed his entry to the first grade by a year so he is a year older than most of his peers. The school district administered an IQ test and an achievement test and Jimmy's scores on these tests were as follows:

Jimmy's First Grade IQ Test
(Composite Scaled Score: 101)

Test	Quantitative	Verbal	Nonverbal	Composite
No. items	40	40	40	
No. items attempted	40	39	40	

Raw Score	32	32	39	
Age Score: Standard Score	98	84	117	101
Age Score: percentile	45	16	86	52

Jimmy's First Grade Achievement Tests

Scores Reported	Grade-Based Percentiles
Reading: Total	72
Language: Total	56
Math: Total	56
Reading, Language, Math Core: Total	61
Social Studies	63
Science	67
Word Analysis	53
Math Computation	45

In third grade, the school district administered another battery of aptitude and achievement tests. These are Jimmy's results:

Jimmy's Third Grade IQ Test
(Composite Scaled Score: 98)

Scores	Percentile (grade-based)	Percentile (age-based)
Nonverbal: Sequences	97	88
Nonverbal: Analogies	99*	90*
Total: Nonverbal	99	92
Memory	17	16
Verbal	6	5
Total	65	45

* Perfect score on subtest.

Jimmy's Third Grade Achievement Scores

Scores	Grade-Based Percentile
Reading	75
Language	52
Math	89
Total Score	75
Science	78
Social Studies	48

At first glance, these test scores are those of a typical child. Despite IQ scores around 100, Jimmy has been performing at or above grade level in all areas. And, standing alone, these test scores certainly do not suggest a need for intervention. Nonetheless, close consideration of Jimmy's chronological age and sub scores suggest that further testing may be appropriate.

Jimmy's first-grade scores reflect a significant discrepancy between verbal and nonverbal aptitude. His age-based 84 standard score placed him in the 16th percentile on verbal aptitude and his 117 standard score placed him in the 86th percentile on nonverbal aptitude. Jimmy placed 1 standard deviation below the mean on verbal aptitude and 1 standard deviation above the mean in nonverbal aptitude. This seeming inconsistency in Jimmy's aptitude, however, did not translate into any significant deficits or inconsistencies in his performance in first grade. In fact, his reading scores were well above average. Therefore, the low verbal aptitude score seemed oddly inaccurate.

Jimmy's third-grade test scores reflect a similar discrepancy between verbal and nonverbal aptitudes. His age-based score on the nonverbal aptitude section of the exam was in the 92nd percentile; he received a perfect score on one part of that exam. By contrast, his age-based score on the verbal aptitude section was in the 5th percentile. That is more than a 3 standard deviation discrepancy between verbal and nonverbal aptitude. Despite a low verbal aptitude, his reading scores were well above average.

In third grade, Jimmy also started to have some difficulty in school. He scored less than proficient on the school district's writing assessment in both the third and fourth grades and struggled with writing assignments in class. Based on his parents' concerns, the school district administered an achievement battery in the spring of fourth grade. He scored above the 90th percentile in reading but scored in the 15th percentile in writing. His writing skills were equivalent to that of a child in the second grade.

After receiving those scores, the school district convened an evaluation meeting and indicated a willingness to label Jimmy as "learning disabled" in writing so that he could get extra help with written expression. Jimmy's parents were happy for him to get extra help but were concerned that "learning disability" may not be the correct category for Jimmy. Why would a child be such a strong reader if his verbal aptitude were so low? And why would he have such an enormous vocabulary? The verbal aptitude score seemed to be inaccurate given Jimmy's strong reading skills, yet Jimmy clearly struggled in written expression.

Jimmy's parents began to wonder if Jimmy had a hearing/listening problem that might be producing this odd profile. Jimmy did not start talking in sentences until age three and he had unusual speech patterns. He has a large vocabulary, but he has trouble with basic syntax and speech patterns. He often misunderstands oral instructions and information. He also says to his parents that he wishes the classroom teacher would write down instructions instead of talking so much.

Jimmy's parents visited an audiologist who made two testing recommendations. The audiologist said the verbal aptitude test that the school district had administered had a significant auditory component. She administered a different verbal aptitude test, which had no auditory component, and on the new test, Jimmy scored in the 95th percentile in verbal aptitude. Further, the audiologist conducted an auditory processing test and learned that Jimmy was in the 2nd percentile for auditory processing. Thus, the audiologist reported that Jimmy was missing most oral instruction in the classroom, and he was using his strong reading skills as a compensatory strategy. Because writing instruction is very auditory in nature, the audiologist was not surprised that Jimmy struggled in that academic area. She said his classroom profile would be similar to that of a student with a profound hearing impairment.

While this story is a complicated one, it reflects that one should look closely at test scores, including subtests, and ask if they make sense. A student with a low verbal aptitude will not typically score above average in reading. In Jimmy's case, the verbal aptitude test was understating his genuine verbal aptitude—it was measuring his weak auditory processing skills rather than his verbal aptitude.

This story also reflects the importance of consulting with a child's parents to get the full picture. Jimmy's odd syntax and delayed speech were consistent with an auditory processing deficit.

Although the school district was trying to be helpful by classifying Jimmy as learning disabled in writing, that diagnosis would have misled the IEP team in considering the kinds of support to provide Jimmy to help him succeed. The audiologist suggested that Jimmy wear a personal listening device in the classroom, which allows communication to go directly from the teacher to Jimmy's ear through a Bluetooth device. That auxiliary aid would never have been suggested if the team hadn't realized that Jimmy had an auditory processing deficit. It is always important to remember that the purpose of the classification process is to later develop an effective IEP. A misclassification of a child's disability can make it difficult for the IEP team to do its job successfully.

B. RE-EVALUATION

The IDEA requires re-evaluations to occur every three years, if the IDEA already has been covering the child, unless the parent and the school district agree that a re-evaluation is unnecessary. Further, either the parents or the school district can request a re-evaluation before the three years have elapsed if there is reason to believe such a re-evaluation is necessary. *See* 20 U.S.C. § 1414(a)(2). A re-evaluation can be a crucial document to revise an IEP to make it more effective, even if the parents and school district agree on the underlying disability classification. The same rules that apply to initial evaluations apply to re-evaluations—they must also be valid and reliable and conducted by trained and knowledgeable personnel.

If the school district has previously evaluated a child and determined that the child qualifies for a Section 504 plan, but not an IEP, a parent can also request a re-evaluation to change that classification. The rules are unclear in this situation. Technically, the IDEA "Child Find" rules apply because the child is not yet on an IEP. But, because the child is on a Section 504 plan, the school district is arguably required to do periodic re-evaluations for the purpose of updating the Section 504 plan. If the parent can afford a private evaluation, and less than three years has elapsed since the last evaluation, it can be a good strategy for the parent to obtain his or her own evaluation and bring it to the school district's attention, because the school district may object to doing a re-evaluation shortly after conducting an initial evaluation.

Below is an example of a report that might be used to transfer a child from a Section 504 Plan to an IEP, as part of a re-evaluation process. It considers how the student's educational program needs modification in light of his progress and continuing challenges.

NAME: Steven Fletcher
BIRTH DATE: 12/16/2007
AGE: 8 years, 11 months
GRADE: 3.4
SCHOOL: Hartford School
EVALUATION DATES: 11/2/2014; 11/09/2016
EVALUATORS:

Reason for Referral

Ms. Lynne Fletcher referred her son, Steven, for a re-evaluation. Steven, currently a third-grade student, has a history of difficulty with speech and language, as well as with the development of reading and writing skills. Although Steven was evaluated one year earlier, Ms. Fletcher wanted an updated evaluation that would include additional recommendations to meet his current educational needs and address his continued reading challenges.

Background Information

Steven lives with his biological parents and one younger sister who is 5 years old. His father is a sales person and his mother is a school teacher. There is no known family history of reading and writing difficulties. Steven has attended Hartford School since kindergarten and generally earns A's in all school subjects. The school district provided him with speech and language therapy starting at age three but then was dismissed from services at the age of 6 in first grade. With the exception of speech and language development, his developmental milestones were reached within normal limits.

Although generally healthy, Steven has a history of ear infections, allergies (nuts, watermelon, strawberry, and dog saliva), and asthma. He has taken the medications, Proventil for his asthma, as well as Benadryl and EpiPen as needed. In 2015, concerns were noted about his vision and he was seen by Amy L. Richman, O.D. and prescribed a bifocal correction to address mild myopic and accommodative refractive concerns. In addition to glasses, Dr. Richman recommended an occupational therapy evaluation to address concerns regarding his fine-motor coordination. After the occupational therapy evaluation, Steven had sessions to improve his strength and motor skills and was also assigned home exercises to improve his hand strength, manual dexterity, and visual tracking.

Throughout his school years, Steven has required extra assistance in learning to read and has received instruction in the Spalding method, a systematic phonics approach, since kindergarten. He has received additional tutoring in this method during the summer months, as well as receiving a great deal of support from his parents at home to assist with his challenges in learning to read and write. He has had difficulty with letter orientation (p-q, b-d) since the first grade and often uses an index card when reading, to keep his place in the text. Although the p-q confusion is now resolved, Steven still has a tendency to reverse the letters "b" and "d."

Steven has had a Section 504 plan in school since the age of 6. This plan addresses his visual challenges for reading going from distance to near (board to desk reading), eye tracking for reading (staying on the lines when reading text), as well as his health needs for asthma and food allergies (nuts, strawberries, watermelon, and dog saliva).

Steven reports that he enjoys sports, likes swimming and soccer, and likes doing projects at school. He notes that he finds it more difficult when the teacher "just talks" and he has to "just listen." He mentioned that even though he is in third grade, his teacher sometimes gives them tasks to do that are for "students in fifth grade."

Prior Evaluations

In October of 2015, Ms. Fletcher requested a speech/language evaluation. The school district's Speech/Language Pathologist conducted an informal observation of Steven (10/24 and 10/ 29/2015) and concluded: "Steven's speech-language skills do not impede his ability to progress in the general education classroom, socialize/interact with peers, or express himself clearly." Any observed errors were considered to be unremarkable due to the fact that they were isolated instances.

In November of 2015, the school district's psychologist, Dr. Shirley White, also administered the following tests:

Beery-Buktenica Developmental Test of Visual-Motor Integration, Sixth Edition (VMI)

Gray Oral Reading Test, 5th Edition (GORT-5)

Woodcock-Johnson III Normative Update Tests Cognitive Ability (WJ III COG)

Woodcock-Johnson III Normative Update Tests of Achievement (WJ III ACH)

Parent Interview

Dr. White provided the following summary and conclusions: "Steven exhibited strengths in nonverbal conceptual thinking, auditory processing and verbal comprehension. He had weaknesses in processing speed, long-term retrieval, and reading comprehension, *but they are not severe enough to be considered a learning disorder*. These may, however, be maximized (i.e., his strengths) and minimized (i.e., his weaknesses) with interventions and accommodations designed to support Steven's learning." (emphasis added) Steven also had above average performance on tasks involving visual spatial thinking and in mathematical calculations. A variety of recommendations were made to address his strengths and weaknesses.

Results from the Current Evaluations

Tests Administered

Wechsler Intelligence Test for Children (5th edition) (WISC-V)

Woodcock-Johnson IV

Tests of Cognitive Abilities (WJ IV COG)

Tests of Oral Language (WJ IV OL)

Tests of Achievement (WJ IV ACH) Standard & Extended

(Scores attached to the end of this report).

All tests were scored by age norms.

Test Behaviors

Steven was cooperative during four one hour and a half long testing sessions. Although he maintained attention overall, on several occasions, he would lose his focus, start talking about some other topic, and then have to be re-directed to the task at hand. In general, his attention and interest increased on tasks that involved visual stimuli and decreased on tasks that involved language and lengthy verbal instructions. For one of the testing sessions, Steven forgot to bring his glasses, so only oral tests that did not involve visual stimuli were administered.

Score Interpretation

Throughout this report, the WJ IV results are mostly described using the labels for Proficiency Ranges (i.e., "limited," "average," "advanced," etc.), which are based on the Relative Proficiency Index (RPI). The RPI is an index of the student's predicted quality of performance on tasks similar to the ones tested. For example, an RPI of 71/90 means that the student would be predicted to demonstrate 71% proficiency with similar tasks that average individuals in the comparison group (age) would perform with 90% proficiency. Someone with an RPI of 96/90 or higher would find that task to be easy. An RPI of 90/90 would be at the instructional level (with a range of 82–95/90). An RPI below 82/90 suggests that the person may find similar tasks to be "difficult."

Cognitive and Oral Language Results

Wechsler Intelligence Scale for Children (5th Edition) (WISC-V)

WJ IV Cognitive Battery (WJ IV COG) and WJ IV Oral Language (WJ IV OL)

Wechsler Intelligence Test for Children—5th Edition (WISC-V)

Verbal Comprehension: 108 (70th percentile)

Visual Spatial: 102 (55th percentile)

Fluid Reasoning: 112 (79th percentile)

Working Memory: 103 (58th percentile)

Processing Speed: 105 (63rd percentile)

Full Scale: 107 (68th percentile)

On both the WJ IV COG and the WISC-V, the majority of Steven's abilities fell within the Average range. Both scores of overall intellectual ability indicate that Steven is currently functioning in the average range compared to his age peers (WISC-V SS = 107, 68th percentile; WJ IV COG GIA SS = 95, 37th percentile).

Oral language. Steven demonstrated average proficiency on tasks involving vocabulary knowledge and general information. His ability to engage in conversation and relate and retell stories was typical for his age.

Memory. The results from various WJ IV COG memory tests were inconsistent. Steven had limited proficiency on several tests involving aspects of memory (e.g., Numbers Reversed, Phonological Processing, Story Recall), but average to advanced proficiency on other measures of memory (e.g., Memory for Words, Sentence Repetition). This inconsistency in results suggests that his low scores on certain memory tests may be more related to fluctuations in attention, rather than to weaknesses in memory *per se*.

Processing speed. In contrast to the most recent evaluation (2013), Steven obtained scores within the average range on measures of processing speed. It is most likely that his slow processing speed on the prior examination resulted from problems with vision (he had not yet gotten his glasses), rather than a weakness in processing speed *per se*.

Phonological processing and phonetic coding. Phonological processing tasks involve accessing words through sounds, whereas phonetic coding tasks involve the oral abilities to blend and break apart word parts and speech sounds. *Steven exhibited weaknesses on phonological processing tasks, but not on phonetic coding tasks*. He had difficulty thinking of words that contained certain sounds, as well as rapidly retrieving words that started with a certain sound.

Steven had average to advanced proficiency on two phonetic coding tasks. His RPI of 97/90 on the Phonetic Coding cluster suggests that when average age mates have 90% proficiency blending and segmenting sounds, Steven will have 97% success, and the tasks will be easy for him. His facility with speech sounds was readily apparent. For example, when asked to identify the number of syllables in a word, Steven put his hand on his chin, and counted the number of times his chin dropped. (The chin drops because each syllable contains a vowel sound, which makes a speaker open the mouth). His high score on this cluster can most likely be attributed to his experience with the Spalding method, which involves direct teacher instruction in both blending and segmenting.

Fluid reasoning. Steven obtained scores in the above average range on measures of fluid reasoning. His WISC-V Fluid Reasoning score exceeded 79% of his age peers. This score suggests good aptitude for mathematics.

Woodcock Johnson Tests of Achievement (WJ IV ACH)

Reading

In contrast to his average proficiency on most other cognitive and academic areas, Steven's reading proficiency was limited. His RPI on the Broad Reading cluster was 31/90, suggesting that when typical age peers have 90% success on reading tasks, Steven will have only 31% success. This suggests that classroom, reading tasks will be very difficult. His proficiency in both word reading (Letter-Word Identification test) and his ability to apply phonics (Word Attack) were limited. *His greatest areas of weaknesses, however, were his reading fluency and rate. He had very limited proficiency on the Sentence Reading Fluency test, where he was asked to read a series of sentences as quickly as he could. His RPI was only 13/90, indicating that when average age mates have 90% success reading sentences quickly, Steven will have only 13% success.* He will find classroom, reading tasks to be extremely difficult. On several occasions, Steven misread common words that share a similar appearance, such as "these" for *those*, "farm" for *frame*, and "part" for *pair*. He did not attempt to self-correct any of these errors. Steven lacked confidence in his ability to pronounce less familiar words, as well as apply phonic skills to pronounce phonically regular nonsense words. These low reading scores are surprising in light of the fact that he has been received instruction in a structured reading intervention since kindergarten.

Written Language

Steven's RPI of 74/90 on the Written Language cluster indicates his proficiency in written language was limited to average. Although Steven was able to express his ideas in writing (Writing Samples RPI = 81/90), he had difficulty with spelling and tended to spell words the way they sound, rather than the way they look (Spelling RPI = 65/90). As examples, he spelled the words *some* as "sum," *paying* as "paing," and *digging* as "digin." He reversed the letters "b" and "d' spelling *baby* as "bady." These types of difficulties suggest problems with memory for spelling patterns, related to orthography (the writing system of a language), rather than difficulty sequencing sounds in order, related to phonology.

Mathematics

Steven's proficiency on math calculation and math problem solving tasks was average. His RPI of 93/90 on the Broad Mathematics cluster suggests that when typical age mates have 90% success, Steven will have 93% success. He had advanced proficiency on a task involving solving math facts quickly (Math Facts Fluency RPI = 98/90). Although the majority of Steven's mathematical scores were presently in the average range, this may be more of a reflection of what he has been taught, rather than what he is capable of learning. In fact, his math calculation score in 2013 exceeded 87% of his peers. In other words, his interest in and aptitude for mathematics seem higher than his present performance levels. In general, Steven was more engaged in questions that involved mathematical reasoning and problem solving than he was with tasks involving reading and writing.

Variations and Comparisons

When Steven's WJ IV *Gf-Gc* composite score (based on higher-level measures of reasoning and knowledge) is compared to his other abilities, his reading performance is identified as being significantly discrepant. When his *Gf-Gc* composite score is compared to his WJ IV Reading cluster, only 5 out of 100 students would have a reading score as low. This discrepancy suggests that Steven's aptitude for learning is higher than his current level of reading performance.

Conclusion

Although the majority of Steven's test scores were within the average range, he demonstrated limited proficiency on all reading and spelling tests. What is of greatest concern is the fact that Steven has made insufficient academic progress in reading even with substantial additional assistance from both home and school. Although he has received targeted reading instruction with the Spalding method since kindergarten, he still struggles with using phonics, pronouncing multisyllabic words, and reading at an adequate rate. The persistence and relative severity of his reading difficulties, his limited response to systematic intervention, his slow word perception, and the types of reading and spelling errors he makes, do support the conclusion that Steven has a reading disability (dyslexia), as well as mild attentional challenges, which also interfere with his listening and learning.

Recommendations

School Programming

1. Steven will require specific accommodations in the classroom, such as extended time on reading assignments and shortened homework assignments. Until his reading performance improves, Steven will need adjustments in the difficulty level in both school and homework assignments. Although he is earning good grades, his reading level is below his age peers.

2. Steven would benefit from sitting at the front of the classroom so as to maximize his attention.

3. When possible, break Steven's in-class assignments into smaller, more manageable chunks. Give him one part at a time with instructions to hand each in as it is completed and pick up the next. Each time he hands in a portion of the work, provide reinforcement for completed work. Using this

technique, he will be more likely to stay on task and complete assignments.

4. Steven has average oral language skills, as well as a good foundation of world knowledge. He also completes visually based tasks that require spatial manipulation with relative ease. Provide Steven with hands-on activities, such as completing science projects, so that he can demonstrate his strengths in visual-spatial thinking and reasoning.

5. Because of mild attentional issues, Steven will have difficulty attending to instruction that is delivered primarily in a lecture style. To maximize his attention, incorporate activities into instruction as much as possible.

6. Because of age appropriate language and math skills, Steven should not be retained in third grade regardless of his performance on a high stakes tests. If needed, provide Steven with a reader when he takes this test so that all of his attention can be focused upon answering questions, rather than using effort to decode words.

Initial Instructional Goals

Reading and Spelling

1. To make progress, Steven requires specialized reading instruction. Steven would benefit from participation in an online reading program, Virtual Reading Coach (MVRC) developed by Mindplay. The program begins with an initial reading assessment (RAPS) that determines exactly which skills he should needs to develop and then plans a

prescriptive program based upon the assessment results. Steven should spend 30 minutes a day, 4–5 days a week with this program, ideally for the next 6 months. Steven will need to understand that this program is like working with a serious reading tutor, and is not based on games. It may be necessary to create some type of reinforcement program to reward Steven for daily completion of the activity. For example, he could earn points that could then be traded in for a pizza or movie tickets. So that Steven will not become overwhelmed with homework demands, allow him to substitute 30 minutes daily of MVRC for homework in the Accelerated Reader.

2. Provide Steven with instruction that increases his recognition of common letters patterns, builds his understanding of spelling rules, and shows him how to use structural analysis (breaking words apart into syllables) to make them easier to pronounce. Reading and spelling instruction will be most effective if the patterns taught for reading are taught for spelling at the same time. Teach Steven how to find prefixes and suffixes. An easy strategy to use is based on the REWARDS program. When presented with a multisyllabic word, ask Steven to: (a) circle the prefix, (b) circle the suffix, (c) underline the vowel in the root word, and (d) draw scoops under each part saying: What part? What part? What part? What word?

3. Use a systematic spelling program, such as *Scholastic Spelling* or *Spellography*, that will provide Steven with a solid foundation in common

orthographic spelling patterns, as well as how to spell common high frequency words.

4. To build speed and accuracy in pronunciation of sight words and phonetically irregular words, use one-minute speed drills. Time Steven daily on reading lists of common, irregular words, as quickly as he can. Record and display his daily performance on some type of graph. Also have him practice spelling these words.

5. Determine a strategy that will help Steven remember the orientation of the letters *b* and *d*. Two examples include:

a. Teach Steven how to form the letters b and d using uniquely different stroke sequences. To form a b, have the student start at the top line, write a vertical line down to the baseline and then, starting at the mid-line, make a forward half-circle (clockwise). In D'Nealian handwriting the student is taught to make a vertical line down and then come up from the base with a half-circle counter clockwise). For the letter d, he should start at the mid-line and form a backward circle (counterclockwise), like the movement for starting the letter c, then continue the upward stroke to the top line and back down again.

b. Have Steven make a b with the left hand and a d with the right (forefinger straight up, circle with thumb and other fingers) to form a "bed.". Tell him that the b comes first in the alphabet so check the left hand for b; the d comes after it, so look at the right hand.

Mathematics

1. Teach Steven basic math skills including multiplication of two digit numbers and simple division. Introduce fractions and decimals.

2. Review counting coins up to a dollar.

3. Consider use of an online math program, such as ALEKS, to supplement math instruction. http://www.aleks.com. This program will design a math curriculum to accelerate Steven's mathematical abilities.

4. Provide practice in math facts and math using fun video games. Many of these can be found on www.coolmath.com.

5. Provide review of different types of math problems. A good book to use would be *Math4Today* which provides daily 10 minute worksheets with a variety of math problems geared at a fourth-grade level.

6. To maximize attention, alternate instruction in math skills with games to reinforce and develop those skills.

Signed

Learning Disability Specialist

This report would be very useful to persuade a school district to convert a student from a Section 504 plan to an IEP. It specifically explains what kind of individualized instruction the student needs in order to be academically successful. Further, it specifies the exact area of learning disability. Finally, it compares the current results with prior results, and it tries to develop educational strategies that will keep Steven in the regular classroom while helping him make progress on grade-level assignments.

CHAPTER 6

INDIVIDUALIZED EDUCATION PROGRAMS

§ 6.1 INTRODUCTION

The development of the "Individualized Education Program" or "IEP" is the heart of the IDEA. After the school district determines that a student is eligible for special education and related services, the IEP team meets to formulate an individualized plan for that student. Extensive statutory and regulatory language governs this process as well as two important Supreme Court cases. There are rules governing the composition of the team that writes the IEP, the content of the IEP, and the progress a student is expected to attain with an appropriate IEP.

§ 6.2 THE IEP TEAM

The IEP team should consist of:

i. The parents of a child with a disability

ii. Not less than 1 regular education teacher of such child (if the child is, or may be, participating in the regular education environment);

iii. Not less than 1 special education teacher, or where appropriate, not less than 1 special education provider of such child;

iv. A representative of the local educational agency who—

> I. Is qualified to provide, or supervise the provision of, specially designed instruction to meet the unique needs of children with disabilities;
>
> II. Is knowledgeable about the general education curriculum; and
>
> III. Is knowledgeable about the availability of resources of the local educational agency;
>
> v. An individual who can interpret the instructional implications of evaluation results, who may be a member of the team described in clauses (ii) through (vi)
>
> vi. At the discretion of the parent or the agency, other individuals who have knowledge or special expertise regarding the child, including related services personnel as appropriate; and
>
> vii. Whenever appropriate, the child with a disability

20 U.S.C. § 1414(d)(1)(B).

These requirements are very important. First, the school district must make an attempt to invite the parents of a child with a disability. If the parents are divorced, the school district must follow whatever rules are set forth in a parenting agreement regarding how decisions are made on behalf of the child. If the parents have a serious disagreement about the IEP then they must resolve those differences outside the context of the IEP meeting. The IDEA presumes that the parents speak with one voice. School districts will typically document their efforts to schedule the IEP meeting at a time when at least one parent can attend. Because parents must be able to "meaningfully participate" at IEP meetings, it is very important that school districts make a sincere attempt to acquire their attendance at IEP meetings, although those practices vary enormously by school district. School districts typically plan IEP meetings during (or shortly before or after) the school day, so it can be difficult for parents to attend who have young children at home or have jobs with inflexible work schedules.

Second, it is important that a member of the school district is present who is "knowledgeable about the availability of resources," because the IEP team must be able to create a program that the school district can realistically implement. The IEP team is the decision-making body and the team's determination should not be subject to approval from someone who is not present at the meeting.

Third, it is important for someone to be present who can interpret the available data. Often, that person is the school psychologist, but it can also be the director of special education (who might attend as the person with knowledge about available resources).

Fourth, people can be excused from an IEP meeting with permission of the parent and school district. *See* 20 U.S.C. § 1414(d)(1)(C). In theory, required members of the team should be present for the entire meeting but, in practice, it is not uncommon for people to walk in and out of the meeting and sign a sheet showing they were present.

Finally, parents will need to decide if it makes sense for the student with the disability to attend. Because the program is being devised for the student, their input can be valuable. On the other hand, IEP meetings can be long and boring and may be of little interest to the student. In addition, some students find these meetings upsetting because of the extensive discussion of their deficits. Sometimes, it makes sense to invite the student to attend the part of the meeting where the student's input would be most helpful. As a student gets older, it can make more sense for the student to be in attendance, especially when discussion of transition planning is required. The decision about whether the child attends is typically that of the parents unless the child is 18 or older. When students are 18, they are responsible for their own educational rights and should be the signatory at the meeting unless a power of attorney or guardianship is in place.

§ 6.3 THE INDIVIDUALIZED EDUCATION PROGRAM: GENERALLY

The Individualized Education Program (IEP) is a written document, which contains eight elements. Many states have forms that school districts use to generate this document. Often, this form can be filled out at the IEP meeting with a projector showing the language on a screen as it is being written. Although school districts are not supposed to "pre-determine" the language of an IEP in advance of the meeting, they will sometimes agree to share a draft with a parent before the meeting. School districts also often have "IEP banks," which are available to school district personnel and reflect language that has been used in prior IEPs to offer various kinds of support, which are often found in these kinds of documents. Again, school districts should not have standard IEPs that they use for all children with various impairments, such ADHD or dyslexia, but they can have language that has proved effective for other children and suggest that language at the IEP meeting.

The overall goal of an IEP is to provide all children with disabilities a "free appropriate public education." *See* 20 U.S.C. § 1412(a)(1). The terms "free" and "public" have a fairly straightforward meaning. However, the term "appropriate" is much more ambiguous. The statute does not define "appropriate." That term has been defined through legal interpretations of the IDEA. Those cases will be discussed in *Nutshell* §§ 6.11–6.13 below. For now, this *Nutshell* will explore the elements of an IEP, and then examine the leading cases clarifying whether an IEP satisfies the requirement that it is likely to provide FAPE.

§ 6.4 PRESENT LEVELS OF ACHIEVEMENT AND FUNCTIONAL PERFORMANCE

The first requirement for an IEP is a statement of the student's present levels of academic achievement and functional performance:

> (I) a statement of the child's present levels of academic achievement and functional performance, including—
>
> (aa) how the child's disability affects the child's involvement and progress in the general education curriculum;
>
> (bb) for preschool children, as appropriate, how the disability affects the child's participation in appropriate activities; and
>
> (cc) for children with disabilities who take alternate assessments aligned to alternate achievement standards, a description of benchmarks or short-term objectives;

20 U.S.C. § 1414(d)(1)(A)(i).

Every IEP must list the present levels of achievement and functional performance (PLAAFP), although school districts are only required to conduct a full eligibility evaluation once every three years. The present levels of performance are a crucial aspect of any IEP because it is impossible to set goals if one does not have an accurate sense of the student's present levels of achievement.

Some states offer useful resources on their websites to assist IEP teams to develop present levels of achievement and functional performance. For example, North Carolina provides useful material that conforms with recommended standards in the field of educational psychology. *See* Public Schools of North Carolina, *Training Materials*, http://ec.ncpublicschools.gov/conferences-profdev/training-materials.

The PLAAFP should contain information that is: (1) current, (2) relevant, (3) objective, (4) measurable, and (5) understandable. It should not merely repeat the results of the eligibility evaluation that is conducted every three years. It needs to have recent data tied to an assessment of the student's progress in the general education curriculum. The information should relate both to *academic* achievement, such as progress towards grade-level standards, as well as *functional performance*. Functional performance refers to an ability to engage in routine functions which may not be academic but which can impact educational achievement such as distractibility or social engagement.

Below is an example of an appropriate PLAAFP provided by the state of North Carolina in its training materials:

> KARA
>
> Based on a review of curriculum-based measures and data collected from teacher observations, given one minute to read a 4th grade passage, Kara reads 48 words correctly (70% accuracy). Given a 3rd grade passage, Kara reads 50 words correctly (80% accuracy).
>
> She is able to read basic sight words and uses picture clues to identify words in a text. She decodes simple one-syllable words with short vowels but has difficulty reading words with multiple syllables. She fails to use word attack strategies to read unknown words in a passage.

> Kara's oral reading is below beginning 4th grade reading level. Therefore, she has difficulty reading 4th grade level material independently. Due to these reading deficits, Kara has difficulty completing assignments independently in reading, math, science, and social studies. Her independent work is often incomplete and inaccurate.

See http://ec.ncpublicschools.gov/conferences-profdev/training-materials.

Looking closely at this description of Kara, one can see why it works well in the IEP. First, it starts by telling us what materials were used to develop the PLAAFP. The school did not rely on only one data source; they accompanied the objective data with teacher observations. Kara is in fourth grade, but we learn that she is not able to read at a fourth-grade level. We also learn about both her strengths and weaknesses. She can read one-syllable words but has trouble with multisyllabic words. We are also told the consequences of her reading problems—how it impacts all of her classes. One area of improvement for this PLAAFP would be for it to state the benchmark for a fourth-grade student for comparison. How many words does a fourth-grade student typically read in one minute? What is a typical level of accuracy? These benchmarks would be useful when the IEP team seeks to draft measurable annual goals. Depending on the reading test being used, Kara's current reading scores are probably at about a first or second-grade level.

As will be discussed in *Nutshell* Chapter 9, a procedural violation, such as failing to abide by all of the requirements for stating PLAAFP is rarely legally actionable. In order to be legally actionable, the failure must be fairly egregious. An example of such an egregious violation can be found in *N.S. v. District of Columbia,* 709 F. Supp.2d 57 (D.D.C. 2010). In this case, the parents alleged that the June 2008 IEP for their 8-year-old child failed to include any present levels of academic achievement and functional performance. *Id.* at 63. Dissatisfied with many aspects of the IEP, the parents brought a due process challenge. The school district did not dispute the fact that the IEP failed to include the child's present levels of academic achievement and performance. *Id.* at 67. The Hearing Officer nonetheless rejected the parents' claims that the school district denied their child FAPE by failing to including necessary sections of the IEP. *Id.* at 64. While the lack of present levels was not the only factor that caused the district court to conclude that the IEP was "effectively incomplete," it was a factor considered by the district court judge in reversing the Hearing Officer. *Id.* at 71.

Nonetheless, as is true of many of the examples discussed in this *Nutshell,* the parents in *N.S.* only prevailed after appealing the Hearing Officer's decision to a district court judge. A small percentage of state administrative decisions are appealed; thus, it is not easy to challenge the adequacy of an IEP even when the statement of present levels is quite inadequate.

§ 6.5 MEASURABLE ANNUAL GOALS

The second requirement for an IEP is a statement of measurable annual goals:

> (II) a statement of measurable annual goals, including academic and functional goals, designed to—
>
> (aa) meet the child's needs that result from the child's disability to enable the child to be involved in and make progress in the general education curriculum; and
>
> (bb) meet each of the child's other educational needs that result from the child's disability

20 U.S.C. § 1414(d)(1)(A)(i).

If the PLAAFP was done correctly, the IEP team has a good sense of the student's educational needs. In the previous example, the team knows that Kara is not able to read at grade level. They should therefore develop an annual goal to improve that specific level of performance. Further, that goal needs to be "measurable." Although the goal only needs to be an "annual goal," most school districts also provide benchmarks or short-term objectives for shorter time frames, such as each quarter. For students who take alternate assessments, the IDEA requires "a description of benchmarks or short-term objectives." 20 U.S.C. § 1414(d)(1)(A)(i)(*I*)(cc).

It is ideal for the annual goal to be grade-level performance in the area in which the student has a significant deficit, but it is also important for the annual goal to be one that the student can expect to accomplish during the school year. If a student is exceeding the goal as the school year progresses, the IEP team can always reconvene and raise the goal. It is essential that students be challenged with high expectations. Finally, it is important to remember that goals can relate both to academic and functional performance. Thus, a functional goal could be a student learning to speak to adults without vulgarities.

Goals must be *measurable*. The examples below reflect measurable and non-measurable goals.

Measurable Goals	Non-measurable Goals
Dressing one's self by zipping or buttoning a shirt or coat	Becoming independent
Speaking to adults without vulgarities	Respecting authority
Reading at grade level	Enjoying literature
Repeating instructions accurately	Asking for help when misses information

The measurable goals in the above chart are objective actions that can be evaluated. The non-measurable goals are often too vague and abstract to be measured. The last non-measurable goal is one that is often mistakenly included in IEPs. It is impossible for a student to know that he or she has missed information. If a student never asks a question, does that mean the student has perfect comprehension? On the other hand, if a student constantly asks questions, is the student learning to process information independently? By contrast, if the teacher asks a student to repeat instructions in his or her own words, then the teacher can determine if the student understood the instructions.

In Kara's example, she might have two reading goals: (1) increasing her reading speed and (2) increasing her reading accuracy for multisyllabic words. Below is an example of how those two goals might be worded:

> Goal 1: Given a 4th grade reading passage, Kara will accurately read at least 105 words or more per minute in 4 out of 5 trials.
>
> Goal 2: Given a 4th grade reading passage, Kara will independently read 4–5 syllable words with 95% accuracy in 4 out of 5 trials.

These goals are measurable and appropriate given the academic needs identified in the PLAAFP. Under the IEP goals, Kara's reading speed would improve from 48 words per minute to 105 words per minute. While that level of improvement would be considerable, it would likely still leave her reading more slowly than the typical fourth-grade student. The goals, however, also emphasize that Kara should have 95% accuracy in reading multisyllabic words. That goal is very important if Kara is to comprehend grade-level text. Because reading instruction typically ends by fifth grade, yet students continue to experience thousands of new, multisyllabic words, which they are expected to decode in context, it is very important for Kara to develop strategies for comprehending multisyllabic words. Learning to decode (rather than merely skip) longer words may slow down her reading; thus, the team will have to decide how to balance the fluency goal with the decoding goal.

In the previous example, the goals were defined as being met in "4 out of 5 trials." That kind of language is commonly found in IEPs and can lead to some confusion. Will all the trials take place on one day? Do they take place during a reporting period? Further, the goal does not specify the length of these reading passages. Are they one paragraph, one page, or one chapter? Even if IEP teams do not provide further specificity in the goal, they can find it helpful to discuss what they mean by a "trial" when writing the goals. Such a discussion can avoid later misunderstandings although the people who will be implementing the goals are not always at the IEP meeting. In writing IEPs, it is helpful to remember that the student might move or other people may need to implement the IEP. Thus, specificity can help make it more effective.

As discussed above, it is difficult to bring a successful challenge to an IEP merely because the annual goals do not meet the standards specified in the IDEA. Nonetheless, in the *N.S.* case discussed above, the court suggested that the annual goals did not meet the IDEA's standards. The IEP merely repeated the annual goals from the previous year calling for the student to "master first grade reading standards with 80% accuracy" and "master first grade math standards with 80% accuracy." *N.S.*, 709 F. Supp.2d at 63. N.S.'s parents' educational consultant testified that the math and reading goals were "too broad to provide meaningful guidance." *Id.* at 69. The school district conceded that the IEP had no goals at all for written language.

A comparison between Kara's and N.S.'s reading goals help show why N.S.'s goals were not legally sufficient. First-grade reading standards are likely to include many benchmarks such as fluency and comprehension. One cannot measure fluency with a general "accuracy" rate. Fluidity is a speed measure where one has to take several trials to get an average fluidity measure. Thus, a general 80% accuracy goal for fluidity would be meaningless. Because N.S.'s team had no present levels of performance, it was impossible to determine what goals were appropriate. The team just wrote a generic goal of "80% accuracy" rather than closely considering N.S.'s strengths and weaknesses to determine what specific goals were appropriate. *Id.* at 62.

§ 6.6 MEASUREMENT OF PROGRESS

The third requirement for an IEP is a description of how progress will be measured:

> (III) a description of how the child's progress toward meeting the annual goals described in subclause (II) will be measured and when periodic reports on the progress the child is

> making toward meeting the annual goals (such as through the use of quarterly or other periodic reports, concurrent with the issuance of report cards) will be provided;

20 U.S.C. § 1414(d)(1)(A)(i).

In meeting this IEP requirement, one can think of the rule as stating that the team should determine (1) *how* the student's progress will be measured, (2) *when* the progress will be measured, and (3) *what* is the benchmark for which progress is being measured?

The example in Kara's case can make this requirement more concrete. The year-end goal for Kara is to accurately read at a fluency of 105 words per minute for a passage at a fourth-grade reading level. She is currently reading at 48 words per minute, but she only reads at 50 words per minute at a third-grade reading level. The team should discuss whether she will initially be tested with passages at a fourth-grade reading level or if it make more sense to keep her at a third-grade level for the first two quarters in an attempt to increase her fluency with passages that she already can understand fairly well? This decision can only be made through consultation with the IEP team. However, one could imagine the following progress reporting for Kara:

On a quarterly basis, Kara will be required to read passages at her instructional level with increasing expectations for fluency as follows:

1st quarter: 75 words per minute at third-grade level with 80% accuracy on 4 out of 5 trials

2nd quarter: 105 words per minute at third-grade level with 80% accuracy on 4 out of 5 trials

3rd quarter: 85 words per minute at fourth-grade level with 80% accuracy on 4 out of 5 trials

4th quarter: 105 words per minute at fourth-grade level with 80% accuracy on 4 out of 5 trials

Although it is typical for school districts to provide quarterly reports of progress towards IDEA goals, the IDEA regulations no longer require any particular timetable for reporting. For some goals, such as timely completion of homework, it may make sense to require a weekly report to parents. Because many schools now have some kind of website or online parent portal, such as PowerSchool, which tracks grades, homework, and attendance, some IEPs refer to PowerSchool data as a part of their reporting obligation. Reporting information must be genuinely available to parents so school districts need to ascertain that software programs are genuinely available to parents if they are going to use such programs for reporting purposes. Independent of the IDEA, school districts have a responsibility to communicate with parents in their native language. This requirement would apply to IDEA reporting requirements (and all other notices sent to parents under the IDEA).

§ 6.7 SPECIAL EDUCATION AND RELATED SERVICES

A. DESCRIPTION OF SERVICES

The fourth requirement for an IEP is a description of special education and related services:

> (IV) a statement of the special education and related services and supplementary aids and services, based on peer-reviewed research to the extent practicable, to be provided to the child, or on behalf of the child, and a statement of the program modifications or supports for school personnel that will be provided for the child—
>
> (aa) to advance appropriately toward attaining the annual goals;
>
> (bb) to be involved in and make progress in the general education curriculum in accordance with subclause (I) and to participate in extracurricular and other nonacademic activities; and
>
> (cc) to be educated and participate with other children with disabilities and nondisabled children in the activities described in this subparagraph;

20 U.S.C. § 1414(d)(1)(A)(i).

The seventh requirement for an IEP relates to a description of specific dates, frequency and location of special education services.

> (VII) the projected date for the beginning of the services and modifications described in subclause (IV), and the anticipated frequency, location, and duration of those services and modifications;

20 U.S.C. § 1414(d)(1)(A)(i).

The fourth and seventh requirements (involving dates and frequencies) are usually combined in the IEP document. The special education services will be listed along with who provides these services, how often, and where these services are provided.

Below is an example of how such services might be listed on an IEP for a student named Manuel:

	Consultant Teacher Services	Speech Language Therapy
Service Delivery	Direct services	Individual, Bilingual—Spanish
Frequency	3 times per week	2 times per week
Duration	60 minutes per session	30 minutes per session
Location	General education, English class	Therapy room
Initiation Date	9/1/2018	9/1/2018

B. SPECIAL EDUCATION AND RELATED SERVICES

1. Special Education

The IDEA requires a student to be provided *special education* and *related services.* The regulations define special education as follows:

> Special education means specially designed instruction, at no cost to the parents, to meet the unique needs of a child with a disability, including—
> (i) Instruction conducted in the classroom, in the home, in hospitals and institutions, and in other settings; and
> (ii) Instruction in physical education.

34 C.F.R. § 300.39(a)(1).

2. Related Services

"Related services" is defined very broadly in the following regulation:

> Related services.
> (a) General. Related services means transportation and such developmental, corrective, and other supportive services as are required to assist a child with a disability to benefit from special education, and includes speech-language pathology and audiology services, interpreting services, psychological services, physical and occupational therapy, recreation, including therapeutic recreation,

> early identification and assessment of disabilities in children, counseling services, including rehabilitation counseling, orientation and mobility services, and medical services for diagnostic or evaluation purposes. Related services also include school health services and school nurse services, social work services in schools, and parent counseling and training.

34 C.F.R. § 300.34.

Although this regulation covers audiology services, it does not include services that apply to students with surgically implanted devices, including cochlear implants, for maintenance of that device or optimization of the device's function through mapping (which optimizes the user's access to sound by adjusting the input to the electrodes on the device). The student, however, would be eligible for other services such as speech and language services that are necessary to receive FAPE. Further, school personnel can be required to check an external component of a surgically implanted device to make sure it is functioning properly. 34 C.F.R. § 300.34(b).

> Related services include:
>
> (1) Audiology;
>
> (2) Counseling services;
>
> (3) Early identification and assessment of disabilities in children;
>
> (4) Interpreting services;
>
> (5) Medical services provided by a licensed

physician to determine a child's medically related disability that results in the child's need for special education and related services;

(6) Occupational therapy;

(7) Orientation and mobility services;

(8) Parent counseling and training to assist parents in understanding the special needs of their child; to obtain information about child development; and to help them acquire the necessary skills that will allow them to support the implementation of their child's IEP or IFSP;

(9) Physical therapy;

(10) Psychological services to administer and interpret test results, consult with staff members, plan and manage a program of psychological services, and assist in developing positive behavioral intervention strategies;

(11) Recreation;

(12) Rehabilitation counseling services;

(13) School health services and school nurse services that are designed to enable a child with a disability to receive FAPE as described in the child's IEP;

(14) Social work services in schools to prepare a child's history, provide group and individual counseling, and assist in developing positive behavioral intervention strategies;

(15) Speech-language pathology services; and

(16) Transportation.

34 C.F.R. § 300.34(c).

3. Case Law

In the list of "related services," the IDEA requires a school to provide "nursing services" to enable a child to receive FAPE, but only requires medical services from a licensed physician to determine a child's medically related disability. The issued raised by this distinction was whether a district needed to provide continuous nursing services in order for the student to be able to attend school. Would continuous nursing services fall under the "medical services" category (which is limited to diagnosis) or under the nursing services category (which needed to be provided throughout the school day)?

The Supreme Court answered this question by calling such services "nursing services" in a 7–2 decision in *Cedar Rapids Community School District v. Garret F.*, 526 U.S. 66 (1999). Garret F. was a boy who was paralyzed from the neck down but had typical intellectual functioning. He used a ventilator and a motorized wheelchair, which he controlled through a puff and suck straw. In order to attend school, he required a responsible individual to be nearby to assist him. *Id.* at 69. Until fourth grade, his parents provided the assistant to be with him during the school day but then made a request for the school to provide the nursing services that Garret needed to attend school. The Hearing Officer concluded that the school needed to provide the services because they were nursing services rather than physician services. *Id.* at 71. The lower courts affirmed, finding that the services did not fall under the medical services exclusion.

On certiorari to the United States Supreme Court, the school district urged the Court to use cost as a factor to exclude the requested service as covered by the IDEA. Although the Supreme Court observed that "the potential financial burdens imposed on participating States may be relevant to arriving at a sensible construction of the IDEA," it refused to allow cost to be used to remove an item from the definition of a "related service." *Id.* at 77–78. Because Garret could not remain in school without the requested services, the Court affirmed the lower court decision that the District was obligated to provide the services. *Id.* at 79. Thus, the school district was required to hire an individual to attend solely to Garret during the school day.

The application of the *Garret* decision to situations in which parents have sought to place their children in psychiatric residential facilities has divided the courts. In *Butler v. Evans,* 225 F.3d 887 (7th Cir. 2000), the Seventh Circuit found that parents were not entitled to reimbursement when they placed their child in a psychiatric hospital for several months because the hospitalization was for medical rather than educational reasons. Similarly, the Third Circuit found that the parents were not entitled to reimbursement for placing their daughter in a psychiatric residential treatment center when the parents took the position that their child was not even stable enough to receive an educational evaluation from the school district during the acute phase of her placement. *See Mary Courtney T. v. School District of Philadelphia,* 575 F.3d 235 (3rd Cir. 2009).

On similar facts, the Eighth Circuit in *Independent School District No. 284 v. A.C.,* 258 F.3d 769, 778 (8th Cir. 2001), allowed reimbursement for placement in a residential treatment facility where the court found that the placement was to "correct [the student's] behavioral and emotional problems, not just to keep her off the streets or to force her to sit down with a tutor." Similarly, the Fifth Circuit found in *Richardson Independent School District v. Michael Z.,* 580 F.3d 286 (5th Cir. 2009) that parents might be entitled to reimbursement for nonmedical expenses at a residential treatment facility if the treatment was designed to permit him to receive an education. These cases are difficult to distinguish, but it appears that the parent needs to emphasize the role of the treatment facility to prepare the student to attain an education in order to be successful.

Some commentators have suggested these cases reflect a misunderstanding of the role of appropriate mental health services for a child to be able to attain a meaningful education. *See, e.g.,* Ellen A. Callegary, *The IDEA's Promise Unfulfilled: A Second Look at Special Education & Related Services for Children with Mental Health Needs After Garret F.*, 5 JOURNAL OF HEALTH CARE LAW AND POLICY 164 (2002). Others have criticized the *Garret F.* decision as providing school districts with an insufficient cost defense. *See* Kristie Harding,

Cedar Rapids Community School District v. Garret F: A High Price for Equal Education, 28 PEPPERDINE LAW REVIEW 143 (2000).

C. EXTENDED SCHOOL YEAR

One type of educational service that school districts must make available to some students is what is called an "extended school year." The following regulation governs extended school year services:

> (a) General.
>
> (1) Each public agency must ensure that extended school year services are available as necessary to provide FAPE, consistent with paragraph (a)(2) of this section.
>
> (2) Extended school year services must be provided only if a child's IEP Team determines, on an individual basis, in accordance with §§ 300.320 through 300.324, that the services are necessary for the provision of FAPE to the child.
>
> (3) In implementing the requirements of this section, a public agency may not—
>
> (i) Limit extended school year services to particular categories of disability; or
>
> (ii) Unilaterally limit the type, amount, or duration of those services.
>
> (b) Definition. As used in this section, the term extended school year services means special education and related services that—

> (1) Are provided to a child with a disability—
>
> (i) Beyond the normal school year of the public agency;
>
> (ii) In accordance with the child's IEP; and
>
> (iii) At no cost to the parents of the child; and
>
> (2) Meet the standards of the SEA.

34 C.F.R. § 300.106.

Extended school year services (ESY) are typically offered to students who would regress if summer programming were not available. All students regress to some extent, but significant summer regression can make it difficult for students to attain any educational progress.

It is important to recognize that ESY services are *not* the same as summer school. They are a continuation of the IEP—with its emphasis on individualized instruction—over the summer months. Each state has the authority to create its own standards for ESY services. The federal regulations, as quoted above, provide minimal guidance. Additionally, the IDEA statutory language makes no mention of ESY services.

Many states use what is called a "regression and recoupment" model to determine eligibility for extended school year services, but federal regulations do not require that model. Other states, for example, consider whether a student's behavior during the school year, such as disruptive or self-injurious behavior, make it difficult for the student to make educational progress during the school year. When states use a regression/recoupment model, it is important to try to document regression over breaks such as winter break, spring break, or summer break to demonstrate that a student is eligible for extended school year services. As the regulations indicate, this service is not limited to any particular disability category. Further, school districts have an obligation to make ESY available, and they cannot have an absolute ban on ESY.

D. PROHIBITION ON MANDATORY MEDICATION

It is *not* permissible for a school district to insist that a student take a prescription drug in order to obtain an evaluation or an IEP. The IDEA provides:

> (A) In general
>
> The State educational agency shall prohibit State and local educational agency personnel from requiring a child to obtain a prescription for a substance covered by the Controlled Substances Act (21 U.S.C. §§ 801 et seq.) as a condition of attending school, receiving an evaluation under subsection (a) or (c) of section 1414 of this title, or receiving services under this chapter.

20 U.S.C. § 1412(a)(25).

§ 6.8 LEAST RESTRICTIVE ENVIRONMENT

A. PRESUMPTION TO BE EDUCATED WITH NONDISABLED PEERS

The fifth requirement is an explanation of whether a student is educated with his or her nondisabled peers.

> (V) an explanation of the extent, if any, to which the child will not participate with nondisabled children in the regular class and in the activities described in subclause (IV)(cc);

20 U.S.C. § 1414(d)(1)(A)(i).

This requirement relates to one of the few substantive requirements found in the IDEA—often termed the "least restrictive environment."

> Least restrictive environment
>
> (A) In general
>
> To the maximum extent appropriate, children with disabilities, including children in public or private institutions or other care facilities, are educated with children who are not disabled, and special classes, separate schooling, or other removal of children with disabilities from the regular educational environment occurs only when the nature or severity of the disability of a child is such that education in regular classes with the use of supplementary aids and services cannot be achieved satisfactorily.

20 U.S.C. § 1412(a)(5).

This substantive rule dovetails with the IEP requirement that the IEP must explain why a student is not in the regular classroom for some or all of the day. The least restrictive environment rule (LRE) presumes that a child will be in the regular classroom "to the maximum extent appropriate." If a student is removed from the regular classroom by attending a special class or a special school then that removal needs to be justified in the IEP. Further, because education with nondisabled children is supposed to happen to the "maximum extent appropriate," a student should be removed from the regular classroom as little as possible. Thus, in the example found in *Nutshell* § 6.7 (above), the IEP describes *where* Manuel is receiving services, as well as who delivers those services, and how often they are provided. The consulting services are provided in the regular classroom, while the speech language therapy is provided twice a week for thirty minutes in the therapy room. Because Manuel speaks Spanish and the services need to be provided in Spanish, he is the only student receiving those services. Often, pull-out services are provided in a small group setting.

The word "appropriate" in this rule, like the word "appropriate" in the term "free appropriate public education" is ambiguous. In general, courts have interpreted the least restrictive environment rule to give a preference for an integrated educational setting but differ on the legal standards to determine if a more segregated setting can be justified as "appropriate."

The IDEA regulations offer a little more guidance on how to interpret the LRE requirement. The regulations indicate that a child should only be removed from the regular classroom:

> if the nature or severity of the disability is such that education in regular classes with the use of supplementary aids and services cannot be achieved satisfactorily.

34 C.F.R. § 300.114(a)(2)(ii).

Thus, Manuel was able to receive assistance in his English class through a consultant who came into his classroom. That way of delivering services allowed him to avoid being removed from the regular classroom.

B. RACIAL DISPARITIES

Although the LRE requirement applies to all children in all school districts, empirical data reflect that students in large urban districts, where the student population tends to be disproportionately racial minorities, are most likely to be placed in self-contained and segregated placements compared to students who attend school in less urban districts. *See* Matthew E. Brock & John M. Schaefer, *Location Matters: Geographic Location and Educational Placement of Students with Developmental Disabilities,* 40 RESEARCH AND PRACTICE FOR PERSONS WITH SEVERE DISABILITIES 154 (2015). In the Brock and Schaefer study, all of the students who were studied had developmental disabilities so differing disability categories could not explain these diverse placement decisions. It simply seems that urban districts are less likely to consider it "appropriate" to keep a child with a developmental disability in the regular classroom than would a suburban or rural district.

A serious complication in considering the racial implications of the LRE requirement is that middle-class, white parents often *want* to send their child to a private, disability-segregated school and fight the school district's attempt to provide a more disability-integrated placement at the local school. By contrast, poor, minority parents often resist attempts to send their child to a disability-segregated placement because, in their poor and urban district, that disability-segregated placement is often a very weak academic option. Thus, many of the appellate and Supreme Court IDEA cases brought by parents of middle-class, white children are seeking to have the school district pay to send their child to a disability-segregated placement. In arguing against the parents' request, school districts often argue that the parent's preferred placement is inconsistent with the LRE requirement.

Two contrasting examples can show how the LRE requirement is applied when the parent is seeking a private placement in contrast to a school seeking to place a child in a disability-only segregated setting.

1. C.L.

C.L. has been diagnosed with ADHD, a nonverbal learning disability, and an executive function weakness. *See C.L. v. Scarsdale Union Free School District,* 744 F.3d 826 (2nd Cir. 2014). From kindergarten to third grade, his parents requested that he be classified as disabled and receive services under the IDEA. Although the school district acknowledged he was disabled for the purpose of creating a Section 504 plan, it refused to classify him as disabled under the IDEA. Dissatisfied with his lack of progress under the Section 504 plan and the school district's unwillingness to create an IEP, his parents withdrew him from the public school and enrolled him in a private school for children with disabilities. *Id.* at 834. Because C.L. had been attending a well-funded suburban school and his parents could afford both private schooling and an attorney, it appears that the family was middle-class.

As will be discussed in *Nutshell* Chapter 9, the parents requested a due process hearing to receive reimbursement for their tuition at the private school. In order to prevail, they needed to demonstrate that the school district denied their child FAPE and that the private placement was "appropriate." Their state (New York) has a two-level Hearing Officer process. The parents prevailed at the first level hearing and lost at the second level hearing. They then appealed the administrative decision to a federal district court, which affirmed the administrative decision. The parents then appealed the district court decision to the Second Circuit.

The school district argued that the parents were not entitled to reimbursement because the private placement was a highly restrictive setting only for children with disabilities. The school district did not seek to contend that they had offered the child a FAPE. *Id.* at 838. Thus, the only issue was whether the private placement was "appropriate." The Second Circuit reversed the district court, awarding tuition reimbursement for the parents. While recognizing that the restrictiveness of a private placement can be a factor in determining whether it is appropriate, it is not dispositive. *Id.* at 837. "[W]here the public school system denied the child a FAPE, the restrictiveness of the private placement cannot be measured against the restrictiveness of the public school option." *Id.*

2. Rafael Oberti

Rafael Oberti was born with Downs Syndrome. He has an intellectual disability, a communication impairment, and difficulty with expressive language. *See Oberti v. Board of Education of Clementon School District,* 789 F. Supp. 1322 (D.N.J. 1992). After attending preschool special education classes, the school district recommended Rafael be placed in a segregated, self-contained special education class in another school district. His school district was a low-income school district; and appears that the parents were represented by a nonprofit organization. Rafael's parents rejected the school district's recommendation and sought to have their son placed in the local school's regular classroom. *Id.* at 1325. They filed for due process and the administrative law judge ruled that the school district's proposed placement was appropriate. *Id.* at 1325. On appeal, the district court found that the school district had failed to consider whether Rafael could be in a less restrictive environment with the use of supplementary aids and services. *Id.* at 1337. Unlike the middle-class parents in *C.L.*, the parents in this case were wary of the education that their child would receive in a segregated setting outside of their school district.

Thus, the LRE rule can be an important argument for parents seeking to avoid a highly segregated public setting, while it can also be an argument used by school districts to avoid paying for a segregated private placement when the school district has failed to provide FAPE.

C. CONTINUUM OF ALTERNATIVE PLACEMENTS

Another important regulation relating to the provision of services in the LRE is the regulation regarding a "continuum of alternative placements." It provides:

> (a) Each public agency must ensure that a continuum of alternative placements is available to meet the needs of children with disabilities for special education and related services.

> (b) The continuum required in paragraph (a) of this section must—
>
> (1) Include the alternative placements listed in the definition of special education under § 300.38 (instruction in regular classes, special classes, special schools, home instruction, and instruction in hospitals and institutions); and
>
> (2) Make provision for supplementary services (such as resource room or itinerant instruction) to be provided in conjunction with regular class placement.

34 C.F.R. § 300.115.

This regulation is important; it does not allow a school district to argue that a placement is not "appropriate" merely because the school district has not made that kind of placement available. In Manuel's example, the school district had to have a consultant available who could spend an hour in Manuel's regular classroom three times per week. They could not require Manuel to receive English instruction in a pull-out room separate from the regular classroom merely because they already had that resource available. Similarly, when Manuel received thirty minutes of one-on-one speech and language therapy, the school could not require that he attend another school only for children with disabilities so that he could receive those services. Instead, those services needed to be available at his school so that he could leave the regular classroom for thirty minutes and then return for the rest of the school day in a regular education setting.

D. CASE LAW ON LEAST RESTRICTIVE ENVIRONMENT

1. Introduction

At present, there is no Supreme Court guidance on how to interpret the word "appropriate" in the LRE rule. There is a three-way circuit split on how to interpret this rule. *See* Sarah Prager, *An "IDEA" to Consider: Adopting a Uniform Test to Evaluate Compliance with the IDEA's Least Restrictive Environment Mandate*, 59 NEW YORK LAW SCHOOL LAW REVIEW 653, 664 (2014/2015):

> 1. "The Fourth, Sixth, and Eighth Circuits apply a three-factor test, which focuses on the feasibility of providing special services in a regular classroom setting."
> 2. "[T]he Second, Third, Fifth, Tenth, and Eleventh Circuits employ a two-prong test that mimics the statute's text and turns on 'the school's proper use of supplementary aids and services, which may enable the school to educate a child with disabilities for a majority of the time within a regular classroom, while at the same time addressing that child's unique educational needs."
> 3. "[T]he Ninth Circuit devised its own four-factor balancing test."

2. *Roncker* Test

The Fourth, Sixth, and Eighth Circuit test was developed in *Roncker v. Walter,* 700 F.2d 1058 (6th Cir. 1983). *See DeVries v. Fairfax County School Board,* 882 F.2d 876 (4th Cir. 1989); *A.W. v. Northwest R-1 School District,* 813 F.2d 158 (8th Cir. 1987).

Neill Roncker has a significant intellectual disability. His parents wanted him to attend Pleasant Ridge Elementary School, which is a regular public school that serves both disabled and nondisabled children. Although he would have been in a segregated classroom for his academic subjects, he would have had access to nondisabled children at lunch, gym, and recess. The school district preferred to place him in a county school where he would have had no exposure to nondisabled children. The school district argued that the county program offered a superior academic program as compared to the local elementary school. *Id.* at 1063. The parents argued that the school district sent all children with intellectual disabilities to the segregated placement without consideration of their individual educational needs. *Id.* at 1064. The parents lost before the state administrative proceeding and the district court. However, the Sixth Circuit vacated the district court decision and remanded the case for determination under the correct factors.

These are the three factors articulated by the Sixth Circuit in determining if the mainstreaming presumption can be overcome:

1. "the handicapped child would not benefit from mainstreaming"

2. "any marginal benefits received from mainstreaming are far outweighed by the benefits gained from services which could not feasibly be provided in the non-segregated setting"

3. "the handicapped child is a disruptive force in the non-segregated setting."

Id. at 1063.

Placing great weight on the mainstreaming requirement, as well as the need to provide supplemental services to avoid segregation, the Sixth Circuit also said: "In a case where the segregated facility is considered superior, the court should determine whether the services which make that placement superior could be feasibly provided in a non-segregated setting." *Id.* at 1063. In this case, the Sixth Circuit remanded the case back to the district court to determine if Neill could be provided with additional services to make mainstreaming appropriate.

3. *Daniel R.R.* Test

The Second, Third, Fifth, Tenth, and Eleventh Circuit test was developed in *Daniel R.R. v. State Board of Education,* 874 F.2d 1036 (5th Cir. 1989). *See Oberti v. Board of Education,* 995 F.2d 1204, 1214 (3rd Cir. 1993); *P. v. Newington Board of Education,* 546 F.3d 111 (2nd Cir. 2008); *L.B. v. Nebo School District,* 379 F.3d 966 (10th Cir. 2004);

Greer v. Rome City School District, 950 F.2d 688 (11th Cir. 1991).

Daniel R. is a boy with Downs Syndrome, an intellectual disability, and a speech impairment. Daniel's parents wanted him to be in a regular classroom environment; the school district sought to place him in a segregated special education classroom. The parents sought an administrative hearing where the Hearing Officer determined that the regular education classroom was not an appropriate placement. The district court affirmed.

The Fifth Circuit affirmed the district court but disagreed with the test applied by the Sixth Circuit in *Roncker* as well as the test applied by the lower court in this case. It criticized the *Roncker* case as necessitating "too intrusive an inquiry into the educational policy choices that Congress deliberately left to state and local school officials." *Id.* at 1046. But it also disagreed with the district court's analysis because it required the mainstreamed child "to learn at approximately the same level as their nonhandicapped classmates" and placed "too much emphasis on the handicapped student's ability to achieve an educational benefit," *Id.* at 1046, failing to consider the language and behavior benefits that might be achieved through mainstreaming. *Id.* at 1048.

The Fifth Circuit articulated this two-part test:

> First, we ask whether education in the regular classroom, with the use of supplemental aids and services, can be achieved satisfactorily for

> a given child. . . . If it cannot and the school intends to provide special education or to remove the child from regular education, we ask, second, whether the school has mainstreamed the child to the maximum extent appropriate.
>
> *Id.* at 1048.

Applying that test, the Fifth Circuit affirmed the school district's placement decision for Daniel. In *Daniel R.R.,* the school district was not seeking to place the child in a segregated county school where he would have no contact with nondisabled peers. Instead, like the parents' proposed placement in *Roncker,* he would have access to nondisabled children at lunch and recess. Thus, although the Fifth and Sixth Circuits proposed different rules for assessing conformance with the LRE requirement, they reached similar placement decisions.

4. *Rachel H.* Test

The Ninth Circuit's test was developed in *Sacramento City Unified School District Board of Education v. Rachel H.,* 14 F.3d 1398 (9th Cir. 1994).

Rachel H. has a significant intellectual disability. Her parents wanted her to be educated full-time in a regular second-grade classroom with supplemental services; yet, the district wanted her to spend half of the day in special education classes. Rachel's parents appealed the District's placement decision to a state Hearing Officer. Rachel's parents prevailed before the Hearing Officer and the district court affirmed.

The Ninth Circuit adopted the four-factor balancing test used by the district court. It considered this four-part test to employ factors found in both lines of cases:

> (1) the educational benefits to the disabled student of full-time placement in a regular class;
>
> (2) the non-academic benefits of such placement to the disabled student;
>
> (3) the effect the disabled student has on the teacher and children in the regular class; and
>
> (4) the costs of mainstreaming the disabled student
>
> *See Id.* at 1404.

Deferring to the Hearing Officer's fact finding, the Ninth Circuit found that Rachel could obtain educational benefits in the regular classroom, that her presence did not have a detrimental effect on the teacher or other students, and that Rachel could be kept in the regular classroom in the future with only a part-time aide. A crucial piece of evidence was from Rachel's second-grade teacher who testified that Rachel performed well in the regular classroom. *Id.* at 1401. Although the Ninth Circuit's test may have differed slightly from the Fifth's and Sixth Circuit's tests, it was also the only case in which a regular classroom teacher testified that the child could do well in a regular educational environment. In *Daniel R.R.*, by contrast, the regular classroom teacher testified that Daniel fell asleep in class and seemed to be very stressed by the regular classroom environment. Irrespective of what test if used by the court, that kind of testimony will have a significant impact on the outcome of a case.

§ 6.9 ACCOMMODATIONS FOR STATE OR DISTRICT-WIDE ASSESSMENTS

The sixth requirement for an IEP is a statement of accommodations for state or district-wide assessments:

> (VI)(aa) a statement of any individual appropriate accommodations that are necessary to measure the academic achievement and functional performance of the child on State and districtwide assessments consistent with section 1412(a)(16)(A) of this title; and
>
> (bb) if the IEP Team determines that the child shall take an alternate assessment on a particular State or districtwide assessment of student achievement, a statement of why—
>
> (AA) the child cannot participate in the regular assessment; and
>
> (BB) the particular alternate assessment selected is appropriate for the child;

20 U.S.C. § 1414(d)(1)(A)(i).

As states increasingly require standardized testing to graduate, these statements on IEPs are important. Each state has its own rules for standardized tests that a student may need to take in order to receive a high school diploma. In New York, for example, a student on an IEP has the option of earning an "IEP diploma," which is not recognized as a traditional "standards-based" diploma. *See* http://www.p12.nysed.gov/specialed/publications/iepdiploma.htm. Because an "IEP diploma" is less desirable than a regular diploma, school districts must also make available to students on an IEP the opportunity to meet the standards for a regular diploma. The IEP diploma "is intended for a student with very limited cognitive abilities who can not, because of his/her disability, earn a regular diploma." *Id.* Thus, a decision not to participate in the regular assessment process can have profound consequences and should be weighed carefully by the IEP team.

§ 6.10 TRANSITION PLANNING

The eighth and last requirement is a statement involving transition planning for older students to facilitate their attainment of career or educational goals.

> (VIII) beginning not later than the first IEP to be in effect when the child is 16, and updated annually thereafter—
>
> (aa) appropriate measurable postsecondary goals based upon age appropriate transition assessments related to training, education,

> employment, and, where appropriate, independent living skills;
>
> (bb) the transition services (including courses of study) needed to assist the child in reaching those goals; and
>
> (cc) beginning not later than 1 year before the child reaches the age of majority under State law, a statement that the child has been informed of the child's rights under this chapter, if any, that will transfer to the child on reaching the age of majority under section 1415(m) of this title.

20 U.S.C. § 1414(d)(1)(A)(i).

The IDEA also defines the term "transition services."

> The term "transition services" means a coordinated set of activities for a child with a disability that—
>
> (A) is designed to be within a results-oriented process, that is focused on improving the academic and functional achievement of the child with a disability to facilitate the child's movement from school to post-school activities, including post-secondary education, vocational education, integrated employment (including supported employment), continuing and adult education, adult services, independent living, or community participation;
>
> (B) is based on the individual child's needs, taking into account the child's strengths,

> preferences, and interests; and
>
> (C) includes instruction, related services, community experiences, the development of employment and other post-school adult living objectives, and, when appropriate, acquisition of daily living skills and functional vocational evaluation.

20 U.S.C. § 1401(34).

The transition plan rules are a relatively recent addition to the IDEA. They were not required until 1990. These are some of the kinds of problems that are frequently identified with transition plans:

- a lack of clarity in identifying responsible personnel for providing services,
- a lack of long range planning,
- a lack of yearly revisions,
- limited connections between schools and agencies,
- untimely development,
- not followed,
- do not reflect the unique aspirations of the student, or
- reflect vague or unreasonable aspirations of the student.

See Margaret Condit, *Remember the IDEA: A Call for Courts to Apply a Piecemeal Approach to*

Transition Litigation, 38 THOMAS JEFFERSON LAW REVIEW 6, 23 (2015).

Although it is rare for a court to invalidate an IEP merely because of inadequate transition planning, courts have taken that step in a few recent cases. *See Jefferson County Board of Education v. Lolita S.*, 581 Fed. Appx. 760 (11th Cir. 2014) (post-secondary goals and transition services fell below FAPE); *Dracut School Committee v. Bureau of Special Education Appeals,* 737 F. Supp.2d 35 (D. Mass. 2010) (failure to provide an IEP containing appropriate transition goals denied the student FAPE); *Carrie I. v. Department of Education, Hawaii*, 869 F. Supp.2d 1225 (D. Haw. 2012) (IEP failed to address student's unique needs as he transitioned from an educational setting to adult life). Nonetheless, other courts have distinguished some of these cases finding that adequate transition services were provided even if there were arguable flaws in the transition planning. *See, e.g., D.C. v. Mount Olive Township Board of Education,* 2014 WL 1293534 (D.N.J. March 31, 2014) (distinguishing *Dracut*); *Anthony C. v. Department of Education, Hawaii,* 2014 WL 587848 (D. Haw. Feb. 14, 2014) (distinguishing *Carrie I.*).

§ 6.11 DEFINING FAPE

The purpose of an IEP is to assist a student attain what the IDEA calls a "free appropriate public education." However, the IDEA does not define the term "appropriate." *See* 20 U.S.C. § 1401(9) (requiring that FAPE "include an appropriate preschool, elementary school, or secondary school education in the State involved"). The regulations offer no additional clarity. *See* 34 C.F.R. § 300.17 (also requiring that FAPE "include an appropriate preschool, elementary school, or secondary school education in the State involved").

Thus, the courts have struggled with defining the term "appropriate." Two leading Supreme Court cases have had a significant impact on the interpretation of that term.

§ 6.12 *ROWLEY*

The leading case on defining the term "appropriate" in the term "FAPE" is *Board of Education v. Rowley,* 458 U.S. 176 (1982), which was recently clarified in *Endrew F. v. Douglas County School District RE-1,* 137 S. Ct. 988 (2017).

The *Rowley* case involved the issue of whether the school district should be required to provide Amy Rowley with a sign language interpreter in grade school. Amy is deaf and had learned sign language from her parents (who were also deaf) before attending grade school. But, according to the courts, she also had excellent lipreading skills. The school district acknowledged that she qualified for an IEP as a student who was deaf and provided her with various types of specialized instruction and accommodations. The school district also attempted a trial use of a sign language interpreter in kindergarten, which they suspended after the interpreter indicated that Amy was not benefitting from his services.

When the school district denied the parents' request for a sign language interpreter, the parents filed for due process. The Hearing Officer ruled for the school district finding that "Amy was achieving educationally, academically, and socially without such assistance." *Id.* at 185. The Rowleys appealed that decision to a federal district court. The district court judge found that Amy was doing very well in school but was not provided "an opportunity to achieve [her] full potential commensurate with the opportunity provided to other children." *Id.* at 185–86. The Second Circuit affirmed. The lower courts applied what might be described as an "equal opportunity standard," requiring the school district to maximize the potential of each child with a disability commensurate with the opportunity provided to nondisabled children. The Supreme Court rejected that standard, finding that "Congress sought primarily to identify and evaluate handicapped children, and to provide them with access to a free public education." *Id.* at 200.

The Court recognized that the difficult legal issue was determining "when handicapped children are receiving sufficient educational benefits to satisfy the requirements of the Act." *Id.* at 202. In seeking to answer that question, the Court recognized that there is a wide spectrum of children who are covered by the IDEA. "One child may have little difficulty competing successfully in an academic setting with nonhandicapped children while another child may encounter great difficulty in acquiring even the most basic of self-maintenance skills." *Id.* at 202.

Given the range of students covered by the IDEA, the Court decided to confine itself to a "a handicapped child who is receiving substantial specialized instruction and related services, and who is performing above average in the regular classrooms of a public school system." *Id.* at 202. For such a child, the Court said that the IEP "should be reasonably calculated to enable the child to achieve passing marks and advance from grade to grade." *Id.* at 204. In a footnote, the Court clarified:

> We do not hold today that every handicapped child who is advancing from grade to grade in a regular public school system is automatically receiving a "free appropriate public education." In this case, however, we find Amy's academic progress, when considered with the special services and professional consideration accorded by the Furnace Woods school administrators, to be dispositive.

Id. at 204 n. 25.

Upon receiving this decision from the United States Supreme Court, Amy's parents moved to a school district in Maryland where she had access to a sign language interpreter. Today, Amy has a Ph.D. and is an Associate Professor in the Department of Modern Languages and Literatures at California State University (East Bay), where she is the Coordinator of the American Sign Language Program. *See* https://www.csueastbay.edu/directory/profiles/mll/rowleyamy-june.html.

The *Rowley* decision left a lot of ambiguity in the meaning of an "appropriate" education because it only answered that question in the context of a student who was receiving significant assistance and performing above grade level. Before discussing that ambiguity, it is important to reflect on what the *Rowley* decision was *not* talking about. The only issue in the *Rowley* case was whether Amy's IEP was appropriate; no one questioned whether she qualified for assistance under the IDEA as a "child with a disability."

Nonetheless, as Professor Mark Weber has discussed, some courts misapply the *Rowley* standard to the issue of whether a child is *disabled. See* Mark C. Weber, *The IDEA Eligibility Mess*, 57 BUFFALO LAW REVIEW 83, 105 (2009). As discussed in *Nutshell* Chapter Five, a student with a learning disability might achieve average grades but still have reading fluency far below grade level. *Rowley* covers the level of services that that student must receive, but *Rowley* does not cover the determination of whether the student is disabled. Nonetheless, as Professor Weber has documented, some courts cite *Rowley* to conclude that a student with a learning disability is not disabled because they are advancing from grade to grade. That is a misapplication of the *Rowley* holding.

In *Rowley,* the Supreme Court offered several different formulations of determining whether the IEP was *reasonably calculated* to offer an *appropriate* education:

- "[I]f personalized instruction is being provided with sufficient supportive services to permit the child to benefit from the instruction, and the other items on the definitional checklist are satisfied, the child is receiving a "free appropriate public education" as defined by the Act." *Id.* at 189.
- The "basic floor of opportunity" provided by the Act requires "access to specialized instruction and related services which are individually designed to provide educational benefit to the handicapped child." *Id.* at 201.
- Access should be "meaningful." *Id.* at 192.

This decision raised as many questions as it answered. How does one predict whether an IEP will provide future benefits? How much benefit is enough? What kind of benefits should be expected for a child who is not able to attain grade-level standards? When is the attainment of grade-level standards not sufficient?

In practice, it is usually difficult to demonstrate that the *Rowley* standard has not been met because the IEP only needs to be "reasonably calculated" to attain *some* educational benefit. If the IEP team meets the procedural requirements of the IDEA, and acts in good faith in providing *some* supports for the student, it is hard to argue that the IEP was not reasonably calculated to provide educational benefits. The fact that a child did not make much educational progress is not necessarily proof that the IEP was not *reasonably calculated* to make progress.

In order to prevail under the *Rowley* standard, plaintiffs typically have to show an egregious pattern of not devising an IEP that is reasonably calculated to attain much, if any, educational benefit. For example, the school district might repeat the same goals year after year even though the student is not making any educational progress. A good example of this type of case is *D.B. v. Bedford County School Board,* 708 F. Supp.2d 564 (W.D. Va. 2010).

When D.B. was five years old, the school district determined that he was developmentally delayed and eligible for special education services. He was re-evaluated three years later, and the school district classified him as having ADHD. The eligibility committee ruled out an intellectual impairment (which they called "mental retardation") but apparently never evaluated him for a learning disability despite general cognitive and processing ability scores that were in the low to very low range.

After several years of little educational progress, D.B.'s parents brought a due process hearing, arguing that his IEP was not reasonably calculated to provide any educational benefit. The Hearing Officer ruled in favor of the school district, noting that D.B. had been promoted a grade every year. *Id.* at 584. The parents appealed that decision to a district court judge who concluded that D.B. was "a sad case of social promotion." *Id.* at 584. He could not read, spell, or write. Rather than progressing, the educational records showed regression. "Despite this lack of progress, Defendant insisted that D.B.'s goals essentially be repeated from year to year, and that the inclusion classroom setting served him best." *Id.* at 586. The school provided few direct services; D.B. only received 30 minutes of speech and language therapy twice a week. His behaviors regressed to the point where he would suck his thumb, cry, and beg to go to the resource room to work. *Id.* at 587. Yet, his IEP kept setting as a goal that he would perform at grade-level standards, as if he could "master four areas of literacy using third grade texts when he has not yet mastered reading on the preprimer level and uses a scribe to record his thoughts." *Id.* at 586.

In this case, the deficiency in the IEP stemmed from the deficiency in the eligibility evaluation. "Defendant failed to properly consider specific learning disability; therefore the IEPs defendant prepared for D.B. could not have been 'reasonably calculated to enable the child to receive educational benefits.'" *Id.* at 584. Despite the very poorly crafted IEP, the parents lost before the Hearing Officer and needed to appeal the case to a federal district court. The Hearing Officer had taken the "advancing from grade to grade" language from *Rowley* to conclude the IEP was adequate despite strong evidence of "social promotion."

The Hearing Officer in *D.B.* reflected the Hearing Officers and judges who often find an IEP adequate if the child is seemingly making any educational progress. Some courts described this standard as being whether the IEP is calculated to confer an educational benefit more than *de minimis*. As we will next see, the Supreme Court rejected the *de minimis* standard in 2017 in *Endrew F.*

§ 6.13 *ENDREW F.*

In a unanimous opinion, the Supreme Court offered more clarity to the *Rowley* standard in *Endrew F. v. Douglas County School District RE-1*, 137 S. Ct. 988 (2017).

Unlike Amy Rowley, Endrew F. is a child who is not likely to readily advance from grade to grade. He was diagnosed with autism at age two and his school district had drafted an IEP from preschool through fourth grade. Despite the years of drafting and implementing IEPs, Endrew seemed to be making little educational or functional progress. He "would scream in class, climb over furniture and other students, and occasionally run away from school." *Id.* at 996. Although his parents thought that the IEP needed to be drastically re-written in order for Endrew to make educational progress, the school district largely carried over goals and objectives from one year to the next. His parents filed for due process, arguing that the IEP was not reasonably calculated to enable Endrew to receive educational benefits. His parents lost before the Hearing Officer, the district court, and the Tenth Circuit. The Tenth Circuit applied the *de minimis* test in concluding that Endrew's IEP had been reasonably calculated to enable him to make *some* progress. *Id.* at 997.

The Supreme Court rejected the *de minimis* test as being inconsistent with its other statements from *Rowley,* focusing on the need for the IEP to produce *adequate* educational benefits. It concluded that *any* educational benefit is not the same as *adequate* educational benefits. *Id.* at 998. This is the general approach that the Supreme Court said should govern IDEA cases:

> [A] school must offer an IEP reasonably calculated to enable a child to make progress appropriate in light of the child's circumstances.
>
> *Id.* at 999.

Emphasizing the IDEA's focus on the individual child, the Court offered some examples of what "appropriate progress" might look like. For a student, like Amy Rowley, who is fully integrated in the regular classroom, one would expect the IEP "to enable the child to receive passing marks and advance from grade to grade." *Id.* at 999. Nonetheless, the Court also noted that this standard is not an "inflexible rule." The Court does not hold that every disabled child who is advancing from grade to grade is automatically receiving an adequate educational program. *Id.* at 1000n.2.

For children who are not in the regular classroom, the Court emphasized that "every child should have the chance to meet challenging objectives." *Id.* at 1000. And those objectives are more demanding than *de minimis*. "It cannot be the case that the Act typically aims for grade-level advancement for children with disabilities who can be educated in the regular classroom, but is satisfied with barely more than *de minimis* progress for those who cannot." *Id.* at 1000–01. It would not make sense to set standards so low that children are merely "sitting idly . . . awaiting the time when they were old enough to 'drop out.' " *Id.* at 1001.

On the other hand, the Court was careful to indicate that it was not accepting the "equal opportunity" standard that it had previously rejected in *Rowley*. "Mindful that Congress (despite several intervening amendments to the IDEA) has not materially changed the statutory definition of a FAPE since *Rowley* was decided, we decline to interpret the FAPE provision in a manner so plainly at odds with the Court's analysis in that case." *Id.* at 1001. Finally, the Court emphasized that the crucial inquiry is whether the IEP is *reasonable*, not whether it is *ideal*. *Id.* at 999.

Because the Tenth Circuit applied the *de minimis* standard, the Supreme Court vacated and remanded its decision. It did not indicate whether the IEP offered to Endrew met its standard, although its statements about Endrew's lack of progress in the school's program and comparative progress at a private school suggests it considered his IEP to be inadequate. At the new school, with the development of a behavioral intervention plan, "Endrew's behavior improved significantly, permitting him to make a degree of academic progress that had eluded him in public school." *Id.* at 997. As a child with autism, who had significant behaviors that were impeding his ability to make educational progress, the Court may be implying that the absence of a behavioral intervention plan is indicative of an inadequate IEP. Many of the amicus briefs in *Endrew F.* sought to educate the Court about classroom programs that can be put in place for a child with autism that will allow them to make academic and functional progress. Nonetheless, the Court did not cite any of those briefs or sources, it seems to have understood that genuine educational progress should be the goal for any child, including one with autism. But, the Court's opinion does not say so directly; it is likely that the case settled so that further decisions will not be rendered. The parents were seeking tuition reimbursement rather than a new IEP at their public school so further developments are unlikely.

§ 6.14 POST-*ENDREW F.*

While it is too early to know how the *Endrew F.* decision will impact decisions by school districts, Hearing Officers, and lower courts, there have been a half dozen or so cases decided under the *Endrew F.* standard. In district court cases, the federal court judge generally affirmed the Hearing Officer decisions, which had been rendered before *Endrew F.* was decided.

- District court affirmed Hearing Officer determination that IEP was adequate despite lessening the amount of student's specialized instruction, decreasing the amount of behavioral support, and failing to have speech-language goals. The Court cited *Endrew F.* for the proposition that an IEP merely need be *reasonable* rather than *ideal. See Davis v. District of Columbia,* 2017 WL 1102647 (D.D.C. March 23, 2017).

- District court affirmed Hearing Officer conclusions that a student with dyslexia had an IEP reasonably calculated to make educational progress, relying on evidence that the child made progress in reading and decoding, and that the school modified the IEP in light of the parents' outside expert reports. *See A.G. and J.G. v. Board of Education,* 2017 WL 1200906 (S.D.N.Y. March 29, 2017)

- District court affirmed a Hearing Officer's conclusion that a student with autism did not receive an adequate IEP until February of his kindergarten year but that the IEP was adequate thereafter. The judge emphasized that an IEP need not be perfect in order to be adequate. *See Brandywine Heights Area School District v. B.M.,* 2017 WL 1173836 (E.D. Pa. March 29, 2017).

- District court affirmed a Hearing Officer's decision in favor of the school district for a student with a speech and language impairment, emphasizing that the student, who was in the regular classroom, made sufficient progress to proceed to the next grade even though she did not make progress in all categories. *See E.D. v. Colonial School District,* 2017 WL 1207919 (E.D. Pa. March 31, 2017).

- District court affirmed a Hearing Officer's decision in favor of parents for student with autism, relying on evidence that staff had a lack of training for how to deal with student's disabilities, that there was not a timely and appropriate behavioral plan in place, that physical therapy was terminated without justification, and that his educational placement was inappropriately changed without notice to parents. The Hearing Officer had ruled for the parents under the Eighth Circuit's *de minimis* standard, and the district court affirmed under the *Endrew F.* standard. *See Paris School District v. A.H.,* 2017 WL 1234151 (W.D. Ark. April 3, 2017).

In the only court of appeals decision since *Endrew F.* was decided, the Ninth Circuit reversed the Hearing Officer's decision. *See M.C. v. Antelope Valley Union High School District,* 852 F.3d 840 (9th Cir. 2017).

M.C. is blind and has many developmental delays. M.C.'s guardian ad litem (GAL), a person appointed by the court to protect a child's "best interest," brought this action on behalf of M.C. She offered several arguments for why M.C. had not been provided an adequate IEP.

First, the GAL argued that the school district failed to document the amount of services that M.C. would receive from a teacher of the visually impaired (TVI). The IEP stated that M.C. would receive 240 minutes of TVI per *month*; the district apparently unilaterally changed the number of minutes to 240 minutes per *week* without giving notice to the GAL and supposedly sent a teacher to his school for *300* minutes of TVI per week. The Hearing Officer did not consider this issue, finding that the GAL had waived it. The district court affirmed the Hearing Officer's decision. The court of appeals reversed, however, finding that the guardian was harmed by these actions because she had to bring legal action even to learn what level of service was being provided to M.C. Further, without a formal modification to the IEP, the school district could treat the additional TVI services as gratuitous and cut back on them.

Second, the GAL argued that the school district failed to identify the assistive technology that would be provided to M.C. The Hearing Officer and district court judge found that this omission did not constitute a FAPE violation. The district court judge said it did not "seriously infringe" on the GAL's opportunity to participate in the IEP formulation. The Ninth Circuit reversed, finding that the GAL "had no way of confirming whether [the A.T. services] were actually being provided to M.C." *Id.* at 850.

Third, the GAL sought relief for the failure of the school district to respond to her complaint. Although this issue did not directly relate to a denial of FAPE, it did arguably impact her ability to participate fairly at the hearing. The Ninth Circuit concluded that the Hearing Officer should have refused to go forward with the hearing until the district answered the complaint. The Ninth Circuit remanded the case for a determination of the prejudice suffered by the GAL through that failure and an award of appropriate compensation. *Id.* at 851.

Finally, the GAL argued that the IEP was deficient because it failed to develop measurable goals in all areas of need, including orientation and mobility services. The Hearing Officer and district court had ruled in favor of the school district on these claims. The district court had cited the language from *Rowley* that Congress did not require a potential-maximizing education. The Ninth Circuit remanded that aspect of the decision in light of *Endrew F.*

It is unusual for a court of appeals to reverse both a Hearing Officer and district court judge, because it ordinarily accords deference to the Hearing Officer's factual findings. In this case, however, the Ninth Circuit was very critical of the Hearing Officer's decision. The Ninth Circuit said:

> The district court accorded the ALJ's findings substantial deference because the ALJ 'questioned witnesses during a three-day hearing" and "wrote a 21-page opinion that reviewed the qualifications of witnesses and culled relevant details from the record." But, neither the duration of the hearing, nor the

> ALJ's active involvement, nor the length of the ALJ's opinion can ensure that the ALJ was "thorough and careful." *J.W. ex rel. J.E.W. v. Fresno Unified School District*, 626 F.3d 431, 440 (9th Cir. 2010). And, in this case, the ALJ was neither thorough nor careful.

Id. at 845–46.

The Ninth Circuit's strong criticism of the Hearing Officer is not directly related to the *Endrew F.* decision, but the opinion, in its entirety, may signal a more vigorous review of Hearing Officer decisions in the Ninth Circuit. Most circuits (including the Ninth Circuit) had not used the *de minimus* test before *Endrew F.* was decided. Further, no district court judge has yet reversed a Hearing Officer based on *Endrew F.* Thus, it is too early to assess what, if any, impact the *Endrew F.* decision will have on the development and enforcement of IEPs.

§ 6.15 SAMPLE IEP

Below is a modified, sample IEP that Arizona State University's Professional Learning Library posted on the Internet. It provides an excellent example of how all the pieces of an IEP fit together when there has been a good discussion of present levels of academic and functional performance.

Present Levels of Academic Achievement and Functional Performance (PLAAFP)

I. COGNITIVE/PROCESSING

Harry Potter is a 7-year-old 3rd grader who demonstrates average intellectual abilities and expected achievement levels in the areas of memory, nonverbal reasoning, and visual spatial processing skills. He demonstrates a significant and unusual processing weakness in the area of crystallized intelligence including verbal comprehension, lexical knowledge, and language-based processing skills. According to standardized achievement testing, Harry is achieving below his same age peers, below grade level, and below his expected achievement range in the areas of reading, oral and written language. These delays are significantly impacting his ability to understand, comprehend, and use language in the academic setting manifesting itself as a Specific Learning Disability in the areas of reading, academic oral language, and written expression.

II. EDUCATIONAL IMPACT

A. DISABILITY IMPACT STATEMENT

The identified disability, Specific Learning Disability, impacts Harry's ability to participate meaningfully and demonstrate sufficient progress in the general education curriculum and activities for his current grade level. The impact of this disability is evident in the areas of reading and writing. Harry also requires related services in the area of speech/language in order to demonstrate academic and social progress, due to deficits in receptive/expressive language. Additionally, Harry receives services in the area of occupational therapy to improve fine motor control and handwriting legibility.

B. EDUCATIONAL NEEDS

Harry demonstrates the need for specialized instruction and accommodations in the areas of reading fluency, reading comprehension, and written expression. Related services in the area of receptive and expressive language and fine motor development are required to ensure progress in the general education curriculum. He requires reading materials that are at his instructional level (first grade), extra time for completion of tests, sentence frames for compositions, graphic organizers, and significant scaffolding.

C. ASSISTIVE TECHNOLOGY

Harry participates appropriately in the general education setting without assistive technology or services at this time. His educational needs can be met through special education and related services, and accommodations specified in the IEP. There is no evidence that assistive technology is required at this time in order for Harry to demonstrate progress toward grade-level outcomes and mastery of appropriate IEP goals. Harry communicates effectively with peers and adults in academic and social settings.

D. LACK OF INSTRUCTION IN READING/MATH

Harry previously attended Grand Valley Elementary School, where he was provided with special education services. At Happy Valley Elementary School this year, Harry has been absent eight days.

E. IMPACT OF ELL

Harry is not an English language learner.

III. STUDENT STRENGTHS (ALL ACADEMIC AREAS REGARDLESS OF DISABILITY CATEGORY)

A. MATH

Galileo Benchmark, 11/15/12. Harry scored in the "exceeds" range in the following areas: express whole numbers through six digits using and connecting multiple representations; compare and order whole numbers through six digits by applying the concept of place value; count and represent money using coins and bills to $100.00; apply and interpret the concept of multiplication and division as inverse operations to solve problems; describe the effect of operations (multiplication and division) on the size of whole numbers; record equivalent forms of whole numbers to six digits by constructing models and using numbers; use a symbol to represent an unknown quantity in a given context; create and solve simple one-step equations that can be solved using addition and multiplication facts; identify and describe 3-dimensional figures including their relationship to real world objects;

identify a translation, reflection, or rotation and model its effect on a 2-dimensional figure; determine elapsed time across months using a calendar and by hours and half hours using a clock; convert units of length, weight, and capacity; determine the area of a rectangular figure using an array model; and measure and calculate perimeter of 2-dimensional figures.

General Educator's Observations and Input (in the area of Math), 11/13/12. Harry's classroom teacher reports that he knows and remembers basic addition and subtraction facts; uses strategies successfully to add and subtract single digit numbers; and adds and subtracts multi-digit numbers with and without regrouping.

B. READING

Galileo Pre-Test, 8/11/12. Harry met the standard in these areas: alphabetize a series of words to the third letter; and interpret information of functional documents (e.g., maps, schedules, pamphlets) for a specific purpose.

Special Education Teacher's Input and Observations, 10/5/12. Harry demonstrates the ability to recognize high-frequency words; acquire new vocabulary daily; use pictures for understanding; identify the main idea after reading/listening to text; and identify characters, sequence of events, and setting.

General Educator's Observations and Input (in the area of reading), 11/13/12. Harry demonstrates relative strengths in reading, in the areas of acquiring new vocabulary and using pictures to support his understanding.

Informal Reading Inventory with Special Educator, 10/5/12. Harry observed all punctuation marks while reading a first-grade level expository text. With prompts to pay close attention to inflectional endings and picture clues, Harry demonstrated progress in his accuracy during decoding. When asked questions about the text, Harry identified the table of contents, the title, front cover, back cover, and title page of the book correctly. He knew where to begin reading and directionality.

C. WRITING

Special Education Teacher's Input and Observations, 10/11/12. Harry generates ideas for writing after modeling and scaffolding are provided. He writes to inform, with a clear topic and support, when he uses a graphic organizer and sentence frames. With the help of a graphic organizer, he writes to persuade, using opinion. In a sentence-level Curriculum-Based Assessment administered individually, with models, on 10/6/12, Harry included beginning capitalization and ending punctuation on each of four complete sentences. His sentences all included a subject and a verb. All sentences were in the present tense and included subject-verb agreement.

IV. STUDENT NEEDS (ALL ACADEMIC AREAS REGARDLESS OF DISABILITY CATEGORY)

A. MATH

Galileo Pre-Test, 8/8/12. Harry's developmental score was 572 (approaching benchmark goals). Galileo Benchmark, 10/3/12. Harry's developmental score was 650 (approaching benchmark goals). On this test, Harry scored in the "falls far below" range on questions measuring the following skills: sort whole numbers into sets and justify the sort; express benchmark fractions as fair sharing, parts of a whole, or parts of a set; compare and order benchmark fractions; add and subtract whole numbers to four digits; create and solve word problems based on addition, subtraction, multiplication, and division; demonstrate the concept of multiplication and division using multiple models; demonstrate fluency of multiplication and division facts through 1O; apply commutative, identity, and zero properties to multiplication and apply the identity property to division; collect, record, organize, and display data using tables and graphs; formulate and answer questions by interpreting and analyzing displays of data; solve a variety of problems based on the multiplication principle of counting; investigate and solve problems using vertex-edge graphs; explain the rule for a given numerical sequence; recognize and describe a relationship between two quantities, given by a chart, table, or graph, in which the quantities change proportionally, using words, pictures, or expressions; translate between the different representations of whole number relationships; recognize similar figures; describe and compare attributes of two- and three-dimensional figures; analyze a problem situation to determine the question(s) to be answered; represent a problem situation; summarize mathematical information, explain reasoning, and draw conclusions; and analyze and evaluate whether a solution is reasonable.

General Educator's Observations and Input (in the area of Math), 11/13/12. Harry does not recall basic multiplication facts; has difficulty verbalizing in complete sentences using math vocabulary; requires prompting to explain his thinking; has difficulty solving story problems accurately; and confuses place values. The teacher estimates his current instructional level to be end of first to beginning of second grade.

B. READING

Galileo Pre-Test, 8/9/12. Harry's developmental score was 563 (falls far below benchmark goals).

Galileo Benchmark, 10/4/12. Harry's developmental score was634 (approaching benchmark goals). On this test, Harry demonstrated skills that fall far below expectations in these areas: use knowledge of prefixes to (e.g., un-, re-, in-, dis) to determine the meaning of words; use knowledge of suffixes (e.g., -ful, -ly, -less) to determine the meaning of words; answer clarifying questions in order to comprehend text; extract information from graphic organizers (e.g., webs, Venn diagrams, flow charts) to comprehend text; connect information and events in text to related text and sources; describe characters (e.g., traits, roles, similarities) within a literary selection; sequence a series of events in a literary selection; identify the speaker or narrator in a literary selection; locate specific information by using organizational features (e.g., title, table of contents, headings, captions, bold print, italics, key words, glossary, indices) in expository text; use a variety of sources to answer specific questions and/or gather information; distinguish fact from opinion in persuasive text; and identify persuasive vocabulary.

He also scored far below grade level in the area of applying knowledge of the following common spelling patterns to read words: that drop the final e and add endings such as: -ing, -ed, or -able (e.g., use, using used, usable); with final consonants that need to be doubled when adding an ending (e.g., hop/hopping); that require changing the final y to i (e.g., baby/babies); that end in -tion, -sion, (e.g., election, vision); with complex word families (e.g., -ight, -ought); and that include common prefixes, suffixes and root words.

Special Education Progress Report, 10/5/12. Early in the first quarter, Harry demonstrated proficiency with 18 of 28 recently introduced phonograms. In September, he identified 15 of 21 phonograms correctly during a written phonogram review (71%). His performance has improved dramatically, as he correctly sounded 50 of 70 phonograms during an oral phonogram review with the special education teacher on October 2; and 55 of 70 with the special educator the following day. This brings his overall proficiency to 79%. On August 3, Harry read 79 of 100 Fry's words correctly, and also self-corrected eleven times. When presented with the second hundred Fry's Instant Words, Harry read 57 correctly, and self-corrected four of his errors. When given decoding assistance or text at first-grade level or below, Harry demonstrates the ability to answer questions about the text. After reading "Go Away, Dog," with picture cues, on August 29, Harry answered three wh- questions accurately. He successfully answered five of five similar questions after listening to and discussing "Sylvester and the Magic Pebble" in the whole group setting on September 19. When given decoding assistance to read a story at the "My First Reading Level" on September 21, Harry again answered all five of five questions correctly, orally. After listening to Thumbelina on October 3, Harry was able to answer four of five questions accurately. Finally, on October 5, Harry read "What Will Little Bear Wear?" and then answered eight of ten questions correctly, orally, for an overall score of 80%.

General Educator's Observations and Input (in the area of reading), 11/13/12. Harry has difficulty decoding at the third-grade level and does not actively seek assistance. He does not understand and follow written directions; he does not observe punctuation marks when reading grade-level text; he has difficulty pronouncing grade-level math vocabulary and using it in the correct context. When reading story problems in math, Harry does not demonstrate understanding of the text, including main idea or question.

In an informal reading inventory on 10/5/12, Harry read a portion of a first-grade level expository text with 83% accuracy. He observed punctuation marks. Informal Assessments with the Special Educator, 10/19/12. During small group written phonogram review, Harry wrote 12 of 19 phonograms correctly. When reading the first 100 Fry's Instant Words, individually, Harry demonstrated 85% proficiency. When reading a portion of an expository, first-grade text, Harry demonstrated 76% accuracy overall; and self-corrected four times. He read words with the -s inflectional ending correctly on 17 of 21 occasions. When answering questions about the text, Harry was unable to identify a caption (when asked what it was); and he was unable to identify where a sentence ended. He was unable to identify the spine of the book.

Informal Assessments with the Special Educator, 10/22/12. Harry read a first-grade level narrative passage with 87% accuracy (140/161 words decoded correctly), while observing punctuation marks appropriately. He decoded six of 13 words with inflectional -s and -es endings correctly. With decoding support, Harry answered four of five comprehension questions correctly, aloud, including multiple choice and short answer responses. Harry identified three important details from the text accurately. After listening to a third-grade narrative text, Harry demonstrated 78% accuracy when verbally answering questions about characters, setting, and events from the story, given repeated/rephrased questions and prompts to provide additional information.

C. WRITING

Special Education Progress Report, 10/5/12. Harry demonstrates the ability and willingness to use graphic organizers as directed, although he sometimes has difficulty transferring his ideas from the organizer into a paragraph effectively. On 9/21/12, given an organizer, explicit directions to use it, and a paragraph with sentence frames, Harry completed a paragraph with verbal reminders to use capital letters appropriately, use lower case letters whenever required, and use proper grammar. He used capital letters correctly in eight of 11 instances and employed correct verb tenses and sentence structure in three of five sentences.

On October 3, Harry used two graphic organizers that he had previously completed in class to compose a sentence about omnivores. He was provided a model and the organizers, which were completed in whole group lessons in the classroom, provided correct spelling of key vocabulary. Harry's composition consisted of four sentences, which presented true information and were written neatly and carefully. One of four sentences included correct grammar and sentence structure. Two of four sentences included capital letters at the beginnings and all four sentences were properly punctuated. Harry included one misplaced capital letter. Three of four verbs matched their subjects grammatically. Harry tends to omit "s" from the ends of plurals and verbs. His spelling was 100% correct and the sentences all related to the topic and title of the paragraph. On 10/4/12, Harry told a personal story aloud, with prompting and questioning. He was provided with a word bank of key words he had produced. He completed an organizer with pictures of events from the beginning, middle, and end of his story. Harry wrote a paragraph with three sentences. The paragraph followed a logical sequence with 75% accuracy. Of twenty words, 90% were spelled correctly.

Harry included capitals at the beginnings of two sentences and failed to capitalize a proper noun, although it was provided in the word bank correctly (50%). The paragraph included a topic sentence and related sentences.

D. SPEECH THERAPY

Harry has been seen for speech/language therapy services to address an overall improvement of his receptive/expressive language skills. Harry's prior IEP goals focused on correctly responding to 2-step directions containing sequential concepts with at least 80% accuracy and formulating grammatically correct sentences with at least 80% accuracy. Currently during speech therapy sessions, Harry is demonstrating that he is able to correctly respond to 2-step instructions with an average of 20% accuracy (progressing but goal not met) and is able to formulate his own grammatically correct sentences with an average of 25% accuracy (progressing but goal not met). Harry's prior IEP was written in March of 2012 so it is not expected that Harry would have met his annual goals by this time. Harry is capable of a higher level of accuracy but consistently makes errors by responding too quickly. Harry frequently forgets what has been said to him or responds to sequential directions out of order. Harry relies heavily on prompts/cues from the therapist in order to respond accurately. On his goal for improving his overall syntax skills, Harry demonstrates a higher level of accuracy when picture cues are used. Harry's correct responses have increased to an average of 60% accuracy.

Harry tries to do his best work on all language tasks presented to him but needs to take his time and improve on his ability to respond independently rather than being dependent on the therapist. Harry continues to demonstrate overall receptive and expressive language weaknesses. Harry's difficulty in the area of receptive/expressive language skills may impede his success in the general education setting in the areas of acquiring new information in the areas of reading, writing, spelling and math, appropriately conveying his thoughts and ideas to others, and creating lasting, positive friendships with peers. Harry would continue to benefit from speech therapy services to address an overall improvement of his receptive/expressive language skills. Harry will receive 120 minutes a month of direct speech/language therapy services to be provided in the special education setting.

E. OCCUPATIONAL THERAPY

Fine Motor:

Harry has shown improvements with fine motor control and handwriting legibility. He is doing much better with line placement of his letters. He continues to have some difficulty with letter memory but he is able to easily fix these errors when they are pointed out to him. Harry has also been doing much better with spacing between words. He continues to have some difficulty with grammar, spelling, and sentence formation. Harry has not shown any signs of fatigue during upper extremity strengthening tasks.

Sensory:

Student has been participating in motor lab activities to help with his sensory seeking behaviors in the school setting. Student has been inconsistent with his response to the motor lab this year. Student continues to have a difficult time attending to task when others are present in the room. He does not like to use the "wiggle cushion" in class. His teacher has been consulted and modifications to his classroom set up have been made to help eliminate distractions. His materials are kept in the back of the room where he will walk and get them when he needs this. This helps limit distractions and also gives him numerous breaks throughout the day. His seating was also arranged so he could be in the front of the class but away from other distracting students.

Student has recently shown a disinterest in coming to occupational therapy.

V. ADLS (Assisted Daily Living Skills)

Student does not require assistance with self-care skills in the school setting at this time.

VI. SOCIAL AND EMOTIONAL DEVELOPMENT

Special Education Teacher's Input and Observations, 10/11/12. Harry demonstrates a curious approach to his learning and he uses his background knowledge to aid comprehension, vocabulary acquisition, and performance in science and history. He is very interested in science and enjoys non-fiction books and folktales. Harry generally interacts appropriately with peers. He completes his homework 80% of the time, and always completes his class work. Harry often forgets to bring his homework back to school, and he has difficulty with organization of materials. Harry is easily frustrated and sometimes does not take responsibility for his own actions.

General Educator's Observations and Input (in the area of behavior), 10/14/12. Harry works well with others. He enjoys activities that involve movement and exhibits high energy levels and a positive outlook. Harry enjoys solving math problems independently and focuses on the task at hand. Harry enjoys narrative books with fantastic locations and plots, and many illustrations. He likes to answer straightforward questions, but prefers to let others answer more abstract questions. Harry has difficulty organizing materials and turning in assignments.

Informal Classroom Observation, 10/15/12. During a 20-minute observation in the classroom, Harry was observed to be on-task 20 minutes out of 20. He was never out of his seat when he should not have been, and he did not interrupt or talk out. He began tasks immediately, followed directions, and appeared to understand directions. He was often attentive to discussions and asked appropriate questions. Overall, Harry rarely speaks out of turn, is overly withdrawn, or demonstrates attention-seeking behaviors.

VII. TRANSITION—NOT APPLICABLE AT THIS TIME

VIII. Physical Development

Harry exhibits age-appropriate physical development and motor development. His vitality and physical skills are sufficient to access and progress in the general education curriculum and typical compared to same-age peers.

IX. OTHER INFORMATION

Harry requires text presented at his current instructional level, in order to demonstrate mastery in the areas of reading fluency and comprehension. He demonstrates progress toward reading grade-level text, with significant support and direct instruction. When Harry is accessing grade-level text in order to demonstrate comprehension or math reasoning skills, he requires a reader of select sections to compensate for deficits in the area of reading fluency. Direct and explicit instruction, frequent review, and modeling are necessary in order for Harry to understand and acquire grade-level content vocabulary across the curriculum (including in the areas of math, science, and social studies). Harry needs personalized word boxes, glossaries, or vocabulary books/lists in order to acquire and use grade-level vocabulary in his responses and compositions, and to support his efforts to spell correctly. Lists of subjects/verbs that illustrate agreement are necessary in order to scaffold this skill until the support can be faded to facilitate greater independence. He requires graphic organizers and rubrics/checklists/adult conferencing, or sentence frames in order to write narrative, informative, or persuasive paragraphs. Modeling is required when Harry produces written responses and compositions. Examples and modeling are warranted across the curriculum to compensate for a specific learning disability and deficits in receptive/expressive language. In math, manipulatives or pictures will allow Harry to understand and express concepts more effectively. Harry requires support in order to organize his materials and come to class prepared. The general education teacher and special educator will collaborate to ensure materials and supports are in place to allow Harry to demonstrate progress across the curriculum and school settings. Harry's parents indicate (10/23/12) that Harry completes his homework, although is sometimes hesitant. He is stubborn at times.

Harry enjoys science and related activities. Mr. and Mrs. Potter have had concerns in the area of reading, and see similar difficulties at home as those noted by Harry's teachers.

X. MEASURABLE ANNUAL GOALS

Reading Goal #1

Given a text or a portion of text at his current grade level, Harry will decode words with common inflectional endings (-s, -es, -ed, -ing) while reading aloud in the individual setting, with 90% accuracy as evidenced by informal reading inventories, on four consecutive trials.

Baseline: 46% given first-grade level text

Measurement criteria: 90% on three trials

How will progress toward meeting the annual goal be measured?

Measurement tool: informal reading inventories

Reading Goal #2

Given decoding assistance, or a reader of select sections, and text at the third-grade level, Harry will verbally answer short answer questions with 80% accuracy independently (without prompts), on three consecutive trials. Data will be collected using informal reading assessments administered individually by the special education teacher.

Baseline: 43% after listening to third-grade text.

Measurement criteria: 80% on three trials.

How will progress toward meeting the annual goal be measured?

Measurement tool: informal reading assessments

Writing Goal

When participating in curriculum based writing assessments, Harry will produce a mean of 25 correct word sequences during a three-minute writing sample, on three consecutive trials.

Baseline: five correct word sequences (15 total in three minutes)

Measurement criteria: 25 CWS

How will progress toward meeting the annual goal be measured?

Measurement tool: Primary Level Curriculum-Based Assessments

XI. ACCOMMODATIONS FOR INSTRUCTION AND ASSESSMENT

1. Provide a reader of select sections of grade-level text, as requested by the student, when decoding and fluency are not being assessed, across curricular areas.

2. Review and model use of new content area vocabulary across subjects.

3. Provide fading support of individualized word boxes, glossaries, and/or vocabulary lists for vocabulary acquisition and spelling in responses and compositions across the curriculum.

4. Provide lists and models to illustrate and prompt subject/verb agreement, with fading support.

5. Provide organizational support through graphic organizers, adult conferencing, rubrics or checklists, and/or modeling when Harry is writing responses and compositions.

6. Break instructions and new information into smaller pieces.

XII. PARTICIPATION IN STATE AND PEA-WIDE ASSESSMENTS

The student will participate in PEA-wide assessments with no accommodations or with standard accommodations.

XIII. SPECIAL EDUCATION SERVICES

Special Education Services	Initiation Date	End Date	Frequency/ Amount	Location (LRE Setting)	Provider Position
Reading Decoding	12/13/12	12/12/13	30 min/week	Resource room	Special Education teacher
Reading Comprehension	12/13/12	12/12/13	30 min/week	Resource room	Special Education teacher
Written Expression	12/13/12	12/12/13	30 min/week	Resource room	Special Education teacher
Speech	12/13/12	12/12/13	120 min/ month	Speech	SLP
Occupational Therapy	12/13/12	12/12/13	30 min/ month	OT room	OTR

XIV. PROGRAM MODIFICATIONS OR SUPPORTS FOR SCHOOL PERSONNEL

	Initiation Date	End Date	Frequency/ Amount	Location (LRE Setting)
Collaboration among the general education teacher, Speech Language Therapist, Occupational Therapist and Special Educator will provide consistent implementation or supports and instruction across curricular areas and school settings	12/13/2012	12/12/2013	30 min./ month	School wide
Taking tests in quiet locations	12/13/2012	12/12/2013	As needed	School wide
Opportunity for clarification with the teacher	12/13/2012	12/12/2013	As needed	School wide

XV. PARTICIPATION IN REGULAR CLASS, EXTRACURRICULAR, AND NONACADEMIC ACTIVITIES

Provide an explanation of the extent, if any, to which the student will not participate with nondisabled children in regular class, extracurricular, and nonacademic activities.

Harry will not participate with non disabled peers while receiving direct instruction for speech, OT, and academic support in the special education setting for 120 min. per week . He is included in the general education setting for the remainder of the day. The potential harmful effects of such placement are far outweighed by the benefits to Harry's academic language and motor development through specialized services. These services are best delivered in a separate location with fewer distractions and the opportunity for repeated, targeted practice of skills.

CHAPTER 7

SCHOOL DISCIPLINE

§ 7.1 INTRODUCTION

Discipline of students with disabilities has received increased attention in recent years. On an annual basis, more than 3 million students are suspended from school, with these students overwhelmingly being disabled and/or racial minorities. A 2015 study by the UCLA Center for Civil Rights Remedies found that suspension rates for students with disabilities were much higher than those for nondisabled students. Among secondary students, 18 percent of students with disabilities were suspended as compared to 10 percent of students overall. Even in elementary school, the suspension rate of students with disabilities (5 percent) is more than twice the overall suspension rate. *See* Daniel Losen et al., *Are We Closing the School Discipline Gap?* (The UCLA Center for Civil Rights Remedies February 2015). Moreover, the rate of suspension was particularly high for students with emotional disabilities—a third of all K–12 students with emotional disabilities were suspended at least once during the 2011–12 school year.

Racial disparity in suspensions among students with disabilities has also received significant national attention. A 2012 UCLA study contained the following description of that problem:

> **Most alarming of all is that one out of four Black K–12 students with disabilities was suspended out of school at least one time in 2009–2010. This high risk for suspension is a full 16 percentage points higher than for white students with disabilities.**

Daniel J. Losen & Jonathan Gillespie, *Opportunities Suspended: The Disparate Impact of Disciplinary Exclusion from School* 14 (UCLA Civil Rights Project August 2012)(bolded in original).

Another serious problem that has received significant national attention is the high rate of restraint and seclusion used for students with disabilities. A 2014 ProPublica investigation found that three-fourths of the students who were subjected to restraint and seclusion during the 2012 school year were disabled. *See* Heather Vogell, *Violent and Legal: The Shocking Ways School Kids are Being Pinned Down Isolated Against Their Will,* ProPublica (June 19, 2014). Even though serious injuries and sometimes death can result from these practices, they are still permitted in most states. *See Can Schools in Your State Pin Kids Down? Probably.*, ProPublica (June 19, 2014).

The Executive Office of President Barack Obama released a thorough report on the issues of suspension as well as restraint/seclusion in December 2016. *See* Executive Office of the President, *Report: The Continuing Need to Rethink Discipline* (December 2016). The Report offered the following statistics:

- Students with disabilities constitute 12 percent of the overall school population and:
  - 25 percent of the students with one or more out-of-school suspensions;
  - 76 percent of the students subject to physical restraint; and
  - 59 percent of the students subject to seclusion.
- One out of five boys of color with disabilities received one or more out-of-school suspensions, compared to a rate of one of ten for white boys with disabilities; and
- More than one in five girls with disabilities who are two or more races received one or more out-of-school suspensions, compared to a rate of one in twenty for white girls served by IDEA.

The first major Supreme Court constitutional law case relating to the issue of school suspension did not arise in the disability context. *See Goss v. Lopez,* 419 U.S. 565 (1975). The students involved in this case were high school students in the Columbus Public School system in Columbus, Ohio. During February and March of 1971, they were engaged in various kinds of protest activities while attending Marion-Franklin High School. They were each suspended for up to 10 days and given no opportunity to contest the facts that led to their suspensions. The school district unsuccessfully argued in the lower court that the students had no due process rights because there is no constitutional right to a public education.

Without determining whether children have a right to a public education, the Court said:

> Having chosen to extend the right to an education to people of appellees' class generally, Ohio may not withdraw that right on grounds of misconduct, absent fundamentally fair procedures to determine whether the misconduct has occurred.
>
> *Id.* at 574.

In most situations, due process would constitute giving the student "oral or written notice of the charges against him and, if he denies them, an explanation of the evidence the authorities have and an opportunity to present his side of the story." *Id.* at 581. The Court however, also recognized that "Students whose presence poses a continuing danger to persons or property or an ongoing threat of disrupting the academic process may be immediately removed from school. In such cases, the necessary notice and rudimentary hearing should follow as soon as practicable." *Id.* at 582. For longer suspensions or expulsions, the Court also clarified "more formal procedures" may be required. *Id.* at 584.

Until the IDEA was amended in 1997 to provide special rules for suspensions of more than ten days for students with disabilities, the *Goss* standard was the primary protection for students with disabilities. Like all students who were suspended, they would expect to have some due process rights to contest the suspension with the formality of those procedures increasing if the suspension is longer than ten days.

In 1988, the United States Supreme Court interpreted the IDEA to require some enhanced protections for students with disabilities who faced suspensions for conduct relating to their disabilities. *See Honig v. Doe,* 484 U.S. 305 (1988).

The San Francisco Unified School District had sought to expel two students who were emotionally disturbed from school indefinitely for violent and disruptive conduct related to their disabilities. *Id.* at 312. The plaintiffs prevailed in the lower courts with the courts ruling that the IDEA had no "dangerousness exception" so that a school could not use expulsion procedures to avoid educating a student whose disability made him more prone to dangerous or violent incidents. While recognizing that schools can suspend students with disabilities for up to 10 school days as a "cooling down" period, the Court found that school districts could not use expulsion proceedings as a way to avoid its obligation to education *all* disabled children. *Id.* at 325–26.

The *Honig* Court emphasized the "stay put" rule which is now codified in the IDEA at 20 U.S.C. § 1415(j):

> Except as provided in subsection (k)(4), during the pendency of any proceedings conducted pursuant to this section, unless the State or

> local educational agency and the parents otherwise agree, the child shall remain in the then-current educational placement of the child, or, if applying for initial admission to a public school, shall, with the consent of the parents, be placed in the public school program until all such proceedings have been completed.

The exception referred to in (k)(4) refers to a Hearing Officer having the authority to order a placement in an alternative educational setting for not more than 45 days "if the hearing officer determines that maintaining the current placement of such child is substantially likely to result in injury to the child or others." 20 U.S.C. § 1415(k)(3)(B)(ii)(II). The (k)(4) exception was not explicitly in the IDEA when *Honig* was decided; nonetheless, the *Honig* Court implied such an exception when it stated:

> [The stay put rule] effectively creates a presumption in favor of the child's current educational placement which school officials can overcome only by showing that maintaining the child in his or her current placement is substantially likely to result in injury either to himself or herself, or to others.
>
> *Id.* at 328.

These suspension rules will be discussed more below but, for now, it is important to recognize that all students have some procedural rights when they are subjected to suspension or expulsion and that students with disabilities have special protections because they are guaranteed a right to attend public school under the IDEA. School district officials generally cannot use suspension and expulsion for behavior caused by a student's disability as an excuse to stop educating that student.

§ 7.2 GENERAL PROTECTIONS UNDER THE IDEA

The IDEA contains various protections for students who are excluded from school:

1. If they are excluded from school for less than ten days then they can be treated like all other students.

2. If they are excluded for more than ten school days, then they are entitled to a determination if their behavior was a manifestation of their disability.

3. If their behavior was a manifestation of their disability, then they cannot be excluded from school for more than ten days unless certain exceptions exist. This protection can apply in situations where the student was not yet identified as disabled, but should have been identified as disabled.

4. If behavior was a manifestation of their disability, then school should perform a functional behavioral assessment and establish a behavior intervention plan.

5. If their behavior was not a manifestation of their disability, they are subject to regular school discipline rules but they should continue to receive educational services in another setting during their exclusion from their regular placement.

See generally 20 U.S.C. § 1415(k) (discussed below).

§ 7.3 TEN-DAY RULE

In general, students with disabilities should not have a change in their "placement" without the agreement of the IEP team because the IEP states where educational services are to be delivered. A school suspension is a change in placement so, ordinarily, one would expect such a change not to be permissible under the IDEA. But the IDEA has special rules about school discipline that override that default principle.

The IDEA provides school officials with the ability to remove a child with a disability for up to ten school days on the same basis as it would remove a nondisabled student from the school:

> School personnel under this subsection may remove a child with a disability who violates a code of student conduct from their current placement to an appropriate interim alternative educational setting, another setting, or suspension, for not more than 10 school days (to the extent such alternatives are applied to children without disabilities).

20 U.S.C. § 1415(k)(1)(B).

The IDEA regulations further clarify how one determines if a removal has occurred for more than 10 days. For example, a school could remove a child once per week for an entire semester. But the removals would not be consecutive. Does that kind of pattern of removal invoke the procedural protections for removals of more than 10 days?

The following regulation seeks to answer that question.

> Change of placement because of disciplinary removals
>
> (a) For purposes of removals of a child with a disability from the child's current educational placement under §§ 300.530 through 300.535, a change of placement occurs if—
>
> (1) The removal is for more than 10 consecutive school days; or
>
> (2) The child has been subjected to a series of removals that constitute a pattern—
>
> (i) Because the series of removals total more than 10 school days in a school year;
>
> (ii) Because the child's behavior is substantially similar to the child's behavior in previous incidents that resulted in the series of removals; and
>
> (iii) Because of such additional factors as the length of each removal, the total amount of time the child has been removed, and the proximity of the removals to one another.

> (b)
>
> (1) The public agency determines on a case-by-case basis whether a pattern of removals constitutes a change of placement.
>
> (2) This determination is subject to review through due process and judicial proceedings.

34 C.F.R. § 300.536.

It is easy to determine if a student has been excluded for ten consecutive days. The determination becomes more difficult when there have been multiple exclusions and they cumulatively add up to more than ten days. The regulation refers to whether the student's "behavior" is the same in each incident, although the third factor offers some flexibility in considering whether the various incidents should be linked for the purpose of this rule. Some situations can be easy when, for example, a student is suspended repeatedly for coming to school late or skipping classes. The rule can be more difficult to apply when a student is suspended for talking back, theft, or a physical altercation. Do those incidents involve similar behavior?

The IDEA provides that the school district is allowed to determine whether the exclusions have exceeded ten days although a parent could contest their conclusion. There is little case law on this particular issue and school authorities likely have a fair amount of discretion in interpreting the ten-day rule. There is no requirement that a meeting take place, which includes the parent, to determine if the pattern of exclusions exceeds ten days. If parents disagree with the school district's conclusion, their only recourse is to file for due process to contest that determination.

§ 7.4 MDR MEETING: WHO SHOULD ATTEND

If the school district concludes that an exclusion of a student from school has exceeded ten days then a manifestation determination review meeting [MDR] must be held within ten *school* days. 20 U.S.C. § 1415(k)(E)(i).

These are the individuals who must be present at the MDR:

- A school district representative
- The parent
- Relevant members of the IEP team as determined by the parent and school district

20 U.S.C. § 1415(k)(E)(i).

Despite the fact that the statutory language says the parents *and* the school district should choose the relevant members, courts have interpreted this requirement *not* to mean that the parents and the school district "agree on the identity of all MDR members, or put differently, that parents have a veto on MDR members." *Fitzgerald v. Fairfax County School Board,* 556 F. Supp.2d 543, 552 (E.D. Va. 2008). Instead, it means that parents can add to the list provided by the school district. While some state Hearing Officers in Ohio and Pennsylvania have concluded otherwise in cases that have involved multiple procedural violations, no federal courts have approved that reasoning. *See id.* at 554 n.17. In the Ohio case, the MDR meeting was held a couple of hours after the incident and the parent had no meaningful opportunity to consider who should attend the meeting. *See Maple Heights City School District,* SEA–1921–2006 (Monica R. Bohlen, SLRO, May 8, 2007). In the Pennsylvania case, the notice to the parents was cursory, parents were not give an opportunity to suggest members of the MDR team, and the team did not review the relevant information in the student's file or follow the applicable IDEA criteria. *See Philadelphia City School District,* 47 IDELR 56 (Perry A. Zirkel, Appellate Officer Jan. 10, 2007).

§ 7.5 MATERIAL TO BE REVIEWED AT AN MDR MEETING

The material that the team should review in making its determination includes:

> all relevant information in the student's file, including the child's IEP, any teacher observations, and any relevant information provided by the parents

20 U.S.C. § 1415(k)(1)(E)(i).

The statute does not state *when* these files must be reviewed and does not specify that the *entire* IEP be reviewed—only relevant information needs to be reviewed. The fact that an MDR meeting is quite short could be evidence of only a cursory review of relevant material, but a school district can always argue that the meeting members were given an opportunity to review relevant information in advance of the meeting.

If school district personnel reviews files in advance of the meeting, and has discussions amongst themselves in advance of the MDR meeting, they could possibly be found to have "predetermined" the outcome of the MDR meeting. As discussed in *Nutshell* § 6.3, IEP members are not supposed to predetermine the outcome of a meeting because predetermination would preclude the parent from having an active role in the decision-making process.

This issue was raised, for example, in *Fitzgerald v. Fairfax County School Board,* 556 F. Supp.2d 543, 560 (E.D. Va. 2008). Not only had some members of the MDR team spoken in advance, but the school psychologist also attended the meeting with a draft IEP that already predicted the MDR team would determine that the student's conduct was not a manifestation of his disability. Nonetheless, the district court concluded that other aspects of the record demonstrated that the team had "open-mindedness" rather than "prejudgment." *Id.* at 561. With less evidence of careful consideration of the record at the MDR meeting, it is possible the court would have found otherwise.

On somewhat different facts, another district court judge found that the procedural protections required for a proper MDR had been violated. *See School Board of the City of Norfolk v. Brown,* 769 F.

Supp.2d 928 (E.D. Va. 2010). In this case, the school district conducted an MDR review on March 3, 2009, which the state Department of Education concluded was in violation of federal law. A second MDR was then held on July 9, 2009, which the student's guardian alleged did not comply with the IDEA. The guardian filed for due process and a Hearing Officer concluded that the MDR had multiple procedural failings, which caused the student to be denied FAPE.

The flaws consisted of:

1. The second MDR did not consider all of the issues that are supposed to be the subject of the MDR.

2. Several people who were present at the first MDR did not attend the second MDR.

3. The student's guardian was denied participation by being misinformed about the purpose of the second MDR meeting.

4. The team failed to consider a report based on a psychiatric evaluation conducted following the behavior, which led to the student's suspension.

Id. at 947.

In sum, "no formal discussion of the issues ever occurred 'with all of the relevant information, at the same time, in the same room with the correct legal standard in place.'" *Id.* at 946 (quoting the Hearing Officer). In affirming the Hearing Officer's decision, the district court judge concluded: "it appears that the second MDR was approached with a closed mind and the outcome was predetermined, Student's parent was denied parental participation, and no meaningful discussion took place." *Id.* at 948. The judge did note, however, that it was not necessarily a violation of the IDEA for different team members to be present at each MDR meeting, implicitly agreeing with the other judge's observation that the school district can determine who it wants to send to the MDR meeting, so long as the parents also have an opportunity to bring people to the meeting.

§ 7.6 ISSUES TO BE RESOLVED AT MDR MEETING

These are the two questions that the MDR team is required to consider:

> 1. If the conduct in question was caused by, or had a direct and substantial relationship to, the child's disability; or
> 2. If the conduct in question was the direct result of the [school district's] failure to implement the IEP.

20 U.S.C. § 1415(k)(E)(i).

The scope of the inquiry to determine if conduct was a manifestation of the student's disability is narrower under the 2004 IDEA Amendments than under previous versions. The team does *not* discuss whether the IEP was appropriate or whether the child's disability impaired his or her ability to understand the consequences of his or her behavior or the effect of the child's disabilities on the child's overall ability to conform his or her conduct to the rules. Nonetheless, the team should determine if the conduct in question was caused by, or had a direct and substantial relationship to, the student's disability. That inquiry requires a close consideration of the conduct that occurred and the student's specific manifestations of his or her disability.

This inquiry can be especially difficult when the parent and the school district disagree about what conduct precisely occurred. When the exclusion from school is for more than ten days, a school district is required to hold a hearing under *Goss v. Lopez*. (That rule applies to all students, not merely students with disabilities.) The *Goss* hearing will result in some fact finding as to what conduct actually occurred. But if the conduct is a manifestation of the student's disability, then a lengthy suspension cannot take place and no *Goss* hearing is needed. Thus, the MDR team needs to meet to determine if the conduct was a manifestation of the student's disability before any fact-finding has occurred about the incident itself.

A recent Pennsylvania case reflects this problem. *See Bristol Township School District v. Z.B.*, 2016 WL 161600 (E.D. Pa. Jan. 14, 2016). The student in this case was engaged in some roughhousing in the school hallway. When the student refused to stop this behavior, a teacher intervened, and the student allegedly twisted the teacher's arm causing him to be injured. *Id.* at *3. The teacher alleged that the student had also taken a "threatening stance" during the incident. *Id.* at *3. The teacher did not come to work the day after the incident, and "his occupational health doctor diagnosed him with a shoulder sprain and prescribed physical therapy." *Id.* at *9. The assistant principal initially suspended the student for one day due to a failure to follow an adult directive but then expanded the suspension when he determined that the student had engaged in a simple assault. *Id.* at *11–13. Because the student was on an IEP, the school district understood it needed to hold an MDR. If the conduct were not found to be a manifestation of the student's disability then the school district would also need to hold a suspension hearing.

The incident occurred on March 17, 2015. Initially, the school district scheduled the suspension hearing and the MDR on March 25th, 2017. The student's parents were told over the telephone that the March 25th hearing was a suspension hearing; they did not learn until they arrived at the meeting that it was also an MDR. Due to this miscommunication, the school district rescheduled the MDR for March 31st and the suspension hearing for April 8th. So, the school district was in violation of the ten-day rule due to miscommunication.

At the scheduled meeting, the student, his parents, a school psychologist, two teachers, and the special education supervisor were present. The special education supervisor conducted the meeting, and the MDR team did not have a discussion of the underlying facts. The special education supervisor recorded on the applicable form that the student was suspended for assault, had refused a directive, and that the teacher had sustained injuries. The team did not consider the student's account of the incident, which suggested that the teacher was not injured and that the student had merely impulsively responded to a teacher trying to interfere with his roughhousing with his girlfriend. The team also did not discuss the student's disability with any specificity to see how it might have caused him to fail to respond to a directive or even engage in aggressive behavior. The student had severe ADHD and took a variety of medications, some of which had a decreasing effect on his ability to concentrate and act non-impulsively as the day progressed. The incident had occurred at the end of the school day. The team only considered broad, general characteristics of ADHD—not this student's manifestation of ADHD.

Further, there was evidence of predetermination because the special education supervisor had completed the forms in advance of the meeting. The special education supervisor:

> convened the manifestation determination with a prefabricated document that encompassed solely her views and conclusions and <u>then</u> asked if anyone objected, which is materially different than, say, for efficiency, filling in background information gathered ahead of time in order to facilitate meaningful discussion about the appropriate answers to the two

> crucial questions at the heart of the manifestation determination, questions that [special education supervisor] had already answered "no" to.

Id. at *31.

The district court judge affirmed the Hearing Officer's conclusion that the MDR was defective because the team did not have enough specific information about the conduct in question to conduct a proper manifestation determination. The school district unsuccessfully argued that the Hearing Officer was improperly requiring the MDR team to engage in a disciplinary hearing.

This case reflects how difficult it can be for parents and school districts to conduct MDR's when the underlying facts are in dispute. Sometimes, parents will take the position that they don't acknowledge that the underlying conduct occurred but, if it did occur, then it was a manifestation of the student's disability. In this case, there was no evidence that the student had been physically aggressive in the past, and it was hard to argue that physical aggression would be a manifestation of his disability. On the other hand, the parents could argue that his ADHD caused him to engage in uninhibited behaviors, such as to pull an arm away and not follow directions. Thus, the parents needed to have an opportunity to dispute the school district's factual account in order to succeed at the MDR. Here, the MDR was too cursory to permit an adequate discussion, and therefore, the parents prevailed at the due process hearing and in the district court.

§ 7.7 IF CONDUCT IS FOUND TO BE A MANIFESTATION OF THE STUDENT'S DISABILITY

A. DEFAULT RULE

1. General Principles

If the MDR team determines that the misconduct was a manifestation of the student's disability, then the student should be kept in their regular educational placement unless the team agrees that a change in placement is appropriate. Further, the student should have a Functional Behavioral Assessment (FBA) and a Behavioral Intervention Plan (BIP) that will assist the child. The following rule explains those requirements:

> Determination that behavior was a manifestation
>
> If the local educational agency, the parent, and relevant members of the IEP Team make the determination that the conduct was a manifestation of the child's disability, the IEP Team shall—
>
> (i) conduct a functional behavioral assessment, and implement a behavioral intervention plan for such child, provided that the local educational agency had not conducted such assessment prior to such determination before the behavior that resulted in a change

> in placement described in subparagraph (C) or (G);
>
> (ii) in the situation where a behavioral intervention plan has been developed, review the behavioral intervention plan if the child already has such a behavioral intervention plan, and modify it, as necessary, to address the behavior; and
>
> (iii) except as provided in subparagraph (G), return the child to the placement from which the child was removed, unless the parent and the local educational agency agree to a change of placement as part of the modification of the behavioral intervention plan.

20 U.S.C. § 1415(k)(1)(F).

If the student already had a Behavioral Intervention Plan, it should be modified to address the behavior that caused the disciplinary incident. The purpose of these rules is to create or modify a BIP that will be effective in assisting the student to avoid the problematic behavior.

2. Functional Behavioral Assessment

Although the IDEA requires a Functional Behavioral Assessment (FBA) for any student whose behavior has been found to be a manifestation of his or her disability, the statute does not define that term. Many states also refer to FBA's in their state regulations but do not always define the term.

New York State has created a document describing an FBA:

What is a Functional Behavioral Assessment?	A functional behavioral assessment (FBA) means the process of determining why a student engages in behaviors that impede learning and how the student's behavior relates to the environment.
When must an FBA be conducted?	A student's need for an FBA must be considered whenever: • a student with a disability is exhibiting persistent behaviors that impede his or her learning or that of others, despite consistently implemented general school-wide or classroom-wide interventions; • the student's behavior places the student or others at risk of harm or injury; • the Committee on Special Education (CSE) or Committee on Preschool Special

	Education (CPSE) is considering more restrictive programs or placements as a result of the student's behavior; and/or • the student is subject to disciplinary actions and a determination has been made that the behavior is related to the student's disability.
What must an FBA include?	The FBA must include, but is not limited to: • identification of the problem behavior; • definition of the behavior in concrete terms; • identification of the contextual factors that contribute to the behavior (including cognitive and affective factors); and • formulation of a hypothesis regarding the general conditions under which a behavior usually occurs and probable

	consequences that serve to maintain it.

What information must an FBA include?	The FBA must:
	• provide a baseline of the student's problem behaviors, across activities, settings, people and times of the day, with regard to:
	  ○ frequency (how often a behavior occurs)
	  ○ duration (the length of time the behavior lasts)
	  ○ intensity (how severe the behavior is)
	  ○ latency (how long it takes for a behavior to begin after a specific verbal demand or event has occurred)
	• include the information on why the student engages in behaviors that impede learning and how the student's behavior relates to

	the environment in sufficient detail to form the basis for a behavioral intervention plan for the student that addresses: o antecedent behaviors; o reinforcing consequences of the behavior; o recommendations for teaching alternative skills or behaviors; and o assessment of student preferences for reinforcement.
What information is an FBA based on?	The FBA must, as appropriate, be based on multiple sources of data (such as structured interviews, behavior rating scales, standardized assessments, checklists) and must include, but is not limited to: • information obtained from direct observation of the

	student; • information from the student, the student's teacher(s) and/or related service provider(s); and • a review of available data and information from the student's record and other sources including any relevant information provided by the student's parent. The FBA cannot be based solely on the student's history of presenting problem behavior.
Is a FBA the same as a Behavioral Intervention Plan?	When an individual behavioral intervention plan is developed for a student with a disability, it must be based on the results of an FBA. The results of the FBA must also be considered at meetings of the CSE or CPSE for the development of a student's individualized education program (IEP).

Is consent required to conduct an FBA?	Yes. An FBA for a student with a disability is an evaluation requiring parent consent pursuant to the requirements in section 200.5(b) of the Regulations of the Commissioner of Education.

See The University of the State of New York, New York State Education Department, Office of P–12 Education, Office of Special Education, *Functional Behavioral Assessments* (May 2011).

As described in the above document, the creation of a Functional Behavior Assessment is a time-consuming, scientific process. The primary purpose is to identify the behavior that is impeding the student's learning and create baseline data about how often that behavior occurs. By identifying the antecedent event that triggers the inappropriate behavior, it is possible to create a Behavior Intervention Plan to encourage alternative responses.

The state of New Mexico has provided some examples of Functional Behavior Assessments using different kinds of data collection instruments. One is called an "ABC Observation Form" (Antecedent, Behavior, Consequence), where the team tries to understand what antecedent behavior triggers the failure to comply with school rules.

Here is a sample ABC Observation Form, modified from a New Mexico example.

Behavior of concern: Mars/destroys school property	Date: 10/10/2003 Time: 9:25–10:10 a.m.	Date: 10/10/2003 Time: 1:05–1:45 p.m.
Context of Circumstances	Cindy is in Reading group working at a table with two other students.	Cindy is in Math class. Teacher is giving examples of 2-digit subtraction on the board
Antecedent (what happens just prior to incident)	The students take their books and materials to the table. Students are supposed to share a bucket of crayons.	The teacher asks for a volunteer to come to board and solve the problem. Cindy jumps out of seat and says aloud, "Ooh, me, please."
Behavior	Cindy starts scribbling on the desk. Another student calls	When Cindy is not selected, she throws her math book on the floor,

	out to the teacher about it.	wrinkling several pages.
Consequence	Teacher stops the lesson and goes over to Cindy's desk to ask her why she did that. Cindy says she doesn't know.	Teacher gives Cindy a disapproving look but continues the lesson. Cindy picks up the book.
Comments or other observations.	Cindy was pleased with receiving teacher's attention.	Cindy needs constant eye contact from teacher to correct her behavior.

See New Mexico Public Education Technical Assistance Manual: Addressing Student Behavior (undated).

It would be good to supplement this form with more data and interviews with both the teacher and the student Cindy; nonetheless, it is a helpful in trying to understand the circumstances that trigger Cindy's inappropriate behavior. Because the teacher tried two different responses to Cindy's inappropriate behavior, it also provides some data on what kinds of interventions might be effective.

3. Behavioral Intervention Plan

The State of New York has also provided a description of the content of a Behavioral Intervention Plan.

What is a behavioral intervention plan?	A behavioral intervention plan is a plan that is based on the results of a functional behavioral assessment (FBA) and, at a minimum, includes a description of the problem behavior, global and specific hypotheses as to why the problem behavior occurs and intervention strategies that include positive behavioral supports and services to address the behavior.
When must a behavioral intervention plan be developed?	The Committee on Special Education (CSE) or Committee on Preschool Special Education (CPSE) must consider the development of a behavioral intervention plan for a student with a disability when the:

	• student with a disability is exhibiting persistent behaviors that impede his or her learning or that of others, despite consistently implemented general school-wide or classroom-wide interventions; • student's behavior places the student or others at risk of harm or injury; • CSE or CPSE is considering more restrictive programs or placements as a result of the student's behavior; and/or • student is subject to disciplinary actions and a determination has been made that the behavior is related to the student's disability.

What information must a behavioral intervention plan include?	A behavioral intervention plan must identify:
	• the baseline measure of the problem behavior, including the frequency, duration, intensity and/or latency of the targeted behaviors.
	  ○ Such baseline must, to the extent practicable, include data taken across activities, settings, people and times of the day.
	  ○ The baseline data must be used as a standard to establish performance criteria and against which to evaluate intervention effectiveness;
	• intervention strategies to be used to alter antecedent events to prevent the occurrence of the behavior, teach individual alternative

	and adaptive behaviors to the student, and provide consequences for the targeted inappropriate behavior(s) and alternative acceptable behavior(s); and • a schedule to measure the effectiveness of the interventions, including the frequency, duration and intensity of the targeted behaviors at scheduled intervals.
For a student whose behavior impedes his or her learning or that of others, what information must be included in the IEP?	The individualized education program (IEP) must indicate if a particular device or service, including an intervention, accommodation or other program modification is needed to address the student's behavior that impedes his or her learning or that of others. A student's need for a behavioral intervention plan must be

	documented in the IEP and such plan must be reviewed at least annually by the CSE or CPSE.
How often must progress monitoring of a student's behavioral intervention plan occur?	The implementation of a student's behavioral intervention plan must include regular progress monitoring of the frequency, duration and intensity of the behavioral interventions at scheduled intervals, as specified in the BIP and on the student's IEP. The results of the progress monitoring must be documented and reported to the student's parents and to the CSE or CPSE and must be considered in any determination to revise a student's behavioral intervention plan or IEP.

The Behavioral Intervention Plan builds on the knowledge gained from the Functional Behavior Assessment by developing intervention strategies that modify the response to the antecedent event. Information needs to be collected to ascertain if the intervention is effective. In the examples above, the data suggest that Cindy engages in the destruction of property when she does not get sufficient attention from the teacher, but Cindy does not appear to understand why she misbehaves. A Behavioral Intervention Plan would seek to assist Cindy in learning to engage in more positive activities when she desires the teacher's attention rather than property destruction. It would also assist the teacher in finding less direct ways to give Cindy attention to stop the behavior loop. One key element of a behavior plan is that it seeks to use *positive* rather than *negative* reinforcement. Cindy could earn points, for example, towards lunch with a special person such as a special adult or guest (e.g., another teacher, the principal, grandparents, school resource officer, etc.) She would be given choices that reinforce positive behavior including the option of being given a minute to calm herself down. If the baseline data collected in the FBA suggests that Cindy engages in inappropriate behavior four or five times a day, then the BIP would seek to lessen those incidents over time.

Here are some examples of positive behavior interventions for a child with ADHD:

- *Set positive expectations*. Teacher: "I play with kids who share. I spend time with students who are working."

- *Give ample preparation for transitions and routine.* Teacher: "Time to clean up in 5, 4, 3, 2, 1 minutes."
- *Praise other students who are displaying appropriate behavior.* Teacher: "Sarah and Joe are cleaning up well. Good job, you will be ready for a snack when you finish cleaning up."
- *Praise student.* Make eye contact or smile at student when behaving well. Pass the student a note when student is working well independently without an adult and write a cheerful comment, specific comment or compliment about behavior.
- *Provide clear simple cues coupled with clear short phrases when a student is not behaving.* For example, when a student is not cooperative, the teacher can use a hand signal or facial expression followed with "We are quietly putting blocks away."
- *Offer directives in the form of a choice.* For example, when a student is not making an appropriate decision, the teacher can say: "You can sit near me and listen to the story and put a star on your chart or you can take a quiet minute to relax and try again." In this example, the student is given space and time to comply.
- *Provide clear limits when misbehavior occurs.* For example, when a student is being angry or disruptive, the teacher can say: "Please take a quiet minute or go take a time out. If

you can take a quiet minute, you can earn extra stars." If the student continues to act disruptively, then the teacher can say: "I gave you a choice but you were not able to be calm. You now need to take a five minute time out." If the student continues to be disruptive, the teacher can seek assistance from an aide who will take the student elsewhere for a time out. The teacher will therefore not continue to give the student the desired attention.

- *After misbehavior, the student returns to a "clean slate."* For example, when a student successfully returns to class, the teacher says: "I can see that you are calm now. Let's try to earn that star. I know you can do it!"

B. EXCEPTIONS

Irrespective of whether the student's behavior is a manifestation of his or her disability, school districts can place a child in an "alternative education setting" for no more than 45 days when one of three criteria are met.

> Special circumstances
>
> School personnel may remove a student to an interim alternative educational setting for not more than 45 school days without regard to whether the behavior is determined to be a manifestation of the child's disability, in cases where a child—
>
> (i) carries or possesses a weapon to or at

> school, on school premises, or to or at a school function under the jurisdiction of a State or local educational agency;
>
> (ii) knowingly possesses or uses illegal drugs, or sells or solicits the sale of a controlled substance, while at school, on school premises, or at a school function under the jurisdiction of a State or local educational agency; or
>
> (iii) has inflicted serious bodily injury upon another person while at school, on school premises, or at a school function under the jurisdiction of a State or local educational agency.

20 U.S.C. § 1415(k)(1)(G).

With respect to the first exception, the term weapon is "a . . . device . . . that is used for, or is readily capable of, causing death or serious bodily injury, except that such term does not include a pocket knife with a blade of less than 2 ½ inches in length." 18 U.S.C. § 930(g)(2).

With respect to the second exception, controlled substances are defined in 21 U.S.C. § 812(c), but do not include drugs legally prescribed to the student (unless the student is seeking to misuse them by selling them to others).

With respect to the third exception, "serious bodily injury" is defined as:

> bodily injury which involves—
> (A) a substantial risk of death;
> (B) extreme physical pain;
> (C) protracted and obvious disfigurement; or
> (D) protracted loss or impairment of the function of a bodily member, organ, or mental faculty

18 U.S.C. § 1365(h)(3).

Thus, in the case discussed in *Nutshell* § 7.6, *see Bristol Township School District v. Z.B.*, 2016 WL 161600 (E.D. Pa. Jan. 14, 2016), the student was reported to have twisted the teacher's arm in a way that resulted in some pain and a need for physical therapy. The teacher, however, was also reported to have engaged in arm wrestling two weeks later. The school district was seeking to suspend the student for a significant period of time consistent with school rules regarding causing physical harm to a teacher, but they could not invoke the serious bodily harm rule because there was no evidence that the physical injury, which allegedly occurred, caused a "protracted loss or impairment."

If a student is sent to an alternative educational setting, the IEP team determines that placement. *See* 34 C.F.R. § 300.531. When the student is in an alternative educational setting, he or she is entitled to receive educational services "so as to enable the child to continue to participate in the general education curriculum, although in another setting, and to progress toward meeting the goals set out in the child's IEP." 34 C.F.R. § 300.530(d)(1)(i).

§ 7.8 IF CONDUCT IS NOT FOUND TO BE A MANIFESTATION OF STUDENT'S DISABILITY

When the MDR determines that the conduct is not a manifestation of the student's disability then the school district can apply its regular discipline rules to the student. Nonetheless, the student is still entitled to receive appropriate education services. As with students who are placed in alternative educational settings, the situation is governed by the following regulation:

> Services.
>
> (1) A child with a disability who is removed from the child's current placement pursuant to paragraphs (c), or (g) of this section must—
>
> (i) Continue to receive educational services, as provided in § 300.101(a), so as to enable the child to continue to participate in the general education curriculum, although in another setting, and to progress toward meeting the goals set out in the child's IEP; and
>
> (ii) Receive, as appropriate, a functional behavioral assessment, and behavioral intervention services and modifications, that are designed to address the behavior violation so that it does not recur.

34 C.F.R. § 300.530(d).

Further, the school district has the option of conducting a Functional Behavioral Assessment to modify, if appropriate, the student's Behavioral Intervention Plan.

CHAPTER 8
STATE ADMINISTRATIVE COMPLAINT

§ 8.1 INTRODUCTION

The IDEA provides students and their parents with a number of mechanisms to assert that a school district is not IDEA compliant with respect to a student's education. The most widely discussed mechanism is filing a due process complaint with the student's school of residence and requesting an impartial due process hearing, which will be discussed in *Nutshell* Chapter 9.

The IDEA, however, also includes another type of dispute resolution process: filing an administrative complaint with the state. Each state must have a procedure to allow an individual or organization to file a signed, written complaint regarding an IDEA violation that occurred not more than one year prior to the date that the state receives the complaint. The complaint can include issues involving a specific child, but it need not do so. Within 60 days of receiving the complaint, unless certain exceptions are met, the state must complete an investigation that can include an on-site investigation. Although no hearing is held, the state may collect information to resolve the complaint, and the complainant may submit information, either orally or in writing, about the allegations of the complaint. The school district is also provided with an opportunity to respond to the complaint.

The key difference between complaints filed under those provisions and due process hearings is that there is no opportunity to assess the credibility of witnesses. The kinds of issues resolved in a complaint are often ones in which the facts can usually be determined from a paper record. The remedies also differ somewhat. In the complaint resolution process, the state may order corrective action such as compensatory services or monetary reimbursement where it finds a failure to provide appropriate services. Additionally, the state may order future provisions of services for all children with disabilities. Unlike the resolution of a due process hearing, the state is not likely to order remedies that require subjective determinations such as the provision of a publicly-funded private education for an individual child in the future. By contrast, the state is *likely* to order training for school staff when systemic violations are found to exist. Such systemic remedies are unlikely as part of the resolution of a due process complaint. Despite the inability to assess issues that require weighing the credibility of expert witnesses, the state investigators can sometimes find that Individualized Education Programs are inadequate or inappropriate in the complaint resolution process.

Another important difference is that an administrative complaint can only assert issues that occurred within a year of filing the complaint. 34 C.F.R. § 300.153(c). By contrast, a due process complaint can allege a violation that occurred not more than two years before the date the parent knew or should have known about the alleged action that forms the basis of the due process complaint. 34 C.F.R. § 300.507(a)(2). Finally, another important difference between administrative complaints and due process complaints is that administrative complaints cannot be appealed to a federal or state court. Due process decisions however, can be appealed to state or federal court. *See* 34 C.F.R. § 300.516 (rules for civil actions). Because of the differing remedies and appellate options between a complaint and due process, parents need to think closely about their options before pursuing a particular remedy.

§ 8.2 ADOPTION OF STATE COMPLAINT PROCEDURES

The IDEA regulations require each State Educational Agency (SEA) to adopt complaint procedures. These procedures should specify that the state agency has the authority to issue a corrective action plan or require appropriate services in the future for students with disabilities. The following regulation governs these procedures:

> Adoption of State complaint procedures.
>
> (a) General. Each SEA must adopt written procedures for—
>
> (1) Resolving any complaint, including a complaint filed by an organization or individual from another State, that meets the requirements of § 300.153 by—
>
> (i) Providing for the filing of a complaint with the SEA; and

> (ii) At the SEA's discretion, providing for the filing of a complaint with a public agency and the right to have the SEA review the public agency's decision on the complaint; and
>
> (2) Widely disseminating to parents and other interested individuals, including parent training and information centers, protection and advocacy agencies, independent living centers, and other appropriate entities, the State procedures under §§ 300.151 through 300.153.
>
> (b) Remedies for denial of appropriate services. In resolving a complaint in which the SEA has found a failure to provide appropriate services, an SEA, pursuant to its general supervisory authority under Part B of the Act, must address—
>
> (1) The failure to provide appropriate services, including corrective action appropriate to address the needs of the child (such as compensatory services or monetary reimbursement); and
>
> (2) Appropriate future provision of services for all children with disabilities.

34 C.F.R. § 300.151.

Unlike due process complaints, an organization or an individual can file these complaints. Each state has a protection and advocacy organization like Disability Rights Ohio or Disability Rights Florida, which sometimes files complaints about systemic problems such as a lack of special education services at a juvenile facility or the overuse of seclusion and restraint.

§ 8.3 STATE COMPLAINT PROCEDURES

> Minimum State complaint procedures.
>
> (a) Time limit; minimum procedures. Each SEA must include in its complaint procedures a time limit of 60 days after a complaint is filed under § 300.153 to—
>
> (1) Carry out an independent on-site investigation, if the SEA determines that an investigation is necessary;
>
> (2) Give the complainant the opportunity to submit additional information, either orally or in writing, about the allegations in the complaint;
>
> (3) Provide the public agency with the opportunity to respond to the complaint, including, at a minimum—
>
> (i) At the discretion of the public agency, a proposal to resolve the complaint; and
>
> (ii) An opportunity for a parent who has filed a complaint and the public agency to voluntarily engage in mediation consistent with § 300.506;
>
> (4) Review all relevant information and make an independent determination as to whether the public agency is violating a requirement of Part B of the Act or of this part; and

(5) Issue a written decision to the complainant that addresses each allegation in the complaint and contains—

(i) Findings of fact and conclusions; and

(ii) The reasons for the SEA's final decision.

(b) Time extension; final decision; implementation. The SEA's procedures described in paragraph (a) of this section also must—

(1) Permit an extension of the time limit under paragraph (a) of this section only if—

(i) Exceptional circumstances exist with respect to a particular complaint; or

(ii) The parent (or individual or organization, if mediation or other alternative means of dispute resolution is available to the individual or organization under State procedures) and the public agency involved agree to extend the time to engage in mediation pursuant to paragraph (a)(3)(ii) of this section, or to engage in other alternative means of dispute resolution, if available in the State; and

(2) Include procedures for effective implementation of the SEA's final decision, if needed, including—

(i) Technical assistance activities;

(ii) Negotiations; and

(iii) Corrective actions to achieve compliance.

> (c) Complaints filed under this section and due process hearings under § 300.507 and §§ 300.530 through 300.532.
>
> (1) If a written complaint is received that is also the subject of a due process hearing under § 300.507 or §§ 300.530 through 300.532, or contains multiple issues of which one or more are part of that hearing, the State must set aside any part of the complaint that is being addressed in the due process hearing until the conclusion of the hearing. However, any issue in the complaint that is not a part of the due process action must be resolved using the time limit and procedures described in paragraphs (a) and (b) of this section.
>
> (2) If an issue raised in a complaint filed under this section has previously been decided in a due process hearing involving the same parties—
>
> (i) The due process hearing decision is binding on that issue; and
>
> (ii) The SEA must inform the complainant to that effect.
>
> (3) A complaint alleging a public agency's failure to implement a due process hearing decision must be resolved by the SEA.

34 C.F.R. § 300.152.

As these rules provide, an individual or entity cannot use the complaint procedure for the same issues involved in a due process hearing. The state will set aside any aspect of a complaint that is being resolved in a due process hearing; the due process decision is binding on the complaint resolution process.

When a due process hearing is filed, the parties are required to engage in a resolution meeting or mediation, as discussed in *Nutshell* Chapter 9. An administrative complaint does not trigger that requirement although a state may choose to establish alternative dispute resolution processes, such as mediation, available to parties involved in an administrative complaint. If you check a state's special education website, it will usually indicate whether it makes alternative dispute resolution processes available to resolve a state complaint. These services are usually offered for free to the parties (at the public's expense).

§ 8.4 FILING A COMPLAINT

> Filing a complaint.
>
> (a) An organization or individual may file a signed written complaint under the procedures described in §§ 300.151 through 300.152.
>
> (b) The complaint must include—
>
> (1) A statement that a public agency has violated a requirement of Part B of the Act or of this part;
>
> (2) The facts on which the statement is based;
>
> (3) The signature and contact information for the complainant; and

> (4) If alleging violations with respect to a specific child—
>
> (i) The name and address of the residence of the child;
>
> (ii) The name of the school the child is attending;
>
> (iii) In the case of a homeless child or youth (within the meaning of section 725(2) of the McKinney-Vento Homeless Assistance Act (42 U.S.C. 11434a(2)), available contact information for the child, and the name of the school the child is attending;
>
> (iv) A description of the nature of the problem of the child, including facts relating to the problem; and
>
> (v) A proposed resolution of the problem to the extent known and available to the party at the time the complaint is filed.
>
> (c) The complaint must allege a violation that occurred not more than one year prior to the date that the complaint is received in accordance with § 300.151.
>
> (d) The party filing the complaint must forward a copy of the complaint to the LEA or public agency serving the child at the same time the party files the complaint with the SEA.

34 C.F.R. § 300.153.

Because these kinds of investigations do not involve a hearing where the credibility of witnesses can be evaluated, they tend to involve issues where a state investigation can determine if a violation took place without making a credibility evaluation. Based on a review of state complaints in Ohio, common issues typically include:

(1) who should be in attendance at IEP meetings,

(2) lack of parent communication/progress reports,

(3) poor scheduling of IEP meetings,

(4) inadequately written IEPs,

(5) need for continuum of placements,

(6) improper use of seclusion and restraint,

(7) obligations of charter schools, and

(8) failing to conduct evaluations/child find.

See Ruth Colker, *Special Education Complaint Resolution: Ohio*, 29 OHIO STATE JOURNAL ON DISPUTE RESOLUTION 371 (2014).

§ 8.5 AN EXAMPLE OF THE COMPLAINT PROCESS

To provide a sense of the difference between the complaint resolution process and the Hearing Officer due process resolution, it is helpful to consider a concrete example of a complaint investigation.

On October 15, 2013, a parent filed a complaint with the Office for Exceptional Children at the Ohio Department of Education involving two issues regarding her child's treatment in the Athens City School District. *See CP 0173–2013, Findings Letter*, OHIO DEP'T EDUC. (Dec. 13, 2013), http://www.edresourcesohio.org/wp-content/uploads/2014/01/CP-0173-2013.pdf. The parent complained that the school district unilaterally changed her son's aide from a one-on-one to a shared aide and also deprived him of transportation so that he could not attend a school field trip. Both issues involved the question of whether the school district was following the existing IEP. However, the parent was not seeking a revision of the IEP. Monica Drvota, Assistant Director, Procedural Safeguards, Office for Exceptional Children, was assigned to investigate the complaint.

With respect to the first issue, the investigator read the IEP for the current year and the previous year, interviewed the parent and the Special Education Director, and received written statements from the six aides who provided services in the student's classroom. The basic facts were not in dispute. The student had been receiving one-on-one services from the same male aide since the 2009–2010 school year, although the IEP did not specify that the services had to be one-on-one. During the 2013 school year, the school district changed the assistance so that the student began to receive services from a new, female aide; she was also assisting another student in the classroom so the services were no longer one-on-one.

The parent argued that the child, who has autism, was regressing with this change in personnel. The IEP, however, did not specify that a particular individual would be the aide. Further, the IEP stated that the student would receive "attendant services" but did not specify they would be one-on-one services, and although the student was no longer assigned an aide to receive services on a one-on-one basis, the staffing of the classroom included eight teachers and nine students. In a due process complaint, the parent might have argued that the IEP needed to be *revised* because the student was no longer making adequate progress, but the issue in this complaint investigation was merely whether the IEP, as written, was being followed. The oral assurances that the mother claimed she received that the prior male aide would continue to be the student's aide on a one-to-one basis were not memorialized as part of the IEP. Thus, in a complaint investigation, the school district was successful and no modifications were required with respect to the first issue.

With respect to the second issue, the investigator read the relevant IEP language, and then proceeded to interview the parent and the Special Education Director. The IEP stated that the student received transportation as a related service. Both the parent and school district agreed that the school district had refused to provide transportation for a school field trip. The school district took the position that the parent should provide transportation and the school district would reimburse the parent for transportation. However, that is not what the IEP said. Accordingly, the investigator found in favor of the parent/student on this issue. The relief that was ordered, however, was only prospective (i.e., for the future). The school district was required to develop and sign a memorandum regarding the contents of two IEP regulations that were relevant to the resolution of this issue. Had this matter been raised in a due process complaint, it is possible that the Hearing Officer would have ordered compensatory education for the lost opportunity to participate in a field trip, but such relief is unlikely in a complaint investigation. The decision in this matter was final, and neither the school district nor the parent had a right to appeal.

The state's letter of findings was issued on December 13, 2013, two months after the parent filed the complaint. The resolution made the parent aware that there was a difference of opinion between her and the school district with respect to how her son was progressing in the classroom. The mother took the position that the student was "sad, showing signs of depression, won't dress himself and does not want to go to school." The school staff took the position "that the student is happy and does not seem depressed." That kind of difference of opinion could not be resolved through the complaint investigation process. The transportation issue (which was likely of far less importance to the parent), however, could be resolved in favor of the parent through the complaint investigation process, although no compensatory relief is likely to be ordered. The fact that the parent chose the complaint investigation process does not preclude the parent, in the future, from asking that the IEP be amended to provide more appropriate services for the student if evidence can demonstrate that he is regressing with the new aide.

In contrast to due process hearings, which will be discussed in *Nutshell* Chapter 9, this example shows how the administrative complaint process can lead to a quick resolution of an issue in which the facts are not contested. Nonetheless, the scope of issues and types of remedies may be narrow under this procedure. Although comprehensive empirical data throughout the country do not exist, it appears that parents may have a somewhat higher success rate using the complaint process than due process. *See* Ruth Colker, *Special Education Complaint Resolution: Ohio*, 29 OHIO STATE JOURNAL ON DISPUTE RESOLUTION 371 (2014) (finding that parents prevailed on all issues in 36 percent of complaints and 30 percent of due process cases). In making strategic decisions about which process to select, parents and others may want to investigate the varying success rates in their communities before making strategic decisions about which procedure to pursue.

CHAPTER 9

DUE PROCESS RESOLUTION

§ 9.1 PRIOR WRITTEN NOTICE

When parents and school districts have a disagreement, the school district must provide parents with written notice, in their native language, of the reasons underlying the school district's decision. As described below in the applicable regulation, there can be more forms of disagreement that trigger this requirement. The parent may believe their child is disabled, the parent may prefer a different educational placement, or the parent may believe that the proposed IEP does not provide FAPE. The regulation uses the adjective "prior" because the notice must be provided to the parent before the contested action takes place. This notice gives the parent the opportunity to file for due process and, as will be discussed in *Nutshell* § 9.2, freezes the current educational placement.

> Prior notice by the public agency; content of notice.
>
> (a) Notice. Written notice that meets the requirements of paragraph (b) of this section must be given to the parents of a child with a disability a reasonable time before the public agency—
>
> (1) Proposes to initiate or change the identification, evaluation, or educational placement of the child or the provision of

FAPE to the child; or

(2) Refuses to initiate or change the identification, evaluation, or educational placement of the child or the provision of FAPE to the child.

(b) Content of notice. The notice required under paragraph (a) of this section must include—

(1) A description of the action proposed or refused by the agency;

(2) An explanation of why the agency proposes or refuses to take the action;

(3) A description of each evaluation procedure, assessment, record, or report the agency used as a basis for the proposed or refused action;

(4) A statement that the parents of a child with a disability have protection under the procedural safeguards of this part and, if this notice is not an initial referral for evaluation, the means by which a copy of a description of the procedural safeguards can be obtained;

(5) Sources for parents to contact to obtain assistance in understanding the provisions of this part;

(6) A description of other options that the IEP Team considered and the reasons why those options were rejected; and

(7) A description of other factors that are relevant to the agency's proposal or refusal.

34 C.F.R. § 300.503.

The content of this written notice is important to parents if they do decide to file for due process because they will have the rationale for the school district's decision. Each state has its own rules with respect to how this regulation is implemented. Most states require the written notice to occur within 10 days of the disagreement. In some cases, courts have found a failure to provide written notice as a factor in determining if a child did not receive FAPE, because this notice can be important to the parents' meaningful participation.

§ 9.2 STAY PUT

When the parent and school district disagree about the child's educational placement, and the parent has filed a due process complaint, the school district must maintain the student in his or her current educational placement during the pendency of the due process hearing, unless the special rules regarding school discipline are applicable as discussed in *Nutshell* Chapter 7.

The applicable regulation states:

> Child's status during proceedings.
>
> (a) Except as provided in § 300.533, during the pendency of any administrative or judicial proceeding regarding a due process complaint notice requesting a due process hearing under § 300.507, unless the State or local agency and the parents of the child agree otherwise, the child involved in the complaint must remain in his or her current educational placement.

> (b) If the complaint involves an application for initial admission to public school, the child, with the consent of the parents, must be placed in the public school until the completion of all the proceedings.
>
> (c) If the complaint involves an application for initial services under this part from a child who is transitioning from Part C of the Act to Part B and is no longer eligible for Part C services because the child has turned three, the public agency is not required to provide the Part C services that the child had been receiving. If the child is found eligible for special education and related services under Part B and the parent consents to the initial provision of special education and related services under § 300.300(b), then the public agency must provide those special education and related services that are not in dispute between the parent and the public agency.
>
> (d) If the hearing officer in a due process hearing conducted by the SEA or a State review official in an administrative appeal agrees with the child's parents that a change of placement is appropriate, that placement must be treated as an agreement between the State and the parents for purposes of paragraph (a) of this section.

34 C.F.R. § 300.518.

One challenge in applying this rule is defining what constitutes an "educational placement." Cases from the Third and Fourth Circuits show how this issue can be challenging to resolve.

In *AW v. Fairfax County School Board,* 372 F.3d 674 (4th Cir. 2004), the student challenged his junior high school placement during a Manifestation Determination Review (MDR). AW was in the gifted and talented program at his elementary school. He was suspended from school for two weeks and the school district instituted proceedings to expel him from school due to a threatening note he had placed in the computer file of a student he disliked. *Id.* at 676–77. On the ninth day of AW's suspension, the school held an MDR and determined that his disability had not caused the infraction of school rules, and he was eligible to be disciplined like any other student. When a school district administrator reviewed the expulsion request, he or she rejected the expulsion recommendation and instead concluded that AW should be transferred to the gifted and talented program at another elementary school for the remainder of the school year. AW was kept in his original school while his parents used due process to challenge the transfer decision. Their due process argument was unsuccessful and AW was transferred to the other elementary school where he attended their gifted and talented program while his parents appealed the MDR in federal court. On appeal, his parents argued that the school district should not have transferred AW to the other elementary school while the MDR was being appealed.

On appeal, the school district argued that transferring AW to another elementary school did not constitute a change in "educational placement" because the educational program at the two schools was identical. His parents argued that "educational placement" refers to the exact classroom to which AW had been previously assigned. The Fourth Circuit ruled for the school district, concluding that "the term 'educational placement' is not the location to which the student is assigned but rather the environment in which educational services are provided." *Id.* at 682. Because the two settings were "materially identical," and did not significantly differ in the length of the commute, the Fourth Circuit concluded that the stay put rule was not violated. *Id.* at 683. A major factor in the court's decision was that the new educational environment was not more restrictive than the prior educational environment; the court emphasized that Congress was particularly concerned with students being segregated or excluded from school during the pendency of their due process complaints; such factors were not affecting AW.

The Third Circuit distinguished *AW* in *D.M. v. New Jersey Department of Education,* 801 F.3d 205 (3rd Cir. 2015) by ruling in favor of the student. E.M.'s IEP stated that she would receive her education at the Learning Center for Exceptional Children (LCEC), a private school for students with disabilities, but would also attend classes in an integrated setting at Today's Learning Center (TLC), a private school for regular-education students that shared classroom space with LCEC.

The school was not able to comply with this IEP because the state Department of Education refused to certify TLC to educate public school students with disabilities. E.M.'s parents sued the Department of Education, arguing that its interpretation of the scope of LCEC's approvals is "incorrect, arbitrary, and capricious." *Id.* at 212.

Although this case had an unusual procedural posture—the parents were suing the state Department of Education rather than the school district—the Third Circuit found that it was a case proceeding under the IDEA, so that the stay put rule applied. While recognizing case law, such as *AW,* where the courts found that the term "educational placement" did not refer to the specific school the child attended, the Third Circuit found those cases distinguishable. In each of those decisions, "an alternative location provided sufficient services to satisfy the requirements of the student's IEP." *Id.* at 217. In this case, the Third Circuit concluded that E.M. was entitled to stay put at a program that reflected the education identified in her IEP—a program that allowed mainstreaming. *Id.* at 218. The Third Circuit, however, also noted that these cases are very fact specific because a court has to determine if a change in location affects the services required to satisfy the IEP. All the courts, however, seem to agree that "educational placement" does not necessarily mean the particular institution or classroom where the IEP is implemented.

§ 9.3 FILING A DUE PROCESS COMPLAINT

The following regulation generally describes how a parent can file a due process complaint. Each state has a procedure for filing an *expedited* complaint when it is important for a matter to be resolved quickly. Cases involving school discipline, for example, are typically resolved through an expedited process, although the parent is never compelled to seek an expedited process.

> Filing a due process complaint.
>
> (a) General.
>
> (1) A parent or a public agency may file a due process complaint on any of the matters described in § 300.503(a)(1) and (2) (relating to the identification, evaluation or educational placement of a child with a disability, or the provision of FAPE to the child).
>
> (2) The due process complaint must allege a violation that occurred not more than two years before the date the parent or public agency knew or should have known about the alleged action that forms the basis of the due process complaint, or, if the State has an explicit time limitation for filing a due process complaint under this part, in the time allowed by that State law, except that the exceptions to the timeline described in § 300.511(f) apply to the timeline in this section.
>
> (b) Information for parents. The public agency must inform the parent of any free or

> low-cost legal and other relevant services available in the area if—
>
> (1) The parent requests the information; or
>
> (2) The parent or the agency files a due process complaint under this section.

34 C.F.R. § 300.507.

§ 9.4 DUE PROCESS COMPLAINT

The following regulation specifies the content that a parent must include in a due process complaint. If the school district believes the complaint does not meet these criteria then they can file a motion that the complaint is not *sufficient*. Because the school district has to explain the reasons for their actions, the sufficiency rule seeks to provide some balance between parents and school districts. Both sides should be familiar with the other sides' position in advance of the due process hearing if these rules are followed.

> Due process complaint.
>
> (a) General.
>
> (1) The public agency must have procedures that require either party, or the attorney representing a party, to provide to the other party a due process complaint (which must remain confidential).
>
> (2) The party filing a due process complaint must forward a copy of the due process complaint to the SEA.
>
> (b) Content of complaint. The due process

complaint required in paragraph (a)(1) of this section must include—

(1) The name of the child;

(2) The address of the residence of the child;

(3) The name of the school the child is attending;

(4) In the case of a homeless child or youth (within the meaning of section 725(2) of the McKinney-Vento Homeless Assistance Act (42 U.S.C. 11434a(2)), available contact information for the child, and the name of the school the child is attending;

(5) A description of the nature of the problem of the child relating to the proposed or refused initiation or change, including facts relating to the problem; and

(6) A proposed resolution of the problem to the extent known and available to the party at the time.

(c) Notice required before a hearing on a due process complaint. A party may not have a hearing on a due process complaint until the party, or the attorney representing the party, files a due process complaint that meets the requirements of paragraph (b) of this section.

(d) Sufficiency of complaint.

(1) The due process complaint required by this section must be deemed sufficient unless the party receiving the due process complaint notifies the hearing officer and the other party

in writing, within 15 days of receipt of the due process complaint, that the receiving party believes the due process complaint does not meet the requirements in paragraph (b) of this section.

(2) Within five days of receipt of notification under paragraph (d)(1) of this section, the hearing officer must make a determination on the face of the due process complaint of whether the due process complaint meets the requirements of paragraph (b) of this section, and must immediately notify the parties in writing of that determination.

(3) A party may amend its due process complaint only if—

(i) The other party consents in writing to the amendment and is given the opportunity to resolve the due process complaint through a meeting held pursuant to § 300.510; or

(ii) The hearing officer grants permission, except that the hearing officer may only grant permission to amend at any time not later than five days before the due process hearing begins.

(4) If a party files an amended due process complaint, the timelines for the resolution meeting in § 300.510(a) and the time period to resolve in § 300.510(b) begin again with the filing of the amended due process complaint.

34 C.F.R. § 300.508.

When the school district challenges the complaint is not being sufficient, the Hearing Officer often allows the parent to amend the complaint to comply with the rules. The only difficulty that can arise in this case is the two-year statute of limitations. That is usually not a problem though because parents often try to file soon after a disagreement has occurred. However, a delay in refilling a sufficient complaint could cause a statute of limitations problem.

§ 9.5 SCHOOL DISTRICT RESPONSE TO A COMPLAINT

Typically, the school district has provided the parent with prior written notice so the parent understands the school district's position. If the school district has not yet provided prior written notice, then it must respond to the complaint with the same kind of information that would have been contained in the prior written notice, as described below.

> LEA response to a due process complaint.
>
> (1) If the LEA has not sent a prior written notice under § 300.503 to the parent regarding the subject matter contained in the parent's due process complaint, the LEA must, within 10 days of receiving the due process complaint, send to the parent a response that includes—
>
> (i) An explanation of why the agency proposed or refused to take the action raised in the due process complaint;

> (ii) A description of other options that the IEP Team considered and the reasons why those options were rejected;
>
> (iii) A description of each evaluation procedure, assessment, record, or report the agency used as the basis for the proposed or refused action; and
>
> (iv) A description of the other factors that are relevant to the agency's proposed or refused action.
>
> (2) A response by an LEA under paragraph (e)(1) of this section shall not be construed to preclude the LEA from asserting that the parent's due process complaint was insufficient, where appropriate.
>
> (f) Other party response to a due process complaint. Except as provided in paragraph (e) of this section, the party receiving a due process complaint must, within 10 days of receiving the due process complaint, send to the other party a response that specifically addresses the issues raised in the due process complaint.

34 C.F.R. § 300.508(e).

§ 9.6 AVAILABLE RELIEF

A. GENERAL PRINCIPLES

The IDEA does not permit parties to seek financial compensation for injuries sustained from failing to have an adequate education. The most common remedies sought under the IDEA are for compensatory education for previous lost educational opportunities and tuition reimbursement when the parent removed the child from a public school and placed the child in a private school. While the statute does not specifically state that a Hearing Officer can order compensatory education, there is decades of case law establishing that remedy.

The more controversial remedy is reimbursement for a school placement. The default principle under the IDEA is that special education services are principally provided at public schools. The school district is not required "to pay for the cost of education, including special education and relates services, of a child with a disability at a private school or facility if that [school district] made FAPE available to the child and the parents elected to place the child in a private school or facility." 34 C.F.R. § 300.148.

Nonetheless, if a school district is *not* providing a student with FAPE, then a Hearing Officer can award tuition reimbursement to parents if:

1. At the most recent IEP Team meeting that the parents attended prior to the removal of the student from the public school, the parents informed the IEP Team that they rejected the school district's proposed placement because it did not provide the student with FAPE; and
2. The parents provided the school district at least 10 business days notice that they intended

to remove their student from the public school, place their child in a private school, and seek reimbursement from the school district.

34 C.F.R. § 300.148.

Even if those conditions are satisfied, the Hearing Officer has the discretion to conclude that the parents acted unreasonably and that reimbursement is not appropriate. It is important for parents to be aware of these notice requirements if they plan to seek reimbursement as part of their due process complaint. Thus, it is prudent for the parents to document their compliance with the reimbursement rule when they file their due process complaint.

B. PRIVATE SCHOOL REIMBURSEMENT CASE LAW

Two Supreme Court cases have clarified the rules regarding a Hearing Officer ordering reimbursement for the placement of a child at a private school when the parent contends that the school district was not providing FAPE.

Before Congress amended the IDEA to provide the ten-day notice rule, the Supreme Court decided *School Committee of the Town of Burlington v. Department of Education,* 471 U.S. 359 (1985). In *Burlington,* a unanimous Supreme Court concluded that the IDEA did vest the authority in the Hearing Officer to require a school district to reimburse parents for the cost of sending their child to a private school if the court ultimately determines that the school district's placement did not provide FAPE and the parents' placement was appropriate. The "stay-put" rule did not preclude parents from unilaterally transferring their child to a new school because, otherwise, parents would be in the unacceptable position of having to keep their child in a program that they believed did not provide FAPE. Nonetheless, as the Court noted, a parent would only be entitled to reimbursement when they demonstrated the school district's proposed program did not provide FAPE *and* their private placement was appropriate.

Congress amended the IDEA in 1997 to require parents to provide the school district with ten-day notice before making a private placement and seeking reimbursement. That rule raised the question of whether a Hearing Officer could order reimbursement for private education if the student had not "previously received special education and related services" from a public school, as required by the IDEA:

> Reimbursement for private school placement
>
> If the parents of a child with a disability, who previously received special education and related services under the authority of a public agency, enroll the child in a private elementary school or secondary school without the consent of or referral by the public agency, a court or a hearing officer may require the agency to reimburse the parents for the cost of that enrollment if the court or hearing officer finds that the agency had not made a free

> appropriate public education available to the child in a timely manner prior to that enrollment.

20 U.S.C. § 1412(a)(10)(C)(ii).

The Supreme Court resolved that question in the affirmative in *Forest Grove School District v. T.A.*, 557 U.S. 230 (2009). In *Forest Grove,* the school district took the position that the student was not disabled and therefore, offered him no special education and related services. The parents gave the school district notice that they disagreed with the result, filed a due process complaint, and transferred their child to a private school. The Supreme Court interpreted 20 U.S.C. § 1412(a)(10)(C)(ii) merely to *permit* reimbursement in those circumstances. "[I]t does not foreclose reimbursement awards in other circumstances." *Id.* at 241. The various rules regarding reimbursement were "elucidative rather than exhaustive." *Id.* at 242.

§ 9.7 RESOLUTION PROCESS REQUIREMENT

The IDEA employs two alternative dispute resolution processes to help achieve settlement and avoid a due process hearing—a resolution meeting or mediation.

The IDEA requires both parties to attend a resolution meeting unless both parties agree to waive this requirement or both parties agree to engage in mediation. Neither party can unilaterally avoid these requirements; although, in practice, both parties need to engage in the processes in good faith for a settlement to occur.

> Resolution process.
>
> (a) Resolution meeting.
>
> (1) Within 15 days of receiving notice of the parent's due process complaint, and prior to the initiation of a due process hearing under § 300.511, the LEA must convene a meeting with the parent and the relevant member or members of the IEP Team who have specific knowledge of the facts identified in the due process complaint that—
>
> (i) Includes a representative of the public agency who has decision-making authority on behalf of that agency; and
>
> (ii) May not include an attorney of the LEA unless the parent is accompanied by an attorney.
>
> (2) The purpose of the meeting is for the parent of the child to discuss the due process complaint, and the facts that form the basis of the due process complaint, so that the LEA has the opportunity to resolve the dispute that is the basis for the due process complaint.
>
> (3) The meeting described in paragraph (a)(1) and (2) of this section need not be held if—
>
> (i) The parent and the LEA agree in writing to waive the meeting; or
>
> (ii) The parent and the LEA agree to use

the mediation process described in § 300.506.

(4) The parent and the LEA determine the relevant members of the IEP Team to attend the meeting.

(b) Resolution period.

(1) If the LEA has not resolved the due process complaint to the satisfaction of the parent within 30 days of the receipt of the due process complaint, the due process hearing may occur.

(2) Except as provided in paragraph (c) of this section, the timeline for issuing a final decision under § 300.515 begins at the expiration of this 30-day period.

(3) Except where the parties have jointly agreed to waive the resolution process or to use mediation, notwithstanding paragraphs (b)(1) and (2) of this section, the failure of the parent filing a due process complaint to participate in the resolution meeting will delay the timelines for the resolution process and due process hearing until the meeting is held.

(4) If the LEA is unable to obtain the participation of the parent in the resolution meeting after reasonable efforts have been made (and documented using the procedures in § 300.322(d)), the LEA may, at the conclusion of the 30-day period, request that a hearing officer dismiss the parent's due process complaint.

(5) If the LEA fails to hold the resolution meeting specified in paragraph (a) of this

section within 15 days of receiving notice of a parent's due process complaint or fails to participate in the resolution meeting, the parent may seek the intervention of a hearing officer to begin the due process hearing timeline.

(c) Adjustments to 30-day resolution period. The 45-day timeline for the due process hearing in § 300.515(a) starts the day after one of the following events:

(1) Both parties agree in writing to waive the resolution meeting;

(2) After either the mediation or resolution meeting starts but before the end of the 30-day period, the parties agree in writing that no agreement is possible;

(3) If both parties agree in writing to continue the mediation at the end of the 30-day resolution period, but later, the parent or public agency withdraws from the mediation process.

(d) Written settlement agreement. If a resolution to the dispute is reached at the meeting described in paragraphs (a)(1) and (2) of this section, the parties must execute a legally binding agreement that is—

(1) Signed by both the parent and a representative of the agency who has the authority to bind the agency; and

(2) Enforceable in any State court of competent jurisdiction or in a district court of the United States, or, by the SEA, if the State

> has other mechanisms or procedures that permit parties to seek enforcement of resolution agreements, pursuant to § 300.537.
>
> (e) Agreement review period. If the parties execute an agreement pursuant to paragraph (d) of this section, a party may void the agreement within 3 business days of the agreement's execution.

34 C.F.R. § 300.510.

A resolution meeting often looks like a mini IEP meeting since it must include a school district representative, some members of the IEP team, and the parents. If the parent chooses to bring an attorney to the meeting then the school district can also bring an attorney. Sometimes, the parties will request a mediator for a resolution meeting through the state education agency. If so, it is very similar to the mediation option described in *Nutshell* § 9.8.

The resolution meeting is supposed to occur within 15 days of the parent filing a due process complaint and some decision should be reached within 30 days. Once the resolution period has ended, a due process decision is supposed to be rendered within 45 days. In practice, it is often difficult to schedule the resolution meeting and due process hearing within those time frames, and the parties often agree to extensions.

§ 9.8 MEDIATION ALTERNATIVE

Mediation.

(a) General. Each public agency must ensure that procedures are established and implemented to allow parties to disputes involving any matter under this part, including matters arising prior to the filing of a due process complaint, to resolve disputes through a mediation process.

(b) Requirements. The procedures must meet the following requirements:

(1) The procedures must ensure that the mediation process—

(i) Is voluntary on the part of the parties;

(ii) Is not used to deny or delay a parent's right to a hearing on the parent's due process complaint, or to deny any other rights afforded under Part B of the Act; and

(iii) Is conducted by a qualified and impartial mediator who is trained in effective mediation techniques.

(2) A public agency may establish procedures to offer to parents and schools that choose not to use the mediation process, an opportunity to meet, at a time and location convenient to the parents, with a disinterested party—

(i) Who is under contract with an appropriate alternative dispute resolution entity, or a parent training and information center or community parent resource center in the State established under section 671 or 672 of the Act; and

(ii) Who would explain the benefits of, and encourage the use of, the mediation process to the parents.

(3)

(i) The State must maintain a list of individuals who are qualified mediators and knowledgeable in laws and regulations relating to the provision of special education and related services.

(ii) The SEA must select mediators on a random, rotational, or other impartial basis.

(4) The State must bear the cost of the mediation process, including the costs of meetings described in paragraph (b)(2) of this section.

(5) Each session in the mediation process must be scheduled in a timely manner and must be held in a location that is convenient to the parties to the dispute.

(6) If the parties resolve a dispute through the mediation process, the parties must execute a legally binding agreement that sets forth that resolution and that—

(i) States that all discussions that occurred during the mediation process will remain confidential and may not be used as evidence in any subsequent due process hearing or civil proceeding; and

> (ii) Is signed by both the parent and a representative of the agency who has the authority to bind such agency.
>
> (7) A written, signed mediation agreement under this paragraph is enforceable in any State court of competent jurisdiction or in a district court of the United States.
>
> (8) Discussions that occur during the mediation process must be confidential and may not be used as evidence in any subsequent due process hearing or civil proceeding of any Federal court or State court of a State receiving assistance under this part.

34 C.F.R. § 300.506.

The mediation process is similar to the resolution process except that a mediator is *always* present to help the parties resolve the dispute. The 30-day timeline also applies to this process as in the resolution process, and the mediator must be provided free of charge by the state. States usually have a rotating list of mediators that they use for this process, listed by geographical region. Although no statistics exist on this process, anecdotal evidence suggests that most parties choose mediation (rather than the resolution process) and most parents do not file for due process at the completion of the mediation process. It is hard to know if that is because the parents feel their issues have been satisfactorily resolved or if they do not have the resources to handle a due process hearing. It is also not uncommon for parties to engage in a successful mediation but for the parent to be dissatisfied with the resolution and file for due process at a later time on a related matter. Because IEPs are created on an annual basis, it is easy for disputes to re-emerge even when they seem to have been preliminarily resolved.

§ 9.9 IMPARTIAL DUE PROCESS HEARING

Impartial due process hearing.

(a) General. Whenever a due process complaint is received under § 300.507 or § 300.532, the parents or the LEA involved in the dispute must have an opportunity for an impartial due process hearing, consistent with the procedures in §§ 300.507, 300.508, and 300.510.

(b) Agency responsible for conducting the due process hearing. The hearing described in paragraph (a) of this section must be conducted by the SEA or the public agency directly responsible for the education of the child, as determined under State statute, State regulation, or a written policy of the SEA.

(c) Impartial hearing officer.

(1) At a minimum, a hearing officer—

(i) Must not be—

(A) An employee of the SEA or the LEA that is involved in the education or care of the child; or

(B) A person having a personal or professional interest that conflicts with the person's objectivity in the hearing;

(ii) Must possess knowledge of, and the ability to understand, the provisions of the Act, Federal and State regulations pertaining to the Act, and legal interpretations of the Act by Federal and State courts;

(iii) Must possess the knowledge and ability to conduct hearings in accordance with appropriate, standard legal practice; and

(iv) Must possess the knowledge and ability to render and write decisions in accordance with appropriate, standard legal practice.

(2) A person who otherwise qualifies to conduct a hearing under paragraph (c)(1) of this section is not an employee of the agency solely because he or she is paid by the agency to serve as a hearing officer.

(3) Each public agency must keep a list of the persons who serve as hearing officers. The list must include a statement of the qualifications of each of those persons.

(d) Subject matter of due process hearings. The party requesting the due process hearing may not raise issues at the due process hearing that were not raised in the due process complaint filed under § 300.508(b), unless the other party agrees otherwise.

> (e) Timeline for requesting a hearing. A parent or agency must request an impartial hearing on their due process complaint within two years of the date the parent or agency knew or should have known about the alleged action that forms the basis of the due process complaint, or if the State has an explicit time limitation for requesting such a due process hearing under this part, in the time allowed by that State law.
>
> (f) Exceptions to the timeline. The timeline described in paragraph (e) of this section does not apply to a parent if the parent was prevented from filing a due process complaint due to—
>
> (1) Specific misrepresentations by the LEA that it had resolved the problem forming the basis of the due process complaint; or
>
> (2) The LEA's withholding of information from the parent that was required under this part to be provided to the parent.

34 C.F.R. § 300.511.

Each state must have a list of Hearing Officers, although states vary in how they make Hearing Officers available to hear due process complaints. Some states have individuals who work on a contract basis as Hearing Officers; these individuals typically have other jobs in addition to this role. Other states have individuals who work for the state as Administrative Law Judges (ALJ's) and they conduct these hearings as part of their ALJ duties. In California for example, these ALJ's also serve as mediators (but not on cases before them as Hearing Officers).

Massachusetts offers an additional process called the "advisory opinion process." *See* http://www.mass.gov/anf/hearings-and-appeals/bureau-of-special-education-appeals-bsea/advisory-opinion-process.html. Under this process, parties each give a one-hour presentation to a Hearing Officer who offers a nonbinding opinion about the case. This process often leads to the parties reaching a settlement without undergoing a full due process hearing. For further discussion, *see* Reece Erlichman, Michael Gregory, & Alisia St. Florian, *The Settlement Conference as a Dispute Resolution Option in Special Education*, 29 OHIO STATE JOURNAL ON DISPUTE RESOLUTION 407 (2014).

§ 9.10 HEARING RIGHTS

Hearing rights.

(a) General. Any party to a hearing conducted pursuant to §§ 300.507 through 300.513 or §§ 300.530 through 300.534, or an appeal conducted pursuant to § 300.514, has the right to—

(1) Be accompanied and advised by counsel and by individuals with special knowledge or training with respect to the problems of children with disabilities, except that whether parties have the right to be represented by non-attorneys at due process hearings is

determined under State law;

(2) Present evidence and confront, cross-examine, and compel the attendance of witnesses;

(3) Prohibit the introduction of any evidence at the hearing that has not been disclosed to that party at least five business days before the hearing;

(4) Obtain a written, or, at the option of the parents, electronic, verbatim record of the hearing; and

(5) Obtain written, or, at the option of the parents, electronic findings of fact and decisions.

(b) Additional disclosure of information.

(1) At least five business days prior to a hearing conducted pursuant to § 300.511(a), each party must disclose to all other parties all evaluations completed by that date and recommendations based on the offering party's evaluations that the party intends to use at the hearing.

(2) A hearing officer may bar any party that fails to comply with paragraph (b)(1) of this section from introducing the relevant evaluation or recommendation at the hearing without the consent of the other party.

(c) Parental rights at hearings. Parents involved in hearings must be given the right to—

(1) Have the child who is the subject of the hearing present;

> (2) Open the hearing to the public; and
>
> (3) Have the record of the hearing and the findings of fact and decisions described in paragraphs (a)(4) and (a)(5) of this section provided at no cost to parents.

34 C.F.R. § 300.512.

The Hearing Officer process does not provide for extensive discovery. Parents are entitled to receive a copy of their child's educational records, and they can request emails and other written records that the school district may have regarding their child's educational performance. The parties exchange their documents five days before the hearing takes place, and sometimes they agree to have a common set of exhibits such as the child's prior evaluation reports and IEPs. To the extent that both parties are relying on the same documents, the hearing can go more smoothly if they use a common set of materials. The parent typically has the burden of proof, so the parent must be prepared to create an appropriate set of materials for the hearing.

A court reporter attends the hearing and creates a transcript that is provided to the parents at no cost. Each state has its own set of policies for how the Hearing Officer is compensated. The parent, however, is never responsible for paying the Hearing Officer.

This regulation is unusual in that it allows a parent to be accompanied by "individuals with special knowledge or training with respect to the problems of children with disabilities." In other words, a non-lawyer can assist the parent at the hearing. However, a parent cannot obtain "attorney fees" from the school district if they prevail to pay this non-lawyer to assist them. In each state, there are individuals who are special education advocates who attend IEP meetings and assist parents at due process hearings. Congress created this option to reduce the cost for parents to seek assistance in the special education process. One would expect the competency of these advocates to vary, as there is no licensing entity that monitors their qualifications. Of course, parents may choose to attend a due process hearing without the assistance of a lawyer; however, they are unlikely to prevail if they proceed without any assistance from a lawyer or advocate.

When parents proceed *pro se* (i.e., without a lawyer) before a Hearing Officer, they sometimes want to appeal the Hearing Officer decision on a *pro se* basis in federal court. The default rule is that non-attorneys are not allowed to represent others, such as their children, in federal or state court. Thus, school districts have challenged parents proceeding *pro se* to appeal an adverse Hearing Officer decision, contending that such an appeal would constitute the unauthorized practice of law. The Supreme Court considered that argument in *Winkelman v. Parma City School District*, 550 U.S. 516 (2007). The Supreme Court concluded that parents could appeal an adverse Hearing Officer decision in federal court because their rights, along with their child's rights, are protected by the IDEA. The *Winkelman* decision is broad and it does not limit parents' ability to proceed *pro se* in cases where they are, for example, seeking tuition reimbursement. The right to a free, appropriate, publicly-funded education, the Court ruled, is a right of the parents as well as that of the child. *Id.* at 533. Thus, parents can proceed *pro se* at all stages of IDEA litigation, not just at the Hearing Officer stage.

§ 9.11 BURDEN OF PROOF

As in any legal matter, parties need to meet their burden of proof. For some years, the lower courts were divided on whether the parent or school district had the burden of proof in these cases. The Supreme Court resolved this issue in *Schaffer v. Weast,* 546 U.S. 49 (2005). It concluded that the standard rules for litigation apply in these cases—the party filing the administrative action has the burden of proof. The Court emphasized that the disclosure rules that precede the due process hearing do not put the school district at an evidentiary advantage, and it is therefore reasonable to place the burden of proof on a parent who may be bringing the administrative action. The Court noted, however, that the school district would bear the burden of proof in cases where it seeks an administrative hearing. When a parent seeks an Independent Educational Evaluation (IEE), for example, the school district must file for due process if it wants to deny the parent's request. There are also some circumstances where the school district brings a due process action for the purpose of asking the Hearing Office to declare their proposed IEP to be valid, because the parents will not agree to its contents. This is sometimes called a "reverse" due process hearing and would require the school district to have the burden of proof. That is an unusual situation, however, and typically, the parent is the one who files the due process complaint and has the burden of proof.

The *Schaffer* case left open the option of a state deciding to place the burden of proof on the school district. In 2008, New Jersey decided to place the burden of proof on school districts. By contrast, the D.C. school board voted in 2007 to change its practice so that the burden of proof would be on the parent. Empirical studies have found that parents are not more likely to prevail in states in which the school district has the burden of proof. The Supreme Court in *Schaffer* predicted the burden of proof would not be especially significant since cases are rarely in "equipoise" (i.e., a perfect tie) so that the burden of proof matters. Nonetheless, school districts fought New Jersey's change in its allocation of the burden of proof, and parents fought D.C.'s change in its allocation of the burden of proof.

§ 9.12 HEARING DECISIONS

Hearing decisions.

(a) Decision of hearing officer on the provision of FAPE.

(1) Subject to paragraph (a)(2) of this section, a hearing officer's determination of whether a child received FAPE must be based on substantive grounds.

(2) In matters alleging a procedural violation, a hearing officer may find that a child did not receive a FAPE only if the procedural inadequacies—

(i) Impeded the child's right to a FAPE;

(ii) Significantly impeded the parent's opportunity to participate in the decision-making process regarding the provision of a FAPE to the parent's child; or

(iii) Caused a deprivation of educational benefit.

(3) Nothing in paragraph (a) of this section shall be construed to preclude a hearing officer from ordering an LEA to comply with procedural requirements under §§ 300.500 through 300.536.

(b) Construction clause. Nothing in §§ 300.507 through 300.513 shall be construed to affect the right of a parent to file an appeal of the due process hearing decision with the SEA under § 300.514(b), if a State level appeal is available.

(c) Separate request for a due process hearing. Nothing in §§ 300.500 through 300.536 shall be construed to preclude a parent from filing a separate due process complaint on an issue separate from a due process complaint already filed.

(d) Findings and decision to advisory panel and general public. The public agency, after deleting any personally identifiable

> information, must—
>
> (1) Transmit the findings and decisions referred to in § 300.512(a)(5) to the State advisory panel established under § 300.167; and
>
> (2) Make those findings and decisions available to the public.

34 C.F.R. § 300.513 (boldface type not in original).

The highlighted language is extremely important and has been narrowed over the years. Parents cannot prevail in an IDEA case merely because the school district failed to comply with the procedural rules under the IDEA. They need to demonstrate an adverse effect on the student's IEP, a lack of meaningful participation by the parent in the process, or a deprivation of educational benefit.

Many cases reflect how difficult it is for parents to prevail as a result of procedural violations, because it is hard to demonstrate that these procedural errors affected the child's education. For example, in *A.M. v. New York City Department of Education,* 845 F.3d 523 (2nd Cir. 2017), the Second Circuit concluded that the cumulative effect of the school district's procedural errors did not deprive the student of FAPE. Those procedural errors included a failure to conduct a Functional Behavior Assessment, a failure to provide parental counseling and training services, and a failure to provide transitional support services. Nonetheless, the parents prevailed on *substantive grounds*, because the IEP failed to provide Applied Behavioral

Analysis (ABA) therapy and 1:1 support, which all of the reports indicated the student needed in order to make educational progress.

Parents often argue that procedural errors deny them the ability to *meaningfully participate* in the IEP meeting. For example, in *E.A.M. v. New York City Department of Education,* 2012 WL 4571794 (S.D. N.Y. Sept. 29, 2012), the parents unsuccessfully argued that they were denied a meaningful opportunity to participate due to procedural errors. The parents alleged the following procedural errors: lack of an appropriate general education teacher and the development of goals outside the IEP meeting without input from the parent. Because the student was only in a general education classroom for gym class and "talent" class, the court did not think which general education teacher was selected to attend the meeting had any impact on the parent's ability to participate. With respect to goals, the court concluded there is no requirement that "parents or teachers have the opportunity to actually draft the goals by hand or on the computer themselves." *Id.* at *8. "While a more specific discussion of goals at the [IEP] meeting may have been desirable, the record does not support the conclusion that the lack of such a discussion significantly impeded the Parent's opportunity to participate in the decision-making process." *Id.* at *11.

By contrast, in *McNeil v. Options Public Charter School,* 2013 WL 791199 (D.D.C. March 1, 2013) (attorney's fees issue), the Hearing Officer found that the parent had been denied a meaningful opportunity to participate because the school district failed to perform a Functional Behavior Assessment, a clinical evaluation, and a speech and language evaluation. The lack of "vital evaluative data" deprived the parent of an opportunity to meaningfully participate. *Id.* at *2.

The substantive argument that an IEP deprives a student of FAPE is governed by the *Rowley* and *Endrew F.* standards discussed in *Nutshell* Chapter 6.

§ 9.13 REVIEW OF THE HEARING OFFICER DECISION

> Finality of decision; appeal; impartial review.
>
> (a) Finality of hearing decision. A decision made in a hearing conducted pursuant to §§ 300.507 through 300.513 or §§ 300.530 through 300.534 is final, except that any party involved in the hearing may appeal the decision under the provisions of paragraph (b) of this section and § 300.516.
>
> (b) Appeal of decisions; impartial review.
>
> (1) If the hearing required by § 300.511 is conducted by a public agency other than the SEA, any party aggrieved by the findings and decision in the hearing may appeal to the SEA.
>
> (2) If there is an appeal, the SEA must conduct an impartial review of the findings and decision appealed. The official conducting the review must—

(i) Examine the entire hearing record;

(ii) Ensure that the procedures at the hearing were consistent with the requirements of due process;

(iii) Seek additional evidence if necessary. If a hearing is held to receive additional evidence, the rights in § 300.512 apply;

(iv) Afford the parties an opportunity for oral or written argument, or both, at the discretion of the reviewing official;

(v) Make an independent decision on completion of the review; and

(vi) Give a copy of the written, or, at the option of the parents, electronic findings of fact and decisions to the parties.

(c) Findings and decision to advisory panel and general public. The SEA, after deleting any personally identifiable information, must—

(1) Transmit the findings and decisions referred to in paragraph (b)(2)(vi) of this section to the State advisory panel established under § 300.167; and

(2) Make those findings and decisions available to the public.

(d) Finality of review decision. The decision made by the reviewing official is final unless a party brings a civil action under § 300.516.

34 C.F.R. § 300.514.

These regulations give the state the opportunity to have a one-tier or two-tiered system of review. Most states have a one-tier system and some states, like Pennsylvania, have moved from a two-tier system to a one-tier system. New York State, which has the largest number of due process hearings, has a two-tier system. Most states make their due process decisions available on a state-maintained website after any confidential information has been redacted. *See, e.g.*, New York Office of State Review, http://www.sro.nysed.gov/decisionindex/. Some are even word searchable. *See, e.g.*, California Office of Administrative Hearings, http://www.dgs.ca.gov/oah/SpecialEducation/searchDO.aspx.

§ 9.14 TIMELINES

> Timelines and convenience of hearings and reviews.
>
> (a) The public agency must ensure that not later than 45 days after the expiration of the 30 day period under § 300.510(b), or the adjusted time periods described in § 300.510(c)—
>
> (1) A final decision is reached in the hearing; and
>
> (2) A copy of the decision is mailed to each of the parties.
>
> (b) The SEA must ensure that not later than 30 days after the receipt of a request for a review—
>
> (1) A final decision is reached in the review; and

> (2) A copy of the decision is mailed to each of the parties.
>
> (c) A hearing or reviewing officer may grant specific extensions of time beyond the periods set out in paragraphs (a) and (b) of this section at the request of either party.
>
> (d) Each hearing and each review involving oral arguments must be conducted at a time and place that is reasonably convenient to the parents and child involved.

34 C.F.R. § 300.515.

States have the option of whether to have a second-level review process. Ohio, for example, has a two-tier process. After the first-level decision is rendered, parties are told they have 45 days to appeal the decision. The appeal is merely a paper appeal, and no further live testimony is taken. Parties are also informed that they have 90 days to appeal the second-level Hearing Officer decision. Thus, due process matters can easily take many months in a state with a two-tier process making the "stay put" rule especially important when there is a dispute about a placement.

§ 9.15 CIVIL ACTIONS

> Civil action.
>
> (a) General. Any party aggrieved by the findings and decision made under §§ 300.507 through 300.513 or §§ 300.530 through 300.534 who does not have the right to an appeal under

§ 300.514(b), and any party aggrieved by the findings and decision under § 300.514(b), has the right to bring a civil action with respect to the due process complaint notice requesting a due process hearing under § 300.507 or §§ 300.530 through 300.532. The action may be brought in any State court of competent jurisdiction or in a district court of the United States without regard to the amount in controversy.

(b) Time limitation. The party bringing the action shall have 90 days from the date of the decision of the hearing officer or, if applicable, the decision of the State review official, to file a civil action, or, if the State has an explicit time limitation for bringing civil actions under Part B of the Act, in the time allowed by that State law.

(c) Additional requirements. In any action brought under paragraph (a) of this section, the court—

(1) Receives the records of the administrative proceedings;

(2) Hears additional evidence at the request of a party; and

(3) Basing its decision on the preponderance of the evidence, grants the relief that the court determines to be appropriate.

(d) Jurisdiction of district courts. The district courts of the United States have jurisdiction of actions brought under section 615 of the Act

> without regard to the amount in controversy.
>
> (e) Rule of construction. Nothing in this part restricts or limits the rights, procedures, and remedies available under the Constitution, the Americans with Disabilities Act of 1990, title V of the Rehabilitation Act of 1973, or other Federal laws protecting the rights of children with disabilities, except that before the filing of a civil action under these laws seeking relief that is also available under section 615 of the Act, the procedures under §§ 300.507 and 300.514 must be exhausted to the same extent as would be required had the action been brought under section 615 of the Act.

34 C.F.R. § 300.516.

Section 300.516(e) refers to the exhaustion rule discussed in *Nutshell* Chapter 4. Parties must typically exhaust their IDEA administrative remedies before filing in federal court. As discussed in *Nutshell* Chapter 4, the Supreme Court recently clarified that parties can sue directly in court under Section 504 if they are seeking relief that is generally available outside the classroom like the right to use a service dog. *See Fry v. Napoleon Community Schools,* 137 S. Ct. 743 (2017).

§ 9.16 ATTORNEYS' FEES

Attorneys' fees.

(a) In general.

(1) In any action or proceeding brought under section 615 of the Act, the court, in its discretion, may award reasonable attorneys' fees as part of the costs to—

(i) The prevailing party who is the parent of a child with a disability;

(ii) To a prevailing party who is an SEA or LEA against the attorney of a parent who files a complaint or subsequent cause of action that is frivolous, unreasonable, or without foundation, or against the attorney of a parent who continued to litigate after the litigation clearly became frivolous, unreasonable, or without foundation; or

(iii) To a prevailing SEA or LEA against the attorney of a parent, or against the parent, if the parent's request for a due process hearing or subsequent cause of action was presented for any improper purpose, such as to harass, to cause unnecessary delay, or to needlessly increase the cost of litigation.

(2) Nothing in this subsection shall be construed to affect section 327 of the District of Columbia Appropriations Act, 2005.

(b) Prohibition on use of funds.

(1) Funds under Part B of the Act may not be used to pay attorneys' fees or costs of a

party related to any action or proceeding under section 615 of the Act and subpart E of this part.

(2) Paragraph (b)(1) of this section does not preclude a public agency from using funds under Part B of the Act for conducting an action or proceeding under section 615 of the Act.

(c) Award of fees. A court awards reasonable attorneys' fees under section 615(i)(3) of the Act consistent with the following:

(1) Fees awarded under section 615(i)(3) of the Act must be based on rates prevailing in the community in which the action or proceeding arose for the kind and quality of services furnished. No bonus or multiplier may be used in calculating the fees awarded under this paragraph.

(2)

(i) Attorneys' fees may not be awarded and related costs may not be reimbursed in any action or proceeding under section 615 of the Act for services performed subsequent to the time of a written offer of settlement to a parent if—

(A) The offer is made within the time prescribed by Rule 68 of the Federal Rules of Civil Procedure or, in the case of an administrative proceeding, at any time more than 10 days before the proceeding begins;

(B) The offer is not accepted within 10 days; and

(C) The court or administrative hearing officer finds that the relief finally obtained by the parents is not more favorable to the parents than the offer of settlement.

(ii) Attorneys' fees may not be awarded relating to any meeting of the IEP Team unless the meeting is convened as a result of an administrative proceeding or judicial action, or at the discretion of the State, for a mediation described in § 300.506.

(iii) A meeting conducted pursuant to § 300.510 shall not be considered—

(A) A meeting convened as a result of an administrative hearing or judicial action; or

(B) An administrative hearing or judicial action for purposes of this section.

(3) Notwithstanding paragraph (c)(2) of this section, an award of attorneys' fees and related costs may be made to a parent who is the prevailing party and who was substantially justified in rejecting the settlement offer.

(4) Except as provided in paragraph (c)(5) of this section, the court reduces, accordingly, the amount of the attorneys' fees awarded under section 615 of the Act, if the court finds that—

(i) The parent, or the parent's attorney, during the course of the action or

> proceeding, unreasonably protracted the final resolution of the controversy;
>
> (ii) The amount of the attorneys' fees otherwise authorized to be awarded unreasonably exceeds the hourly rate prevailing in the community for similar services by attorneys of reasonably comparable skill, reputation, and experience;
>
> (iii) The time spent and legal services furnished were excessive considering the nature of the action or proceeding; or
>
> (iv) The attorney representing the parent did not provide to the LEA the appropriate information in the due process request notice in accordance with § 300.508.
>
> (5) The provisions of paragraph (c)(4) of this section do not apply in any action or proceeding if the court finds that the State or local agency unreasonably protracted the final resolution of the action or proceeding or there was a violation of section 615 of the Act.

34 C.F.R. § 300.517.

This rule gives district courts, not Hearing Officers, the authority to grant attorney fees to parents when they are the prevailing party in an administrative action. The school district can also seek attorney fees against the parent if their action is found to be frivolous. It is rare for such a determination to be made, but school districts sometimes inform parents of that possibility if they are going to seek attorney fees from the school. Parents are not entitled to attorney fees if the relief they ultimately obtained was no better than the relief offered to them by the school district in a written offer of settlement. Finally, the attorney fees that are obtained are only for the due process hearing, not the IEP meeting that preceded the due process hearing. An exception, however, is when the Hearing Officer orders a new IEP meeting. Then, the parent can get reimbursed for an attorney attending that meeting.

This rule only applies to attorney fees, not expert expenses that the parent obtained in order to be successful at the due process hearing. *See Arlington Central School District Board of Education v. Murphy,* 548 U.S. 291 (2006). Thus, as the dissent notes, a parent can spend tens of thousands of dollars on experts to prevail at a due process hearing and is not be able to recover any of those costs. Attorney fees can include: reasonable photocopying, postage and parking costs, but would not include the plaintiff's *own* parking expenses. *See Hammond v. District of Columbia,* 183 F. Supp.3d 145 (D.D.C. 2016).

§ 9.17 CONCLUSION

While this chapter has sought to summarize the steps involved in bringing a due process complaint on behalf of a student, it is important to investigate a state's due process practices carefully before proceeding with a complaint. In some states, virtually all due process complaints are resolved so that a hearing is not conducted. In other jurisdictions, like the District of Columbia, there is a high volume of due process hearings and a well-established private bar that often assists parents to bring these kinds of complaints. Within a state, some school districts virtually never have complaints filed against them, whereas, others are often involved in litigation. Because due process hearings are handled at the state level, this chapter could only provide broad guidelines that cover such hearings.

The cases that result in federal litigation are not necessarily representative of typical special education matters. They typically involve a parent's request for reimbursement for private schooling. Only a small percentage of students covered by the IDEA attend a private placement. Most disputes involve more routine matters like whether a child is eligible for special education services or the kinds of services that are provided.

Finally, it is important to remember that most school districts provide services to students on IEPs without disputes with parents and their children. While these IEPs may not be perfect, they typically reflect a genuine commitment on the part of school staff and parents to assist a student made educational progress. This *Nutshell* has tried to provide resources to help make that process better comply with the IDEA. At the end of the day, however, it is the good faith efforts of IEP team members that make the IDEA an effective tool on behalf of students with disabilities.

INDEX

References are to Sections
